09/2017

AN ARMY OF ONE

ALSO BY TONY SCHUMACHER

The Darkest Hour

The British Lion

AN ARMY OF ONE

A JOHN ROSSETT NOVEL

TONY SCHUMACHER

wm

WILLIAM MORROW
An Imprint of HarperCollins*Publishers*

HarperCollins
PUBLISHERS
Since 1817

FIRST EDITION

Designed by Diahann Sturge

Library of Congress Cataloging-in-Publication Data

Names: Schumacher, Tony, 1967- author.
Title: An army of one : a John Rossett novel / Tony Schumacher.
Description: First edition. | New York, NY : William Morrow, an imprint of HarperCollins Publishers, [2017]
Identifiers: LCCN 2016055361| ISBN 9780062499875 (hardcover) | ISBN 0062499874 (hardcover) | ISBN 9780062499905 (ebook) | ISBN 0062499904 (ebook)
Subjects: | BISAC: FICTION / Suspense. | FICTION / Thrillers. | GSAFD: Alternative histories (Fiction)
Classification: LCC PR6119.C3865 A88 2017 | DDC 823/.92--dc23 LC record available at https://lccn.loc.gov/2016055361

17 18 19 20 21   LSC   10 9 8 7 6 5 4 3 2 1

For Anna, who finally brought me home

AN ARMY OF ONE

LIVERPOOL

IT WAS RAINING.

Blowing in left to right off the river. Silver sheets that caught the streetlamps, looking like shoals of tiny fish, twisting and turning in a swell.

The Bear breathed into his right fist, then stretched his fingers before wrapping his hand around the rifle stock again.

He rolled his shoulders and rested his cheek against it. It was so cold it made his face ache. He waited, it warmed; he blinked, then looked down the telescopic sight.

The same peeled-paint door stared back at him.

He moved and the rifle creaked a little. The view in the sight smudged black, then came back into focus. He breathed out through his nose, then shifted his aim a fraction to the right.

The docker was still there, still smoking, still waiting by the car. Hunkered in his coat, looking left and right, making sure whoever was in the warehouse behind him wasn't about to be disturbed.

"Time, time, time." Softly, to nobody but himself, as the crosshairs crept up the docker's chest, then settled on his face, just below his left eye.

The Bear blinked and saw his own eye in the reflection of the sight for a fraction of a second. He tried to focus on it, catching the swirl of a silver iris before it blurred out of view. He breathed in, slow and deep, trying to ignore the pain that was starting to knot in his neck.

He thought about moving position, climbing higher in the empty warehouse. He decided against it. He'd chosen the spot badly, he knew that, but there wasn't much he could do about it now. He felt the pain, enjoyed the pain, lived with the pain, then forgot it.

If his neck was sore tomorrow it would be sore.

His right index finger traced the trigger guard, then folded back into place on the stock. The rifle creaked again, like it was stretching out an ache the same as him.

His mouth was dry. He had a canteen of water in his bag but decided it would have to wait. He listened to the rain dripping through where the roof used to be. High up above him, away in the darkness, off through the holes in the shredded floors of the empty bombed-out building he was hiding in.

He was down in the docks. Surrounded by the warehouses that had taken the worst of the punishment when Liverpool had been bombarded by the German army. Years ago now, back during the fighting that had taken place to gain control of the city during the Battle for Britain. There had been a collapsing clamor to get on the last ships, away down the oil-slicked river as the Nazis had choked the life out of the land all around it.

Back then the Bear had just been Karl Bauer.

Back then the Bear had been normal.

Back then the Bear's hands had just been splashed with blood.

All these years later they were drenched in the stuff. The Bear saw it in his dreams, tasted it in his food, smelled it in the air, and sweated it in his nightmares.

He was blood.

He was Captain Karl Bauer.

He was the Bear.

He'd been a member of the Waffen SS that had thundered through France, then onward through England, before finally hammering on Liverpool's door. What was left of the British army had almost universally scrambled to the few ports up north that were still operating.

The ships hadn't hung around for long. They had slipped out of the river like shy lovers disturbed by the sound of a key in the door.

The River Mersey had slapped against the quayside walls the night the boats left. A sarcastic round of applause under a smoke-smudged sky traced with searchlights, flak blast, and shadows.

The ships headed north, running for the safety of the Atlantic. As far away as they could get, as quickly as they could get there. Most of them hadn't made it; they'd been sunk even before the city surrendered.

Truth be told, from what Bauer had seen, it was a miracle Liverpool had managed to last two days.

A miracle or maybe a nightmare, depending on your point of view. For forty-eight hours, German ordnance pounded from all sides. Across the River Mersey a long line of artillery had lined up and shelled the city center, while from every main road into the city, tanks and armor had rained heavy death.

And rain it had.

Death had been a downpour.

Thousands had died in the tightly packed streets, in a bombardment that blasted tenements and terraces to pieces. There had been no way out for the population as the ring around it squeezed tighter and tighter, until on the final night—it choked.

By the time the Germans switched off their engines, there was barely one brick mortared to another.

It had taken a week for what was left of the population to be driven out of their holes and cellars, blinking into the new dawn of the New Order.

THE BEAR HADN'T stopped for long that first time he visited. There was barely time to catch the breath he'd been chasing since he crossed over the Channel from France a month earlier. He had moved north, pushing harder, crushing harder. Day after day, week after week, carrying the fight to an enemy that was on the ropes but didn't have the sense to go down.

Even when it was over, he didn't have the time to breathe.

He was one of the best of the best. He had shown talents that proved he was needed to wheedle the woodworm. The ones who wouldn't surrender, the ones who had to be hunted.

So he didn't stop.

He never stopped.

When the battle was won, the occupation began. The Bear lived in the ruins he'd created. Picking off resistance wherever he was needed. There was nobody better at it than him, so he was the man who did it.

The hunter, the killer, taking no prisoners.

Eight? Or was it nine years since the first person fell in his sights? He'd lost count of the years, lost count of the deaths, and now none of it mattered or made sense.

He blinked. He was back.

He turned his head and looked to a black corner next to him where a rat was sniffing the air and scratching some rubble. The Bear stared; the rat paused, an eye glinting as it tried to decide if he was a threat.

He wasn't.

The Bear lowered his hand. The rat sniffed his index finger and then darted away as he tried to stroke the top of its head.

He watched it retreating back to the shadows, then settled again, eye to the sight, same as always.

He saw the peeled-paint door opening.

He squinted, watching as first one man, then another, and then another exited through the doorway.

They weren't happy, he could see it, and he knew why.

He smiled.

He shifted the rifle on the rest he had made out of rubble and old rags. He didn't need to worry about the breeze and rain off the river. He was close enough. The bullets he'd polished and cared for would blast through the wind without giving it a second thought.

They just needed the right target for the first shot.

He scrolled through them.

Docker, docker, docker, driver, docker, seaman, too young, too old . . . suit.

One of them was wearing a suit.

Smart, dark, well cut, probably tailored. The man wearing it was walking to the car, squinting in the rain, one hand up to protect his hair.

"Hello," the Bear said quietly, and the rat in the shadows stopped sniffing and looked at him again.

The Bear pulled the trigger.

It felt intimate, the violence passed between them like the brush of a lover's lips.

They were one hundred yards apart, but still locked in an embrace.

Time seemed to stop.

Then there was the telltale spray.

Then the man in the suit dropped down dead.

The Bear breathed out, worked the rifle bolt without moving his elbows or head, then fired again. Like idiots in a silent film, the men from the warehouse were looking down at the body in the suit. One wiped a hand across his own blood-spattered face and stared at it.

The Bear shot him next.

The bolt click-clacked, smooth on its fresh oil.

The Bear breathed out through his nose.

Then shot the kid just behind the ear.

The bolt click-clacked, but this time he heard brass on brass as the ejected cartridge hit another in the rubble near his elbow.

They were ducking now, eyes looking up and around. He could see that a couple of them had pistols in their hands. The streetlamp next to them flickered as the city electricity supply labored under the strain.

One more.

He shot the one crouching on the wrong side of the car.

He deserved to die for being an idiot.

The Bear shifted slightly, trying to mark a target through the side windows of the vehicle. The streetlamp's flicker and the rain made it difficult. He blinked, waited for a shift in a shadow, a sign, something to kill.

Someone shot out the streetlamp.

The Bear waited for his eyes to adjust.

Everything seemed blue, deep blue and black.

He waited.

He sighed. He'd only shot four of them. He'd wanted more. He drifted his aim back to the door, which was still closed, the paint sucking the light out of the sight. He scanned the car again.

Nothing.

He frowned.

Four would have to do.

He thumbed the safety and then, using his elbows, pushed himself up to his feet. He waited a second, the rifle still in his shoulder, his eye near the sight, as he scanned the scene one last time.

Nothing but the pooling blood.

Time to go.

The Bear slung the rifle over his shoulder, then picked up his satchel and StG 44 assault rifle. He turned, took a step, and dropped through a gap in the floorboards down to the floor below. It was almost pitch black, and although his night vision was still weak from the streetlamp, he moved fast. He'd spent long enough beforehand tracing the route out of the warehouse. He knew every broken floorboard, every overhanging beam.

He was the Bear; he didn't make mistakes.

He moved like a slick black cat in the nighttime shadows. Smooth, fluid, light on his toes, with soft words on his lips barely louder than the breath that carried them.

"Four steps, turn right, drop down . . ."

He stopped only once, at the blasted hole in the wall, on the ground floor where he had gained access.

He listened to the falling rain slapping on the cobbles. The alleyway was empty. He tilted his head and opened his mouth. Letting the sounds of the night echo in his mouth.

Nothing.

"Don't forget the doorbell . . ."

He knelt and gently unhooked the almost invisible trip wire from the booby-trapped grenade he had set earlier. He reassembled the grenade quickly and dropped it into his satchel. He picked up his rifle, then stepped through the hole in the wall and out into the dark back alleyway.

"Do not move," a voice barked from behind him. "I mean it . . . do not move one muscle or we will blow your fucking head clean off."

The Englishman sounded like he was about to shit his pants. The Bear weighed the odds as he stared off down the alleyway toward where he had parked his car. He took a breath, quarter-turning his head to the left, looking for a shadow, some clue to where the man behind him was standing.

"Stand still!" Another voice, to his right. "We are police, drop your weapons!"

He was flanked on both sides. He did the calculations and worked out that he would be able to get them both if he dropped to a knee to throw off their aim as he turned. He steadied himself.

"Do as you're told!"

Another one, farther back, judging by the sound of his voice, maybe crouching.

Shit.

He raised his free hand slowly in surrender.

"Okay, I surrender. Let's see where this takes us."

CHAPTER 1

ROSSETT SAT SILENT in the darkness. The sounds of the night set-tled on his shoulders like sorrow, then faded until it was so quiet, he could hear the ticking of his watch drowning out the beating of his heart.

He didn't move.

He barely breathed.

He was alone, patient, staring into nothing. A part of the darkness, as much as it was a part of him.

He knew they were near; they'd come eventually.

He'd be waiting.

"I FIND PUNCHING people rather relaxing." Finnegan rubbed his chin with a hand that looked like a bruised ham and looked across at Hall.

"What?" Hall was tired; the night had been long and his patience was short.

"I'm just saying, I find it relaxing."

Hall shook his head and went back to staring at a poster of the Führer. It was pasted on a sooty black brick wall, right next to where they were parked. Old Adolf was shaking hands with Prime Minister Mosley, who was bending a little at the waist, so as not to look too tall next to his boss.

Hall thought that Mosley looked like a spiv or some sort of ponce with his pencil mustache. He shook his head, embarrassed that that was the best that Britain could come up with to run the country.

Hall frowned. Someone had had a go at ripping the poster off the wall, but only the top left corner had come away. It was hanging limp, damp in the morning air like a mongrel's ear.

GOD SAVE THE KING! was daubed in thick strokes of red paint across Hitler's face. Hall wondered which king they were talking about: the one in England, or his brother, hiding halfway around the world?

"There is something about the 'whump, whump, whump,'" Finnegan started up again. "I don't know . . . it calms me down, makes me feel peaceful."

Hall dragged his eyes away from Hitler and over to the darkened shop on the other side of the road. He willed it to open up for the day so they could get on with what they had gone there to do.

Finnegan kept on talking to nobody but himself.

"When I was a kid, I used to like smacking the sheep's heads my mam would buy to make soup with. I'd take them in the back alley and see if I could break the bones. When my old mam found out she'd try to do the same to me, 'cos I'd gone and ruined the dinner."

"Will you be quiet?" Hall's patience tapped out.

"I'm bored, that's all."

"Be bored quiet."

Finnegan folded his arms and shifted on the leather seat with a squeak. And then a forty-watt bulb across the street saved Hall from more torture.

"Finally," Finnegan said for both of them.

Hall looked around to check nobody was about. Finnegan licked his lips and started to rock slightly, excitement mounting, boredom forgotten, seat creaking softly, as if the springs were getting excited, too.

"Wait till we can see him, all right?" Hall said, trying to put the brakes on his partner.

"Yeah," Finnegan replied, suddenly a man of few words.

"No speeches. Just in and out, there's no need for drama." He looked at his partner. "No drama. Yeah?"

Finnegan's blood was rising; Hall could tell by the sound of the springs creaking faster underneath him. He had another go at reining Finnegan back in.

"Don't kill him. Remember he's an old bloke, he can't pay if he's dead."

"Is that him?" Finnegan pointed toward the shop.

Forty watts can cast a lot of shadows on a dark morning. Both men squinted, looking for movement. Hall checked his watch: 6:50 A.M., nearly opening time.

"Old bastard might just pay and save us the bother," Hall said quietly.

"I hope not," Finnegan replied. "I want to—" He broke off as the silhouette of the shopkeeper appeared at the glass door and turned the CLOSED sign to OPEN. "Here we go."

Finnegan opened the car door.

Hall caught his arm.

"Don't kill him, remember? We just want the money."

Finnegan pulled his arm free and stepped out of the car. The studs in the heels of his shoes cut the quiet of the morning and made it sound colder. He adjusted his coat and pulled up his collar, acting like a gangster in one of the movies they used to show before the war.

From the other side of the car Hall emerged. He also worked his collar, dragging it up so high that he looked like a buzzard waiting for breakfast.

Both men set off across the road toward the shop, breath rising like steam. Finnegan was slightly ahead of his partner, flexing his shoulders and rolling his head on his bull neck as he picked up speed.

The door of the shop opened when Finnegan was five feet from it. He didn't hesitate, his pace certain with the confidence of a man who seldom had to slow down.

In the doorway stood the shopkeeper, openmouthed, carrying a wicker basket of mop heads. The first item for the pavement display he'd put outside every morning, excluding Sundays, Easter, and Christmas, for the last forty-two years, clutched high up on his chest.

Finnegan used the basket to push the old man back into the shop and straight down the center aisle until they slammed into the counter.

Nobody spoke.

A brass bell cheerfully signaled that Hall and Finnegan were inside and the door had closed behind them. Hall paused to turn the sign around to show CLOSED, then checked the street outside.

Finnegan stared, knuckles white on the basket rim as he pushed it into the old man's chest. The wicker creaked, then the old man found the words that shock had scared out of him.

"I ain't paying." In the old man's head, it had sounded more certain than it did on his lips. "I told your boss, and now I'm telling you, I ain't paying."

Over by the door, Hall rolled his eyes.

Finnegan smiled. It was time for the bit he liked second best.

The speech.

"Listen to me." He stared so hard, the old man shut his eyes. Finnegan waited for them to open again before he continued.

"All my life people have told me what ain't happening. Ever since I was a kid. People have told me 'I ain't doin' this' or 'I ain't doin' that.' Do you know what I always say back?"

The basket squeaked and creaked again. Finnegan waited a second. The old man just stared back, eyes scared, breathing quickly in sharp gasps.

"I asked: Do you know what I say?" he asked again.

The old man shook his head.

Finnegan smiled.

"I always say"—his voice dropped to almost a whisper, and the basket strained again as he leaned in even closer—"'You will do what I say.' And do you know what?" Finnegan leaned his head so far forward his lips almost brushed the old man's nose. "They always do . . . in the end."

Finnegan's eyes were hooded, cloaked with the kind of scar tissue that came from being a bad boxer with a sharp skull. Under the scar tissue, black shadows got deeper. He leaned in a tiny bit further, turning up the pressure. The weight of his body distorted the shape of the basket so much, it took on the shape of a closed clamshell.

"I'm going to knock you about a bit now." Finnegan sounded like he was whispering sweet nothings to a lover. "And then, when I'm ready, you're going to tell me where the money is. When you do, I'm going to take it and leave. But that won't be the end of it." He smiled. "Because this time next week, I'm going to come back and repeat the exercise. I'm going to put bruises on your bruises, and then I'm going to take the money all over again. And then maybe, the week after that, if you've learned your lesson, you're going to give me the money and not get a beating." Finnegan paused as he lowered his forehead and rested it against the old man's. "Assuming, of course, you have learned your lesson. If you ain't, if you are as stupid as you look right now, I'm going to kill you. Just like that. And as you lie dying on the floor of this shit-house shop, you'll think to yourself: I wish I'd paid good old Mr. Finnegan. But by then it'll be too late, 'cos you'll be fucking dying and I'll be walking out."

Finnegan eased back and slowly dragged the basket from the old man's hands. He dropped it to the floor and smiled.

"Now, let's me and you get cracking."

"No," said Rossett. "Let's me and you get cracking instead."

Finnegan looked across to the dark corner where Rossett had been sitting. Rossett nodded to the shopkeeper to get out of the way. The shopkeeper slithered around the counter like an eel hiding behind a rock as Finnegan did a half turn.

Hall took a half step forward over by the door.

"Who the fuck are you?"

"I'm your worst nightmare." Rossett kept his eyes on Finnegan as he replied to Hall. "And you two are under arrest for threats to kill, conspiracy to commit murder, and extortion. Oh, and attempting to assault a police officer."

"We haven't attempted to assault a police officer."

"Give it time."

Finnegan shrugged, a little confused, but too dumb to be scared.

"You on your own?"

"Yes."

Finnegan snorted, looked at his partner, then back at Rossett.

"Really?"

"You're not very bright, are you?"

Finnegan frowned, then charged at Rossett like a bull.

Rossett twisted at the waist, flicking the blade of his left hand up into Finnegan's throat as he went past. The big man gasped and a dull reflex drew his hands up to protect himself. He was too late. Rossett's hand was already withdrawing, damage done.

Finnegan stumbled forward. Blinding lights danced in his vision for a second and then he choked. He grabbed at his neck, lungs sucking at a vacuum as his diaphragm twitched and his throat spasmed.

He was wasting his time.

Rossett slammed his left foot into the inside of Finnegan's knee, then took a half step backward as Finnegan fell, his leg twisted out to the side like a newborn deer's. The big man tried to turn as he went down, offering his back as a target. Instead he caught his temple on the corner of some shelves and landed in a stunned, crippled heap.

Finnegan caught the sweet whiff of polish off the well-worn floor. He screwed up his eyes and tried to think himself straight as his breath jammed in his throat like leaves in a drain.

Don't panic. He gulped a quarter breath. Do not panic.

He'd been in enough fights to know panicking got you beaten. He knew the secret was to keep thinking, stay focused, protect your head, and wait for the moment. His breath would come back. He just needed time. Hall would give him that. Hall was always there to cover him. Finnegan just had to wait and protect his head.

Hall would do the copper, no problem.

HALL HAD HIS cutthroat razor out and down at his side.

The copper was good.

Hall had never seen Finnegan put down like that before.

Hall had assumed he wasn't going to be getting involved. But now here he was, razor out of his pocket and his heart pounding in his chest. Slicing up a copper was never going to be a good thing.

Killing one was even worse.

But Hall had a feeling that was what it was going to take. This copper looked like the kind of man who needed killing.

Fuck.

Hall took a few paces toward Rossett and lifted the razor so that he would be able to see it glinting in the dim light. He wanted the copper to focus on it, to worry about it, to watch it coming the way a rat stares into the eyes of a snake.

Hall frowned when the copper didn't seem to notice it.

Rossett stepped away from Finnegan, then walked toward Hall up the aisle as if he were looking for soap on the shelves. He moved fast, but in a way that seemed casual, matter-of-fact, like he was already tired of the fight and just wanted to get it over with.

Hall stopped. Hall started to back up. Hall never backed up.

Hall started to wonder why he was doing it now.

"I'll cut you!" He was surprised at the sound of his own voice.

He never shouted, not ever.

The copper kept coming.

"I mean it!" he shouted again. This time the pitch was so high, he was embarrassed by it.

The copper kept coming, faster, certain.

Like death, black coat open, black suit, black tie, black hair, black eyes.

Death was coming.

Hall swiped with the razor too early, missed, tried to swipe again with a backhand, then felt his forearm being gripped and pushed up into his face. He felt another hand against his elbow. The pressure almost smothered him as he tried to not fall backward onto the floor.

He failed.

He fell backward and cracked his head so hard, he chipped a tooth and bit through his bottom lip.

He couldn't see what was happening, but the weight of the copper pressed down like earth on a coffin. Hall tried to turn his head to get out from under his own arm.

He couldn't.

He tried to pull his other arm around to land a punch. He couldn't. He was locked under, buried in darkness, gravity, death.

He started to panic.

He felt fingers wrap around his hand. Try as he might, he couldn't hold the ivory handle of the razor. He twisted, desperate to get out from under the copper, as he felt the razor slide away from him.

The spare blade, he always carried a spare blade.

Hall struggled to get his free hand under his body and into his back pocket. He squirmed under the copper's weight until he was able to draw his knife. His knuckles scraped on the floor as he slipped, then whipped it to where he thought Rossett's face would be.

It wasn't there.

Hall tried again, lower, and felt the blade dragging through the thick woolen overcoat Rossett was wearing. He pushed harder, trying to angle the knife from a slash to a stab.

Hall heard the slice.

It struck him as strange that he heard it but didn't feel it.

Hall had never considered that having your throat cut wouldn't hurt. He'd always assumed it would hurt like hell. But it didn't, not at first; for a few seconds it just felt strange. Like his face was loose, and the skin around his jaw suddenly didn't fit.

Icy, gasping breath filled his lungs as it washed in through the hole in his throat and then out with a chug of blood onto the floor.

Then, finally, it hurt.

Sharp, high-pitched pain.

Hall was dying. He knew it. He could hear gurgling and the sound of his heels banging on the floor. The pressure on his chest eased. He reached for his throat and felt himself leaking out.

He tried to roll onto his side, but the copper stopped him. Hall gripped at the blood and tried to keep it inside.

He tried to take a breath but felt like he was drowning.

He looked at the ceiling and noticed there was darkness at the edge of his vision. His eyes rolled; he caught a glimpse of Rossett, then the ceiling, then Rossett.

Hall was scared.

He wanted to ask for help.

The ceiling.

Rossett had blood on his face. He was trying to help him, Hall knew it.

Hall knew it was too late.

So dark now.

He wasn't scared anymore.

The darkness became darker still.

He felt like he was sliding into a hole.

Frank Hall died.

ROSSETT SAT OUTSIDE the shop, feet in the gutter, a tuft of white lining on show at the top of his sleeve where the knife had sliced through. Finnegan was cuffed and facedown next to him on the pavement, trussed like a calf at a rodeo.

Rossett stared at the cigarette in his bloodstained fingers.

The paper was dirty red, almost brown.

It tasted bad as it shook.

He'd be sore later. He still wasn't fit. The injuries of the last couple of years were starting to add up. It was getting more and more difficult to keep going to the well, draining himself a little deeper each time.

Maybe he'd come back to work too soon, but what else was he going to do?

Finnegan grunted and flexed at the handcuffs, turning his head so that he could look at Rossett.

"You are dead, copper. I swear to God, you are a dead man."

Rossett ignored Finnegan and stared off into the distance.

Finnegan groaned and flexed again at the cuffs. He tried to roll onto his side to face Rossett but couldn't because of the pain in his busted knee. In the distance the siren of a police car sounded. Finnegan turned his head toward it, then looked back at Rossett.

"You don't know who you're messing with. I'm a dangerous man. Take these cuffs off me and I'll show you—"

"Hush," said Rossett quietly. He put the cigarette back into his mouth and continued staring off into the distance.

BY THE TIME the police car finally made it to them, a few people had interrupted their morning commute to stare at the quiet copper and the handcuffed heavy sitting outside the shop. A slow slick of sticky blood was leaking from the doorway behind them onto the pavement. Rossett ignored it, and the crowd, and just stared into the distance as a sergeant and a young bobby got out of the police car and approached slowly.

The bobby had his truncheon out, ready for trouble, while the sergeant looked past Rossett at the blood on the pavement, then down at Finnegan.

"Who the bleedin' hell are you?" the sergeant said to Rossett.

Rossett held up his warrant card.

"Rossett."

"Rossett?" Finnegan parroted from the pavement. "I got arrested by John Rossett?"

Rossett got up from the curb slowly. His bones were already aching from the fight. He flicked the long-dead stub of his cigarette at Finnegan on the ground and looked at the young bobby.

"Look after him."

"I've read all about you, sir. Can I just say—" The bobby looked starstruck.

"No, you can't." Rossett stepped past him, over the blood, heading back into the shop.

In the small storeroom at the back he found the old man sitting on an old wooden chair next to an even older table. The room was cluttered with stock for the shop. It smelled of bleach, damp cardboard, and forty years of slaving your guts out for pretty much no return. There was a bulb hanging from two twisted wires, and Rossett could see the steam coming off a fresh cup of anemic tea on the table.

"I wasn't expecting that," the shopkeeper finally said, almost to himself.

"Drink some tea."

"The way you killed him."

"It'll help with the shock."

"I wasn't expecting it."

Rossett went to speak, paused, took a look around the storeroom, and tried again.

"What were you expecting?"

"I thought you'd just see them off."

"I'm not a scarecrow."

"You'll make things worse."

"I'm the law. I live by the law, and the law does what it has to do. I have no half measures; I don't scare people. I'm a policeman, I do what I have to do, and I do my job properly. That is who I am."

CHAPTER 2

YOU KILLED A man this morning?"

"Self-defense."

"But you killed him?"

"Yes, sir."

"And you're just sitting here?"

Rossett looked around his office, then back at Kripo Generalmajor Erhard Neumann.

"I think so."

Neumann shifted on the wooden chair he was sitting on. It was uncomfortable, a little too narrow, so he couldn't quite relax. He wondered if that was intentional, a way of keeping people on edge when they sat opposite Rossett in his office. He looked at Rossett, who was staring back at him with eyes that were so blue they were almost silver.

Neumann realized the chair wasn't planned to make people feel uncomfortable. Rossett did that all on his own.

"You were attacked with a razor?"

"Yes."

"Injured?"

"My coat and jacket took most of the damage."

"Most?"

"Most."

"Stitches?"

"In me or the coat?"

Neumann wasn't sure if Rossett was joking, so he waited for a moment to see if there was going to be a smile.

There wasn't.

"In you."

"Just a scratch. I'll live."

"Hmm." Neumann adjusted his balance on the seat. "Someone once told me it would take an army to kill you."

Rossett didn't reply. Instead he folded his hands on top of the paperwork that was piled on his desk. Neumann looked up at the small portrait photograph of King Edward on the wall to his left. It was the picture that hung in every civil servant's office in the country. The king was in full military regalia, staring into the distance with the certainty of someone who was finally in his right place.

On a wall, in a dingy office, with a chest full of medals, holding a hat covered in gold braid.

The medals and the hat were impressive, but it was the Knight's Cross at his throat that caught the eye. It was out of place, wrong, awkward, put there to make a point.

Nazis choking a king and his country.

The portrait was normally placed opposite one of Hitler. The two men looking wistfully across the grime into each other's eyes. In Rossett's office there was a hook, but no Hitler, and even the king hung crooked in his frame.

"Have you heard from Koehler?" Neumann looked like he was talking to the picture.

"Not since he went back to Germany." Rossett looked at the Rolex wristwatch his last boss, Ernst Koehler, had given him the day before he had taken his daughter Anja back to Germany.

Rossett had saved the girl from the resistance, but he hadn't been good enough to save her mother. That was another scar, another black mark on his record, another blemish on his soul.

Koehler didn't see it that way, but Rossett did, and that was all that mattered. He'd failed. Rossett knew what it was like to mourn a wife and child. He'd done his best to save Koehler from suffering the same pain, but ended up saving him only half of it.

After rescuing Koehler's daughter, Rossett had woken up battered, bruised, shot, and stabbed in a military hospital. He'd crossed the line to lawlessness and back trying to save the child—but then, so had Neumann, and that was why he was asking.

Ernst Koehler had nearly taken all of them down. They'd all committed acts that would ensure a firing squad if they ever came to light. But they had saved the girl, and even better than that, they'd gotten away with it.

Getting away with it was one thing, walking away heroes was another. So when Rossett had finally opened his eyes in the hospital, he'd been surprised to find that he wasn't chained to the bed.

He was even more surprised to find out he was a hero all over again.

Not to himself.

But to the Nazis and the Mosley government.

The British Lion had roared, and the papers had loved it. Rossett knew better than to deny the stories. He'd shaken the hands, stared straight ahead, and accepted the bar on his Iron Cross in silence.

On the back of the Rolex was engraved: "To the British Lion, the best of the best, from Anja and Ernst."

Rossett knew it was a lie. Sometimes he thought he could feel the words scratching at his skin, reminding him of what he wasn't, when he was drunk and lying on the floor of his room, staring at the fallen bottle, with the spilled tears on the carpet next to it.

When he was sober, he told himself that the girl was alive and that was all that mattered.

But he didn't believe it.

Neumann interrupted his thoughts.

"So you don't know how Koehler is doing, then?"

"No," replied Rossett.

"Probably for the best."

"I'd imagine so," Rossett concurred.

"Is he coming back?"

"I don't know."

"Would you go and work for him again?" Neumann suddenly seemed embarrassed by his own question. "You know . . . if he came back, would you go back to rounding up the Jews?"

"No."

"You might not have a choice."

"You always have a choice."

Neumann shifted on the chair again, then nodded.

"Yes, I suppose, if you feel that strongly, you would have a choice."

"I'm a policeman now, back to doing what I do best."

Neumann lifted an eyebrow.

"My understanding was that you are office based?"

"I am."

"I wouldn't imagine that suits someone like you."

"I get by."

Rossett's eyes flicked around the desktop for his cigarettes. He spied them peeking out, half crushed under another fresh pile of files that had been dumped that morning.

"I'm told you're nothing but a paper pusher." Neumann went to cross one leg over the other, but decided against it when the chair creaked under him.

Rossett reached for the cigarettes.

"I'm a policeman," he finally said after he lit up and took his first drag.

"You're a celebrity. I read the kids' newspaper they wrote after you saved Koehler's daughter."

"None of that is to do with me, it's all down to the propaganda ministry."

"I heard they are making a film?"

Rossett shrugged.

"Will you be in it?"

Rossett didn't dignify the question with an answer.

"Which actor do you want to play you? I heard they were trying to get

John Mills back from Hollywood, but I think somebody like Roger Livesey or maybe Jack Hawkins? Assuming they would come over here to—"

"What do you want? I'm busy," Rossett lied.

"No, you're not. I checked." Neumann finally risked leaning back and crossing his legs.

"I've work to do."

"You don't. You've paperwork to do."

"It says Detective Inspector on the door, so that means I have detecting to do."

"It doesn't say anything on the door."

"It will when they paint it on." Rossett cursed himself for glancing up at the plain glass pane in the door, then back at Neumann.

"How long have you been down here?"

"Two months."

"Two months and they haven't painted your name on the door?"

Rossett went to reply, but decided it wasn't worth trying to be smart. He took a drag on the cigarette instead.

Neumann tried another angle. "When was the last time you solved a crime?"

"This morning."

"You call cutting a man's throat solving a crime? I'm told that the . . ." Neumann paused, looking for the right word. ". . . the incident this morning was off the books. That you were acting alone, and that there is to be an investigation into what took place."

"You get told a lot about me."

"There's a lot to be told. Such as, senior management are concerned that they can't control you, but they are scared to get rid of you, and that is why they buried you in here."

Rossett moved some files, then slid the ashtray a little closer. Neumann waited to see if he would bite, and when he realized he wasn't going to, tried again.

"What you don't realize is that there are people in Scotland Yard who might want to use what you did this morning as an excuse to get rid of you."

"Rid of me?"

"You embarrass them."

Rossett took another pull on the cigarette and stared at Neumann. The smoke stung his eyes a little. He blinked as he thought about the work he had done for the Germans. The rounding up of the Jews, the clank of the cattle trucks taking them away. The smell of the oil and grease on the rusty locomotive at the head of the train. He could even feel the rough stones of the goods yard digging through the soles of his shoes.

It didn't take much for the memory to come back, the work that shamed him, the killing of the innocents. He knew that whatever embarrassment the Metropolitan Police felt, his was far greater.

He tapped the cigarette against the side of the ashtray and used his thumb to wipe his eye.

"I've done nothing wrong," Rossett lied.

"That's a matter of opinion."

"I've done nothing wrong today."

"Hmm." Neumann didn't sound convinced.

Neumann looked up at the picture of the king again. He couldn't take it anymore. He pushed himself out of the chair, crossed to the photograph, dipped his head an inch, and straightened the frame. He took a half step back and stared at the portrait, his face barely reflected off the grimy glass.

"I want you to come and work with me." It looked like Neumann was talking to the king.

Rossett leaned back in his seat. "You want what?"

Neumann looked at him. "One job. Just try it out, see if you like it."

"With you?"

"Yes."

"No."

"Why?"

"Because I said I wouldn't work for the Germans again."

"I'm a policeman, just like you. The only difference is that I solve crimes committed against Germans or by Germans on British soil."

"You're a Nazi."

"So are you."

Rossett bridled. "I'm not a Nazi."

"You're in the party."

"I had to join."

"So did I."

"You're a German."

"We've already established that." Neumann stepped away from the photograph, checked that it was straight, and crossed Rossett's small office to take up a position by the window. "I can protect you," he finally said.

"I don't need your protection."

Neumann turned to Rossett. "You do. You think you don't, but you do. Those people"—Neumann pointed a finger to the ceiling, as if the top brass of the Met Police were up there looking down—"they stuck you in this office pushing paper for a reason. Do you know what it is?"

Rossett shrugged.

"It is because they hate you. You embarrass them. Sure, you got your medals for being a hero before the war. Sure, you got your name in the papers for being a good party member and working with us after the war. But facts are facts: they hate you because they can't control you. You're violent, you don't play by their rules, you don't bend in the wind, and you're damaged. But they can't stop you because they think they'll upset the Germans, which they will. So they solve the problem by locking you away in here, buried under a pile of paperwork that will never get smaller and matters to nobody."

"That's not true."

"Why were you alone this morning?"

"I work alone."

"Why didn't you take some more men with you? You must have known there would be more than one of them."

"I told you, I like to work alone."

"You're a liar."

Rossett turned in his seat and looked at Neumann, who was still standing by the window. He wanted to object to what Neumann had said, but instead he paused, then relaxed his shoulders a little under the weight of the fact.

It was true.

The reason he was alone was that he didn't trust anyone to back him up. He didn't trust them because they hated him.

He wasn't corrupt.

He'd worked for the Nazis.

He wouldn't bend the rules.

Whatever the reason, they hated him, so he couldn't trust them.

Which meant that Hall was dead. Rossett knew the truth of it. If there had been more police in the shop waiting for Hall and Finnegan, there wouldn't have been a struggle, and Hall wouldn't be dead.

Just another soul scratched on his ledger.

He turned back to his desk and picked up the cigarette pack again. He played with it in his fingers, then noticed the tobacco stains on his hand. He studied his fingers and realized he needed to ease off smoking a little. He put the pack back down and wiped his hand down his face.

"I just want to be a policeman." It sounded pathetic, and Rossett hated himself for saying it.

"Be one with me." Neumann leaned forward and rested his hands on the corner of the desk.

"Why are you bothering with me?" Rossett looked up.

"Because you're the best I can get." Neumann crouched down next to the desk so he was eye level with Rossett and used his first name for the first time. "You'll be a policeman, John. You can fight crime with me, out on the streets again. I can give you that back, and I can protect you from the people who want to get rid of you."

"No."

Neumann pushed back from the desk and wandered back to the rickety chair. He sat down carefully, then leaned forward and rested his elbow on the desk so that he was sitting directly across from Rossett. He took a breath and then he began.

"I got a phone call this morning. From a senior member of the command at Scotland Yard. It may surprise you, but I have friends here. I treat people fairly, I respect you British, and that gets me respect back."

"So?"

"The person who called told me what happened this morning. They told me that you have upset senior members of the London underworld and that you are a marked man. They told me that they can't protect you any longer."

"Protect me?"

"Protect you." Neumann paused, letting the words sink in. "You're hated. Your colleagues hate you, criminals hate you, the resistance hates you. Jesus, everybody hates you . . . except us, the Germans."

"They hate me for doing my job?"

"For doing what you've done, and being the man you are. You've fought the resistance, you've hunted Jews, and on top of that, you're not a bent copper. You haven't changed, you still think it is the old world, and it isn't. The wind blows harder now; people have to bend further . . . but you don't bend at all."

"I don't understand."

Neumann sighed. "This criminal you killed this morning?"

"Hall."

"Hall. Who did he work for?"

"I don't know. I don't care."

"He worked for an organization that, besides being involved in crime, is probably involved in the resistance." Neumann sounded like he was reading his reply off a card.

"So?"

"So." Neumann offered his hand up, like he was passing Rossett an idea. "You have killed one of their men. What do you think will happen?"

"They won't be happy."

"Of course. So you now have some gangsters who want you dead."

"So I'll get them first."

"But these aren't just gangsters, they are resistance. Some of them probably work in this building."

"I don't care."

"Really?" Neumann tilted his head.

"I have the law behind me."

"The only thing you have behind you is a dirty window and a pipe on a wall that carries shit from the upstairs toilets."

Rossett thought about frowning, changed his mind, and just stared back across the table. Neumann continued.

"They are probably getting ready to release Finnegan even as we speak."

"He'll be charged."

"If, and it is a big if, he is charged, it'll probably be with a half-arsed assault on you and he'll get a slap on the wrist."

"He tried to kill me."

"You think the coppers downstairs give a damn about what he tried to do to you? As far as they are concerned, you're no better than me."

"You're wrong."

Neumann flapped his hands in exasperation.

"How many people work for the Met?" He pointed at the ceiling again, and this time Rossett looked up.

"I don't know."

"A few thousand at least. How many of them are happy that the Germans are here?" Neumann pointed at the floor.

"Not many."

"So . . . You worked with us, the Germans. You're their enemy, or at least they think you are. This morning you killed a member of the resistance. A resistance that is probably paying half the coppers in London's take-home pay in bribes."

"He was a gangster."

"What is the difference?" Neumann made to get off the chair again, but then thought better and remained seated. "Most of the resistance are gangsters. Fighting war costs money, and now the Brits aren't getting any from the Americans, they've turned to crime."

Rossett moved his mouth as if he was going to speak, but in the end no words actually came out. He stared at Neumann, judging him, weighing him up the way he would weigh up a suspect before an interview.

Neumann's gray mustache made him look older than Rossett guessed he was. It was the color of the ash on the end of a cigarette, and it aged him to about his mid-fifties. He had the build of a light heavyweight who was finding it tougher to make the weight than he used to. The German was wearing a brown woolen suit, almost a tweed, and it looked decent quality, expensive, same as his shoes.

Rossett took a pull on his cigarette, then looked at his suit cuff. It was worn, almost frayed, the black faded down to the color of an old chalkboard. He rubbed it between his finger and thumb, then looked up at Neumann, who stared back, waiting out the inquisition.

"I don't know," Rossett finally said quietly, then rubbed his eyes with a finger and thumb.

"They want you killed, and these aren't the sort of people who take no for an answer."

Whatever they wanted, Rossett wanted a beer.

He sighed. He suddenly felt tired of talking, tired of fighting.

When he spoke his voice was flat. It sounded like it was coming from the middle of his chest, and Neumann had to lean forward a fraction to pick up all the words.

"I just want it to be simple. I want to see black and white, good and bad, be a copper again. I'm sick of it, I just want to be normal."

"Like before the war?" Neumann's voice was softer, too.

Rossett felt a pressure behind his eyes. He took a breath to ease it, then spoke again.

"Yes."

"The world has changed, John. There's no going back."

"I know that." Rossett felt the tremor in his hands starting up, so he clenched his fists and dropped them into his lap.

"The best you're going to get, all you're going to get, is what I'm offering."

Rossett didn't speak, so Neumann filled the void.

"I can give you back your pride. With me you'll be arresting bad people who have broken the law, pure and simple."

"Germans."

"Germans who commit crime. It's better than what you're doing now. We can be partners; you can be my liaison with the British people who don't want to talk to me. You can cross those bridges, while I protect you from your English bosses and the people who want to stab you in the back." Neumann paused, considering his next words carefully before he finally took a chance on saying them. "I can't offer you your past, John, but I can give you a future that's better than your present."

Rossett looked at the packet of cigarettes and the piles of files that were starting to look like prison walls. He sighed, wiped his hand down his face, then looked up at Neumann.

"It wouldn't be difficult to offer me something better than my present."

"So what do you say?"

Rossett picked up his pen and opened one of the files unconvincingly. "I'll let you know in the morning."

Neumann shook his head. "You need to think about it?"

"I'm one of life's thinkers." Rossett pretended to start reading a crime report.

"That, John, I find hard to believe."

CHAPTER 3

ROSSETT DIDN'T STAY in the little office with its yellow walls, damp drainpipe, and piles of files for long after Neumann left. He was being pushed along by life again, instead of pushing himself, and it made him feel restless and lost, like he was locked in a cell.

He stayed in the pub for longer than he stayed in the office.

A lot longer.

He drank alone, same as usual, nothing but beer and bad Scotch to keep him and his memories company.

He didn't get the tube back to his lodging house. By the time he left the pub it was dark and he was drunk.

Again.

His step was as aimless as the half-tide Thames he walked alongside. He stopped for a while to watch the river as it sat waiting for the tide to turn, hiding under the fog, hoping not to be noticed.

A barge bell was ringing on the swell, lonely, lost in the gray, calling out like it was hoping something else would call back.

Nothing did, so Rossett started moving again to break the spell. He walked, hands in his coat pockets, hat down low, listening to the foghorns down by the docks. They moaned in the night and sounded a million miles away. He stopped. Another match warmed his face as he struck up again, the cigarette smoke lost in the fog as he flicked the match into the murk of the dark water below.

He didn't want to go home.

He ended up sitting at the counter of a half-empty all-night café. Feeling the ache of the alcohol fading, breathing fumes over the waitress, who did her best to stay at arm's length when she leaned in to top up the countless cups of tea he was working his way through. He sat, almost finished a cheese sandwich, and read the faces of the lost and lonely sitting all around him.

Big Ben rang out across the night sky, and told Rossett it was two thirty in the morning.

Another day down.

Another one on the horizon to get through.

The streets were empty except for the sound of distant traffic. He turned into the road where he was renting his latest room and stopped for a moment to stroke a tortoiseshell cat that was sitting on a wall.

The cat dug its head into the palm of his hand. It danced on tiptoes and twisted its body as it closed its eyes and pushed harder. Its fur was smooth and damp with dew. Rossett started walking again, checking over his shoulder to see if the cat was going to follow him.

It didn't.

It sat on the wall, golden eyes watching him walk away. Another lonely soul that didn't want to form a bond, for fear of being let down by life again.

HIS ALARM CLOCK went off at 6:30 A.M.

He knocked it off the table and it continued ringing and rattling on the floorboards, spiteful in its rejection. The bells finally petered out and Rossett rolled onto his back, shielding his eyes with his hand.

He groaned. It was still dark. There was only a hint of yellow light from the streetlamp outside his window. He got out of bed and waited for a thirty-second coughing fit to pass. His body ached, his head ached, and his stomach ached. He stared at the rung-out clock on the floor at his feet, listening to its quick tick echo off the wooden boards.

The view out the window wasn't much, just the streetlamp, his old battered Austin Seven car, and a terrace of sooty brown houses staring back like a solid wall of misery through the early-morning fog.

He crossed to the sink, flicked on the light that was hanging over it, and stared at the fresh bruises on his chest and arms from the fight the day before.

He remembered Hall.

He turned on the tap, and the pipe in the wall rattled with a choking airlock before coughing some water into the sink. He drank from his hand and spat before staring into the mirror again.

Hall had had to die.

Rossett had had no choice.

Kill or be killed.

Rossett filled the dented metal kettle and dropped it onto the two-ring stove in the corner of the room. As the stove hissed some warmth into the bedsit, he did some push-ups to get some heat into his body and some ache out of his muscles.

By the time the kettle had boiled he was blowing hard, lying on his back on the floor staring at the stained ceiling. He was slowing down, he knew it. A life of drinking and smoking, coupled with old wounds, was working against him now. The shootings, the stabbings, the scars on his back and on his front made him feel like he was wading through water.

He wondered when he would be swept away.

THE TOP DECK of the bus was empty except for two office cleaning women on their way to work. They didn't stop talking from Battersea to Vauxhall Bridge, where they got off, their wide backsides bouncing off alternate seats as they headed for the stairs. When they were gone Rossett sat in silence, gently rocking his way to Scotland Yard as the bus rattled down the early-morning streets.

At Scotland Yard he sat alone in the canteen. He drank another cup of tea and pushed the cooked breakfast he had ordered around the plate. He finally settled on hiding the food under a piece of toast, same as he always did, and slid the plate away across the empty table.

The canteen was filling up with early-rising and late-to-bed coppers. Some chatted, some sat alone, but none of them acknowledged him.

Rossett looked at the Rolex and then up at Harding, the admin sergeant who telephoned him once a week to complain about his poor paperwork skills. Rossett had gotten good at avoiding Harding, but obviously not good enough.

"Sergeant."

It was the best Rossett could manage as a greeting.

"Sir."

"What?" Rossett asked, even though he knew what was coming next.

"Sir, this is very difficult for me."

"Say what you've got to say." Rossett tried to sound friendly, failed, and realized it was something he should maybe work on.

"Sir . . . your paperwork. It is late and it is causing a backlog."

"I know."

"You're a month behind."

"I know."

"I'm under a lot of pressure, sir." Harding wrung his hands together as Rossett sipped his tea, all the while staring over the top of the cup. "I know you don't want to be dealing with admin, sir. I know it isn't what you . . ." Harding glanced around. "It isn't what you are good at, I know that." Harding dropped his voice and bent forward a little at the waist. "I respect you, sir, despite what people say. I genuinely respect you. Maybe I can help you?"

"What people say?"

Harding held up a hand.

"I didn't mean to . . ."

Neumann appeared next to Harding, who looked ready to kiss him for helping him out of the hole he had just dug for himself.

"Good morning," Neumann said in his excellent English.

Rossett held up a hand to cut Neumann off so he could continue interrogating Harding. "What do people say?"

"They don't say anything, sir."

"What?" Neumann looked confused.

Rossett held up his hand again. "You said—"

"I didn't mean anything, sir. I only wanted to—"

"What did he say?" Neumann again.

"I didn't, sir." Harding looked like he was going to faint. "I just wanted to know about the paperwork."

"Paperwork?" Neumann smiled.

"Please?" Rossett looked at Neumann and then back at Harding. "You said 'despite what people say.' What did you mean?"

"Please, sir, I just wanted—"

"Have you seen the paperwork on his desk?" Neumann flicked a thumb toward Rossett. "You'd be better off with a box of matches than a filing system."

Harding forced a smile and took a step back from the table. "I'd better be leaving."

"What did you mean?"

"I really must be getting on." Harding nodded at Neumann and headed for the door almost at a run.

Rossett watched him go as Neumann pulled out a chair and sat down opposite Rossett.

"Friend of yours?" he said as he inspected what was left on Rossett's plate.

"No."

"Colleague?"

"No."

Neumann looked up from the plate.

"You're not hungry?"

"No."

Neumann smiled.

"So have you given it some thought?"

"What?"

"About working with me."

Rossett stared at Neumann, then at the door through which Harding had run.

"How much paperwork is there?"

"I don't know . . . I have a secretary, so not much, I suppose."

Rossett paused before answering. "I'll work with you."

"Just like that?"

"Just like that."

"Good, because we've just got our first job together."

"Already?"

"Already."

"I'll need to give some notice, tidy stuff up admin-wise before—"

"You don't. You're coming with me."

Rossett tilted his head.

"I made a call yesterday. It mustn't have trickled down to your friend yet." Neumann waved in the direction of the exit.

"But I hadn't decided what I was going to do."

"No, but I knew which way you would go."

"You knew?"

"I'm a good judge of people."

They stared at each other over the table for a moment until Rossett finally spoke again.

"So anything I have outstanding?"

"My department will make it go away."

"I've a prisoner in the cells, from yesterday."

"Poof." Neumann looked up at the ceiling as he blew out his cheeks, and then smiled at Rossett. "He just went away."

"Just like that?"

"Just like that."

Rossett considered his options. It didn't take long.

"So what's the job?"

Neumann smiled.

"We've got a dead consul in Liverpool."

"Liverpool?"

"Up north, you know it?"

"Yes, I know it, I just didn't expect to be dealing with jobs up there."

"We go where the work is. Besides, the change will do you good."

Rossett found it hard to argue with that, so instead he asked for more detail.

"Dead diplomat?"

"Consul. American. Report says he was shot by a captain from the SS."

"What for?"

"That's what we are going to investigate."

"What else do we know?"

"From what little we have, some British police heard shooting, went to investigate, and arrested the German carrying a rifle."

"They arrested a German with a rifle?" Rossett couldn't hide his incredulity.

"Apparently the officer concerned was on his own, and out of uniform."

"So?"

"There was an old sergeant there who insisted on making the arrest."

"Is he mad?"

Neumann shrugged.

"Maybe he is just one of the old school who thinks being a policeman means enforcing the law."

Rossett felt his face flush.

"Yeah, of course."

"Either way, they heard shooting, searched the area, found a German with a gun and a consul with a hole in his head. The SS officer wouldn't speak to them, and with it being a U.S. citizen, they had no choice but to notify us. All the German had to say was that he thought the consul went for a gun after being challenged. He would have been back in the barracks before the body was cold."

"Indeed." Rossett lifted the piece of cold toast, thought about taking a bite, then tapped it a few times on the edge of the plate, then dropped it back down to cover the food it had been hiding once again.

"So what do we do?"

"We go solve our first case."

———

THEIR FOOTSTEPS ECHOED in the stairwell as they descended toward the car park at the back of Scotland Yard.

"The local police up there want him out of the cells as soon as possible; they have enough trouble on their hands as it is." Neumann was speaking over his shoulder as he led the way.

"With what?"

Neumann slowed slightly, so they were walking side by side.

"Haven't you heard?" he lowered his voice.

"What?"

"About the north, the way things are?"

"I don't read the papers."

"It isn't in the papers." Neumann stopped, rested a hand on Rossett's elbow, and eased him into a corner on the stairwell landing. "My job—our job—requires a lot of traveling up and down the country. We hear things and see things that aren't in the papers. Do you understand?"

"Like what?"

"Not all of Great Britain is as safe and well run as the southeast and London. The rest of the country isn't much of a priority to the government outside of maintaining the coal fields, the docks, and a few bits of industry here and there."

"So?"

"It's in a bad state, John." Neumann leaned in close. "People are hungry, money is scarce. Most of the young men have either been moved to work on the continent or have volunteered to fight out east. Times are hard, so the families that don't have work mostly live on what their young men send back from abroad."

"Is there unrest?"

"There were food riots last year in a few places. It got pretty bad here and there, so much so that the government had to ease rationing to calm things down."

"Doesn't sound good."

"It's not just rioting. Some pockets of the resistance cause problems. Bombs, assassinations, occasional kidnapping, and all that. From what

I've heard, though, support can be thin on the ground for them, what with the reprisals."

"Reprisals?"

Neumann paused and listened to some footsteps on the stairs a few flights above them. Once he was sure they weren't coming closer, he drew close and continued.

"Local commanders can be pretty brutal when they want to impose order. Local government is also having problems with running things—electricity and gas, distribution of food, pretty much everything. Some cities have imposed curfews, but most don't really have a functioning police force to make sure people obey them. The occupying army is spread pretty thin up there as well, so they mostly rely on HDT."

Rossett frowned.

The Home Defense Troops were mostly made up of ex-criminals or old fascists from before the war. Many had simply signed up for the extra rations and the chance to beat people up and throw their weight around. They were the dregs of society given a uniform and a big stick to go with it. They were disliked by most Germans and despised by most British.

"You could have told me this before I took the job." Rossett started to descend the stairwell again.

"It shouldn't affect us," Neumann said, following. "We go in, do what we have to do, and if we need to, bring the prisoner back with us. In and out, simple as that."

"I've heard that before."

WHEN THEY ENTERED the small courtyard car park the overnight fog had lifted. In its place was a soft sheen of drizzle. The sun was behind clouds, unable to make a dent in the late-autumn gloom.

Several cars were parked around the edge of the courtyard, all of them black, except for a dark blue SS Jaguar 2.5 saloon.

Neumann headed for the Jaguar.

"We're going in this?" Rossett stopped short of the long hood.

"We can't go in a Mercedes or an Opal, we'd stand out a mile. And there is no way I'm using your Austin, it's ridiculous."

Rossett pointed at the hood, which actually looked longer than his Austin's.

"You don't think this stands out?"

"It won't be a problem in Liverpool, we'll park it somewhere secure and use a local car if we have to. Do you need to pick anything up from home?" Neumann tossed Rossett the keys.

"We go now?"

"You have other plans?"

"No, but—"

"So we go now."

"How long for?"

"A night at the most. Like I said: in and out."

"Just like that?"

"Just like that." Neumann smiled.

Rossett shook his head and climbed into the Jaguar. The red leather interior smelled new. The seats were deep and comfortable, and the caramel walnut dash was polished to within an inch of its life.

"It belonged to an army general of cavalry. He donated it, just before he went home last year." Neumann got into the passenger seat.

"Donated?" Rossett looked down at his feet, then fired up the engine. It grumbled and settled down to a purr, like a cat that had been woken up and then discovered it was lying in the sun.

"The general had been embarrassed in a brothel in Oxford. As a result of that embarrassment, a significant amount of German stores had been diverted to the black market."

"Speak English." Rossett was fiddling with the controls.

"He was being blackmailed and gave away eight tons of army field rations to keep things quiet."

"All that just for sleeping with a prostitute?" Rossett looked at Neumann. "Pretty much every German over here does it."

"Not with male prostitutes."

"Oh."

"Indeed." Neumann reached around to the backseat and pulled a brown leather briefcase onto his lap. He opened the case and Rossett saw a Luger 9mm pistol on top of some papers. Neumann picked up the pistol, checked the safety, and passed it butt first to Rossett. "You'll need a weapon."

Rossett took the Luger. "Then why didn't you get me one?"

"What?"

Rossett released the pistol's thin magazine from the grip. He checked the breech and started to thumb the rounds out of the magazine into the palm of his hand.

"What are you carrying?" he looked at Neumann.

"A Walther."

"PPK?" Rossett dropped the rounds into his lap and started to disassemble the Luger.

"Yes."

"Hmm."

Neumann started to sort through the paperwork in the case while Rossett worked his way through the pistol. After half a minute Rossett dropped the parts of the pistol and the loose rounds onto the paperwork in the case.

"It's rubbish."

"It's a good pistol," Neumann protested.

"It's unreliable and difficult to work with."

"I would have thought you were made for each other."

"I'll take my Webley."

"An old revolver?"

"It's big and simple."

"Like I said, made for each other."

CHAPTER 4

LIVERPOOL

STURMBANNFÜHRER THEO DANNECKER had a hangover.

He'd first started drinking to help himself sleep about four years ago, and at first, it had helped. Lately, though, it seemed to throw him into a dark tunnel from which he emerged the next morning blinking like a tramp stumbling out of a thicket after being mugged.

He squeezed his temples with both hands, then wiped his hands down his face, aware that his driver was watching him out of the corner of his eye.

Dannecker wasn't a happy man, and it wasn't just the hangover that was making him sad. He was tired. Tired of everything. Tired of being in command, tired of being in the SS, tired of his men, tired of the resistance, the fighting, the uniform, the length of time since he'd been home, the chance that he might make a mistake and end up on the end of a length of piano wire, but most of all, he was tired of the sheer pointlessness of what he did for a living.

He'd served in the Waffen SS for eleven years. First as an enlisted man and then as an officer. He'd been promoted in the field after excelling on the battlefield, then on the streets of occupied Europe.

His last posting had been the frozen tundra out east. In the wilds where what was left of the Soviet military machine had retreated after the fall of Moscow and the escape from the Urals.

Dannecker had traveled for days on the troop train, listening to the wheels on the tracks for hour after hour of head-nodding boredom.

The rattle-clatter had reminded him of when a needle was stuck at the end of a record. Repeating the same rough note, over and over again, for what seemed like an eternity. Hour after hour of clicking track, followed by month after month of the grim brutality of the work he'd been asked to do.

He had done it, though.

He'd suppressed what was left of the tattered and battered Soviet population and made them sorry they were ever born.

He hadn't hated them; he just hadn't cared about them.

They were less than grit trapped in his boot.

He'd done things he wouldn't have been able to imagine years before. He'd shot, stabbed, slashed, and slaughtered his passage to hell.

He'd killed so many times that taking a life was now like taking a sip of cold coffee.

He didn't feel guilt, but he did hate it.

He hated it because he knew it was all so pointless.

And the knowing was the worst.

None of it mattered.

There had been a time when Dannecker had cared about Germany and the Führer, and nothing else. There had been a time that whenever he heard the "Horst-Wessel-Lied" being sung his eyes would mist over, and he would have to get to his feet and link arms with the monster standing next to him.

But all that was gone.

He'd seen through it.

It was a sham, and the madness of it all was now apparent. It was broken; he was broken; the whole Reich was broken. He no longer cared because there was nothing he could do about it. Except try to survive and make it out the other side.

The car thudded through a pothole and his forehead brushed against the cold glass of the side window.

"Shithole," he said quietly to himself.

"Sir?" His driver looked at him.

"I said that this place is a shithole." Dannecker turned to face him.

"Yes, sir." The driver looked away.

"Do you have a cigarette, Muller?"

"No, sir."

"Fuck's sake."

"Sorry, sir."

Dannecker rested his chin in his hand and went back to the window. The car banged through another pothole. This one was filled with oily brown water that erupted and plumed across the pavement and onto two young women walking to work. They threw up their hands, but dropped them quickly when they saw the armored half-track full of Waffen SS soldiers following Dannecker's staff car.

The soldiers on the back of the half-track whistled and shouted at the women, who in turn spun away to look at their dripping reflections in an empty shop window.

Dannecker smoothed the front of his uniform and twisted the driver's mirror around so he could check his appearance. He wiped his hand across his cropped hair, then pulled at the collar of his tunic and adjusted his Iron Cross. He looked over his shoulder out the back window to check that the half-track was still behind them, and then leaned forward to look at the sky out of the windscreen.

Heavy clouds.

England.

Did it ever stop raining?

"May I have my mirror back, sir?"

"Take it, there's nothing in it I want to see."

The staff car pulled in to the curb, while the half-track stopped in the middle of the road to provide cover. The soldiers on the half-track were tumbling down and taking up positions on either side of the street before Dannecker even had his door open. A few of them paused, looked lost, and then followed their colleagues and dodged closer to walls and parked cars. Dannecker stepped out, looked around at the tall office buildings that surrounded Hope Street police station, and placed his cap on his head. He kicked the car door shut with his heel, then bent slightly at the waist to use the reflection in the window to check that his cap was on straight.

Across the street there was a clatter as someone dropped his rifle. Dannecker looked across at Staff Sergeant Paul Becker.

Becker shrugged a what-can-I-do sort of shrug, then glared at the men spread out around him.

Becker dominated the street, all six feet four of him, head held high, a challenge to snipers, unlike his men, who were crouching low and dodging around. Becker slung his StG 44 machine gun over his shoulder and walked around the half-track to join Dannecker.

Dannecker didn't return the salute.

"Who dropped his rifle?"

"Kraus, sir."

"Jesus, where do they find them?" Dannecker didn't wait for an answer from either Jesus or Becker. Instead, he turned and walked up the steps into the police station.

Becker followed his boss.

Same as he always did, without orders and without questions.

CHIEF SUPERINTENDENT JAMES Evans hated his job.

He wasn't scheduled for retirement for another four years, but even if he made it that far, he doubted they'd let him go. Police pensions had been slashed, so even if they did, he probably wouldn't.

He was trapped, and he knew it.

The police force had become a cutthroat world where the wrong word or step could lead to you being sacked, imprisoned, shot, or disappeared.

Either by the Germans or the resistance.

Evans didn't know which was worse, and he hoped he would never find out.

Every day was filled with dread.

Every day was worse than the one before.

Every day he wished he were dead.

He had joined the job just after the 1919 Liverpool police strike. Back when half the force had been sacked overnight for daring to stand up for their rights. Evans had answered an advert in his local paper, then jumped on a train from Wales to Liverpool and never looked back. For six years he hadn't thought about promotion. For six years he'd been happy to be a simple bobby walking the beat. Then one day he met a girl who wanted a husband who was better than a beat bobby, so he'd worked hard and become a detective. It wasn't long before that wasn't good enough, either, so he became a detective sergeant, and then an inspector, with a car and a mortgage that looked like it was never going to go away.

He'd have stayed an inspector if the war hadn't come along, then the invasion. He was the only senior officer who hadn't been part of the final stand as the Germans took control of the city. Many coppers had fought alongside the last troops who held out, and the ones who had survived were long gone, away working on the continent.

Evans hadn't been a coward that day. Surgery on a burst appendix had deprived him of the chance of being a hero, pretty much the same as it had deprived him of dying and getting it over with.

As a result of being alive, he was all that was left of the officer class in Liverpool. He'd been sucked into an unhappy vacuum, and that vacuum had just sucked a Waffen SS major, and the biggest, scariest-looking staff sergeant he had ever seen, to the other side of his desk.

Evans put down his pen. Behind the German staff sergeant, Mrs. Kenny, Evans's secretary, peeked around and lifted one hand to the ceiling in a what-was-I-supposed-to-do gesture.

Evans didn't know what to do, either.

Dannecker sat down and tossed his cap onto Evans's desk. Becker took up position leaning against a filing cabinet. The butt of his StG 44 banged against it, causing Evans to flinch.

"Good afternoon, Chief Superintendent."

"Good afternoon, Major Dannecker."

"You know why I am here?"

"I do, sir."

"Why am I here?"

"I have one of your men in custody."

"Why is that?"

Becker, over by the cabinet, adjusted his position slightly and Evans looked up at him. The big German stared back so blankly, Evans felt like he was falling into a trance. It took him a few seconds to finally drag his attention back to Dannecker.

"He was involved in a shooting; he killed an Amer—"

"Do you know what?" Dannecker cut Evans off by airily waving his hand as he turned his head away. "I really don't care about all of that. Honestly, I'm sorry I asked. Just tell me why he is in your cells."

Evan reached for the pen he'd put down moments ago, swallowed, and then tried again.

"As I was saying, he is accused of—"

"Who do you think you are?" Dannecker interrupted again.

"Excuse me?" Evans looked at Dannecker, then Becker.

"Who do you think you are?" Dannecker said it again, his voice low, his German accent loose around the edges of his clipped English.

"I . . . I don't know." Evans leaned back from his desk an inch. He realized his secretary had retreated and silently closed the door behind her.

He was alone.

He put the pen down again, being careful not to let it make a sound on the desktop.

"Answer the question." Dannecker tilted his head this time.

Evans swallowed. He didn't know what to say, so he said nothing.

Dannecker squinted, then rubbed his right temple with the palm of his hand. When he finally spoke he sounded exhausted.

"I have a terrible headache, and I am very, very tired." He dropped his hand into his lap. "So to speed things up, I'll tell you who you are, Chief Superintendent. That way if you are stupid enough to meet me again under these circumstances, it'll save us some time." Dannecker paused, stared, then smiled.

"You are nobody." Dannecker waited to see if Evans wanted to say anything, then continued when he was satisfied the Englishman didn't. "You are a failed policeman in a failed city. You don't want this job, and I don't blame you. It is a shit job. Only an idiot would want it. The problem you have, though, is that you've made it shitter than it need be. Much, much, shitter."

"Major, I had no choice . . ."

"Considerably shitter." Becker spoke for the first time.

"Even the staff sergeant agrees with me, Chief Superintendent. You have a shit job, and you are doing a shit job of it."

Evans tried again with Dannecker. "What am I supposed to do? Your man committed a . . ." Evans paused, then lifted his hands toward Dannecker. "What am I supposed to do?"

"You telephone me and we sort it out," Dannecker said quietly. "You don't hold him without telling me."

"If . . ." Evans leaned forward, hands still out in front of him, as if he were trying to hand the words he couldn't find over the table. "If it had been an Englishman he'd shot, I could have done that. But this is an American, sir, and a consul at that. The arresting officers contacted London before I could intervene. I had to do something." Evans turned to Becker, desperate for support from someone. "Your man didn't even try to explain to the arresting officers what was going on. If he had, maybe he could have talked himself out of the arrest. But he didn't even try, Major. What were they to do?"

Dannecker broke the silence after a few seconds.

"Where is Captain Bauer?"

Evans swallowed. "I can't release him. Please, I really can't."

"Where is he?"

"Please, Major." Evans was coming apart. "Just wait until your German police liaison officer gets into town, I'm begging you. I'm sure he'll sort things out."

"Liaison officer?"

"I have . . . we have . . . a procedure. I must follow it, sir. It really isn't in my hands. We have to call London, the Home Office. They set the wheels in motion for matters such as this."

Becker shifted over by the filing cabinet, the butt of his assault rifle ringing out again. Both Dannecker and Evans looked at him, then back at each other.

"Who is this liaison officer?" Dannecker's voice was soft now, his hangover back with a sudden solid ache.

Evans scanned the top of his desk and then picked up a piece of paper.

"Generalmajor Neumann, and a Detective Inspector Rossett."

"An Englishman? They're sending an Englishman to question a German?"

The paper fluttered in Evans's hand for half a second like a bird held by one foot. He quickly placed it down on the desk, then laid the palm of his hand flat across it in a poor attempt to hide his nerves.

"According to this he is attached to the Kripo, sir."

"Well, he can unattach and then kiss my arse."

"I don't think Detective Inspector Rossett is the sort of man to do that, sir."

Dannecker tilted his head, unsure if his authority had just been challenged.

"He'll do as he is told."

"If it is the Rossett I think it is, I'm not sure he will, sir."

"And who do you think it is?"

"He's a hero, sir."

"The world is full of fucking heroes; you're looking at two of them now."

"Rossett was famous, sir. He won the Victoria Cross."

Dannecker tilted his head, so Evans elaborated. "It's the highest award for bravery in the British army. They are making a movie about him."

"I've got an Iron Cross."

"With respect, sir."

"It had better be."

"It honestly is, sir . . ." Evans waited to see if Dannecker was going to up the stakes again. He didn't, so Evans continued. "With a great deal of respect, Major, the Victoria Cross is hardly ever awarded, and Rossett's was presented to him by the king himself."

"Which one?"

"The old one."

"So he fought against us?"

"Yes, sir."

"And now he works with us?"

"Yes, sir. I think he's also got an Iron Cross now."

"I don't care," Dannecker interrupted, but sounded less certain than he'd hoped. "He'll do as he is told, and so will you. Release my man."

"Sir, you have to understand, I—"

Dannecker leaned in close to the desk and raised a finger, cutting off Evans midflow. He waited, just a second or two, and then pointed at Becker.

"Look at him."

Evans did as he was told.

Dannecker waited for the Englishman to swallow a knot of nerves, then leaned in even closer across the desk and whispered.

"You are about five seconds away from him pulling out his gun and shooting you in your fat fucking face."

The clock on the wall ticked three times, then Evans picked up the phone on his desk and rang downstairs to the jail.

SEVEN HOURS LATER, Neumann leaned forward a little too far and had to grab the corner of Evans's desk to steady himself.

"You did what?"

"I had no choice. They came into my office, what was I supposed to do?" Evans looked up at Rossett, who was standing where Staff Sergeant Becker had been earlier, but taking up slightly less room.

"You're supposed to be a policeman," Rossett said quietly.

"You don't know what they are like." Evans pointed a finger at Rossett, happy to be arguing with an Englishman for a change. "These men are dangerous, they can do what they want in this city, and for miles around. So don't you judge me, Inspector. I have a family. I have to go home at night." Evans shook his head, his voice fading away. "I do what

I have to do to stay alive. You don't have to deal with them day to day the way I do." He looked down at his desk before adding quietly, "I have a very difficult job."

Rossett turned away to look out the window at the gathering gloom of the Liverpool evening.

Evans's mouth opened, closed, and opened again before he made one last attempt to justify his position, this time to Neumann.

"You don't know what it is like; you have no idea how hard it is here now. This isn't London, this is Liverpool."

"The law is the same," Rossett said quietly, eyes still on the window.

"Not anymore." The fight was gone out of Evans. He took a breath and sighed, deflating as the breath left his body. "This city has fallen apart; it barely functions as a place to live for civilized people. We get no money, the schools have closed, the libraries have closed, the museums have been looted, and the local politicians roll over and do the government's bidding with barely a whimper. And I for one don't blame them, because if you dare to complain . . ." He shook his head and looked at Neumann.

"Do you know how many guns are floating around here? Not just German ones, either. Do you know?" He waited a moment for an answer that didn't come, and then continued. "There were thousands left at the docks in the evacuation, thousands. After the surrender the port was full of men desperate to get out of the country. Most of them bought their passage on a ship with anything they had, including their weapons. It was chaos then, and it is worse now. I've got families and gangs fighting for control of the black market and the brothels. Even the Germans are up to their eyes in crime. My uniformed officers go out on patrol in groups of four at the very least, and even then they won't leave the city center unless they are in a car. We don't have control, and neither do the Home Defense Troops."

"Who does?" Neumann glanced at Rossett, who was still staring out the window.

"Nobody, not really."

"The Germans?" Neumann tried again.

"Just the docks, the airport, and the goods railway to London. The rest can go to hell as far as they are concerned. The running of the city is down to us and the local council, and we can barely cope." Evans glanced at his wristwatch.

"So you don't bother trying," said Rossett.

"What's the point of trying? I've got people who are hungry and poor, I've got an infrastructure that has broken down, half the time the electricity is off or the phones are down. Liverpool is like a desert island and nobody cares, least of all a small group of police constables who aren't paid on a regular basis. This is supposed to be a British-controlled zone, and yet the British either don't care, can't cope, or are corrupt and only interested in London." Evans looked at Rossett.

"Which one are you?" Rossett asked, but Evans ignored the question.

"There is money to be made. Black markets in food, petrol, clothing, women, booze, the lot. I've got gangs running the docks, gangs running the city center, I've got gangs running pubs, clubs, brothels, and drug dens. I'm supposed to police a city with thirty-three bobbies who are mostly too scared to leave their stations."

"Thirty-three?" Neumann shook his head.

"Thirty-three. The budget is gone, and keeping hold of the people we can afford to pay is even worse. Would you want the job?" Evans looked at Neumann and then Rossett. When neither of them replied he shrugged his shoulders. "Exactly. I'm only here because I've got nowhere else to go."

He sank back into his chair. His final statement hanging in the air like a bad smell.

Rossett turned back to the window, which looked out over the street where he had parked the Jaguar. It sat glistening, speckled with drops of rain in the glow of the few streetlamps that were still working. Other than their car the area was deserted, except for the odd pile of rubbish here and there. He suddenly felt tired, and he rested a shoulder against the wall. It had been a long drive through almost constant rain from London, he was hungry, and he needed some sleep.

The room was silent behind him a minute before Neumann finally spoke.

"I still need the SS officer who was arrested."

"Can't we blame the resistance? I can have someone picked up so we have a body to interview and then hand over to the court in London. Between us we can say there was a mistake involving the arrest." Evans leaned back so far in his chair, Neumann briefly thought it was going to tip backward.

"You're asking me to not do my job?" Neumann tilted his head.

"I'm just trying to find a solution that works."

"Just because you've given up doesn't mean we have to," Rossett said to the window, his breath misting it slightly.

Evans tried again with Neumann.

"You don't know these people."

"I'm the law, German law. This SS major will do as he is told." Neumann sounded almost like he was trying to convince himself. "If we don't deal with it in the correct manner, I'll have the American embassy complaining, and the people who sent me here will send me to Moscow next."

Evans looked like he was about to faint. He wiped his eyes again. The docks of Liverpool were full of American ships and cargo. What little work there was in Liverpool that paid decent money relied on those ships. The thought of it being in jeopardy made his stomach churn.

"If the Americans clear off out of the city, it'll be finished. The only reason Liverpool is still here is because of the docks, and those docks are busy with Yank ships." Evans now had his face buried in both hands. His voice was muffled as it pushed its way past his palms.

"So you understand the importance?"

Evans lifted his head just enough so that he could look at Neumann through his fingers.

"I already know the importance, but I have to stay here after you've gone. I have to live here, and I'll not risk my life over this. You do what you have to, you speak to who you have to speak to." He pointed a finger across the desk at Neumann. "But if you try to drag me into this, I'm off. I'll resign and so will half of my men. Sometimes a job just stops being worth it, and this is one of those times."

"We've got a suspect, we know where he is, so we need to go arrest him," Rossett said to Neumann. "I'm tired of this."

"You want to go to an SS garrison and arrest one of them?" Neumann twisted to look at him.

"Yes."

"Two of us?" Neumann hooked his arm over the back of the chair. "We just walk in and stick on the cuffs?"

"It's our job."

Neumann considered the situation for a moment as he smoothed his finger and thumb across his mustache, then looked back at Rossett.

"We may need to plan a method of approach."

"I'm a detective with a corpse, a suspect, and a location for the suspect."

"So you want to do your job?"

"That's why you gave it to me."

Neumann nodded.

"Okay. We go get him tomorrow."

CHAPTER 5

NEUMANN AND ROSSETT checked into the Adelphi Hotel on Liverpool's Brownlow Hill at 8:50 P.M. Rossett left Neumann filling in the register at the front desk and drove the Jaguar around to the secure car park at the rear of the hotel.

Three night watchmen were huddled around a battered, soot-blackened oil drum inside of which Rossett could see an insipid smoky fire burning. All three of the watchmen turned to look at him as he lowered the window.

"I need to park the car." Rossett could smell burning rubber, and he pushed the window back up an inch to try to keep the smoke out.

One of the men, twiglike, wrapped in too-big clothes bundled with a thick leather belt, bent a little at the waist and looked like he was going to snap. He had a salt-and-pepper beard that looked orange in the reflection of the fire. It was so thick it exaggerated his chin's movement as he squinted through the smoke at Rossett and made it look like his face was folding in half.

The old man pointed to the gloom just inside the entrance of the dark warehouse that doubled as a car park.

"Leave it there, I'll park it for you." The fire was lighting the watchman's face from below, catching sooty shadows that danced around his eyes and made the beard seem to move even more.

A flame flickered and popped its head over the rim of the oil drum.

Rossett saw that the light from the fire was pretty much all there was in the garage. He realized that most of the streetlamps outside weren't working, same as outside the police station.

The place was falling apart.

"I'll park it," he replied to the old man.

"We're supposed to do it."

Another one of the watchmen wiped the back of a fingerless glove across his face, smearing a little soot like war paint across the bridge of his nose.

Rossett didn't reply.

"Throw it in the far corner." The first man went back to staring into the fire.

There was no point in arguing.

The Jaguar's headlamps cut through the gloom, sharp, straight edges of white pushing back the night as Rossett entered the garage. It was almost empty except for a few cars covered in thick layers of dirt. Most looked like they hadn't been moved for years.

Rossett parked the Jaguar next to an old Rover saloon in the farthest corner of the warehouse. He got out of the car and noticed that rain was dripping through a hole in the roof and slapping onto the concrete floor. He looked up at the sky through the hole for a moment, then locked the Jaguar.

Rossett strolled the hundred yards back to the hotel slowly, through a rain so fine it was almost mist. It was as if a cloud had descended to take a look around Liverpool's empty streets, and then stayed the night.

A tram clattered past. Rossett watched as sparks bounced off its roof. It swung around a street corner, then headed away from the hotel. There was a pub on the far side of the road. The lights were off, and the only movement was the slow swing of the sign hanging above the door.

The city was dead.

He stopped at the bottom of the steps that led up to the entrance of the hotel, sparked up a cigarette, then watched the streets. Always the copper, first one way, then the next, eyes everywhere, taking it in, the lay of the land. A shop front was illumined, way off to his left. The light from the window display dashed the wet pavement with a watery yellow of mattes and glosses.

Rossett saw movement. There and then gone. He stepped back into the shadows and watched as another tram clattered past. He didn't move an inch as the tram whined away into the night and the street fell silent again.

More movement, a shadow at first, then a figure. All Rossett could make out was a bundle of rags tied in the middle. It was a kid, the first person he'd seen since he'd left the garage, sifting through a rubbish bin, picking out random items and dropping them on the ground, then moving on to the next one, coming closer.

A girl, nothing more than a child. She almost looked Victorian. Like she'd fallen through a time tunnel and landed in the twentieth century. The night made her black and white. She stopped, staring at the orange tip of Rossett's cigarette as it glowed in the shadows.

Rossett realized she was scared and took a step forward so that she could see him under the light outside the hotel.

She didn't move.

He raised a hand.

She watched.

He lowered his hand, then took another drag on the cigarette.

She weighed him up. He watched her; she reminded him of a fawn in a forest, peeking through the trees, always on edge, unable to relax as its nose twitched the air sniffing for danger.

She took a chance and lifted her hand.

Rossett nodded.

She approached but stopped short, maybe fifteen feet away. Her eyes looked too big for her face, and a thin slit of a mouth became thinner as she tried to size him up.

"Got any spare change?" Her voice had a touch of phlegm about it.

"What are you doing out so late?" Rossett wafted the cigarette at the sky in case she hadn't noticed how dark it was.

"Out?"

"Yes."

"I live out." The old coat she was wearing was so big, Rossett only got a hint of the shrug that had just happened underneath it.

"You've no home?"

"No."

"No parents?"

She looked up the street, then back at hm. "Me mam's dead, it was the Germans. Me dad . . . I dunno."

"You don't have anyone to look after you?"

"No." She pulled at her sleeve, then wiped her nose with the heel of her hand. "I don't need no one."

"Everyone needs someone."

"I don't." She pulled her sleeve down.

Rossett was in danger of agreeing with her, but instead he flicked the cigarette away and buried his hands in his coat pockets. "Where do you sleep?"

"Why?"

"I'm worried about you."

"Why?"

"You're a kid."

"I'm not gonna let you touch me."

Rossett bridled. "I don't want to touch you."

"I know what you perverts are like."

"I'm not a pervert."

"Talkin' to kids outside hotels? You're not touchin' me."

Rossett pulled his warrant card. "I'm a policeman."

The girl squinted at the card, then gave the shrug Rossett was becoming all too familiar with. "Policemen is worse."

"Worse?"

"Policemen took me mam."

"What?" Rossett pocketed the card.

"Policemen took me mam. The Germans said they wanted her, so the police come round and took her to them."

"When?" Rossett said quietly.

"Last year."

"Did they say why they wanted her?"

"No."

"They must have had a reason?" He realized he sounded defensive and felt embarrassed about it.

"They were loadin' the wagon."

"They have a wagon?"

"The Germans tell them to fill it up."

Rossett stared at the kid. Her big eyes blinked at him as she jutted out her chin and hooked a thumb through the piece of string that was tying her coat.

"You've been on your own since then?"

The shrug again.

"There's other kids." She looked off into the distance as she wiped her nose again.

Rossett followed her gaze, then looked at the ground. "I'm sorry," he said finally, and he meant it.

She looked at him. "Got any change?"

"Isn't there anywhere you can go?"

"The church, but they make you go to school."

"You should go to school."

"Why?"

"For your future."

She snorted, wiped her nose again, then held out the wiping hand toward Rossett. "Got any change?"

Rossett dug in his pocket, thumbed through some coins, and then handed them over. "Here."

The girl didn't need asking twice. She was so quick Rossett barely felt the brush of her fingers in his palm. It was like a sparrow had landed and then left, and when he looked down he saw that the money had gone.

She smiled.

He smiled back. "I can get you a room here, for the night, maybe two?"

"I'm not going to touch you." That the kid should have to be so defensive against such an innocent offer made him scared to think about what she had been through.

"I can help you."

"I don't want help. Not from no copper, anyway." She started backing away. "You lot killed me mam."

She headed off the way she had come, and Rossett watched her go without trying to stop her.

Like she had said, his lot had killed her mam.

ROSSETT'S ROOM WAS small, dark, and damp.

The window was open a few inches. Rossett tried to close it, but the swollen frame was jammed against old paint and refused to budge. He stepped back and looked at the curtains. He doubted they would meet in the middle when they were pulled across.

He sighed.

He took off his overcoat and threw it onto the wooden chair in the corner of the room.

The lamp by his bed, which was the only source of light, flickered as the coat landed. Rossett stared at it for a moment, then stamped his foot on the floor. The light flickered again, this time for longer, before finally settling down again.

He crossed back to the window and saw that the girl was digging in another bin, this one a little farther down the road. Another lonely tram rattled past, this time going in the opposite direction. On the top deck there were two people sitting behind condensation-covered windows in the yellow light of the cabin. They seemed to ripple as they passed.

Rossett sat down on the corner of the bed. He ran his hand across the top sheet. It felt gritty, dusty, and he lifted his palm to check for dirt.

He had one arm back in his overcoat when there was a knock at the door. He opened it and found Neumann, staring off down the corridor, hands in his pockets.

"Do you want to get something to eat?" The German looked tired; his eyes were red, as if he had just been rubbing them. "If I stay in that room all night there is a good chance I'll kill myself."

"I was just going to the garage to get a rope," Rossett replied flatly.

"Shall we go the bar instead?"

"I'm guessing it'll be as depressing as this room, but yeah, let's go to the bar."

THE BAR WAS in the hotel basement, and Rossett had been correct.

It was as depressing as his room.

Neumann went to the counter as Rossett took a seat in one of the threadbare red velvet booths. The booths ran around three sides of a small, dusty, disused dance floor. Above the dance floor was a large crystal chandelier. Most of the bulbs had blown and Rossett could see cobwebs and dots of dead flies like they were trapped in time.

The velvet he was sitting on felt damp through his trousers, so he shifted and tested it with the palm of his hand. He couldn't decide if it was just cold or if the seat was actually wet, so he gave up trying and sat back down. The booths had once been ornate, their woodwork surrounds gilded. Now they were chipped and faded, and black and brown bruises could be seen poking through from underneath the old paint.

Neumann put two pints of beer and two glasses of watery Scotch on the table, then slid in next to Rossett.

Rossett had to resist the urge to huddle for warmth. Instead, he nodded thanks and picked up the whiskey.

"Cheers."

Neumann picked up his own glass.

"Cheers."

Both of them pulled the same face as they sipped at the whiskey.

"What is that?" Rossett managed to say after a few seconds.

Neumann didn't answer; he was too busy rubbing his chest with the heel of his hand. Rossett caught the eye of the barman and pointed at Neumann, then at the Scotch.

The barman gestured apologetically at the empty shelves behind him.

Take it or leave it.

Rossett shook his head and took a sip of the beer. It wasn't much better. He looked at Neumann, who was still wheezing.

The German took a deep breath. "Is that a secret way of killing Germans?"

Rossett picked up his own glass and sniffed it, then shook his head at the barman again.

"If it was, we would have won the war."

"If we'd known you had that, we wouldn't have started it." Neumann picked up his beer with one hand and slid the remaining Scotch as far away as he could manage. "You might want to brush your teeth before you light up one of those cigarettes of yours."

Neumann looked around the bar and its scattering of customers, who were spread almost as thin as the cheap carpet.

"This is the worst part of the job," said Neumann.

"Bad alcohol?"

"Bad hotels." Neumann took a drink, paused, and added, "And bad alcohol."

"It's better than what I used to do with Koehler."

"Working with the Jews?"

Rossett ignored the question and scanned the bar. There were eight other people in there, seven customers and the barman, all men. Nobody seemed to be enjoying the experience, least of all the barman. He was wearing an overcoat, sitting on a stool, reading a newspaper so thin he was having trouble holding it up in the draft from under the door.

"I hate Liverpool." Rossett said it so softly, he was almost surprised when Neumann replied.

"You've been here before?"

"Yeah."

"When?"

Rossett let out a long sigh and stared at his beer. "My wife." He took a sip, then wiped his top lip clear of suds. "She was from here."

"I didn't know."

"Why would you?"

"Is it a problem for you? Being here?"

"No." Rossett didn't sound as convincing as he had hoped.

"How did you meet her?"

"I was up here tracing a suspect. He had a little . . . trouble when he was arrested, and she worked in the hospital we had to take him to."

"She was a nurse?"

"Yes." Rossett took another sip of beer.

Neumann spoke again. "You must have been a fast worker."

Rossett looked at him, so Neumann elaborated. "You must have got to know her quickly to make such an impression."

"Yeah, well." Rossett shrugged. "I spent a week there while my suspect was recovering, so we had a while to get to know each other."

"You put him in hospital for a week?"

"What?"

"You put him in hospital for a week?"

"No."

"No?"

"No. It was three weeks, but I only hung around for a week. I had to get back to London."

Neumann shook his head. "A little trouble?"

Rossett ignored him, and continued speaking. "I wrote to her, and visited a few times. We got to know each other and then . . . well, you know."

"What?"

Rossett shrugged. "We fell in love."

"Wow."

"Yeah, wow."

"So you got married?"

"Yeah, six months later."

"Whirlwind romance."

"Sort of."

"She moved to London with you?"

"Yeah." Rossett adjusted the position of his pint glass by a few inches.

Neumann waited for him to speak again. He didn't.

"Do you want to go visit her family while you are in town? We can make time for it if you do."

"No."

"I can't imagine that you get much time to see them. It wouldn't be a problem, John. It'll be a good chance to catch—"

"They blame me."

"Blame you?"

"For her death." Rossett paused. "And my son's."

Neumann was silent.

"When I got out of the prisoner-of-war camp, after my family were killed by the bomb, I wrote to her family."

"And?"

"They replied—well, her mother replied, saying that if she hadn't married me she wouldn't have been in London, and she wouldn't have been killed by the bomb."

"That's hardly fair."

"It's true."

"But still not fair."

"Yes, well, they never approved of the marriage. Her dying just fed the fire."

"Oh" was all Neumann could think to say.

"Yeah." Rossett lit a cigarette.

"What about your own family?"

"I don't have one." Rossett shrugged, took another slug of beer, and then dragged the conversation away from places best left in the dark. "So this a regular part of the job?"

"What?" Neumann sounded relieved.

"Places like this?"

"Sadly, yes."

"Jesus," Rossett said. "I wish you would have told me."

"The worst part is the time on your own away from your family."

"You get used to it."

"Of course, I'm sorry, I didn't mean to . . ." Neumann held up a hand. "Forgive me."

Rossett waved away the apology with a waft of the cigarette. "You got kids?"

"Son, Dieter, he's in Africa with the Luftwaffe. My daughter, Leni, is at university in Berlin, studying chemistry."

"Wife?"

"Ex-wife, in Berlin, living in my house."

"Was it the job?"

"The job?"

Rossett pointed at himself, the drinks, and then around the room in fast succession. "Being a policeman."

"No. It was another man."

"Ah."

"She fell in love with Hitler," Neumann said.

"Oh."

Neumann sighed and rubbed his chest again. "She was what we used to call 'an enthusiastic party member.'"

"I see."

"As Kripo I'm a member, and I have to wear the badge." Neumann tapped his lapel, where the party swastika had been until they had arrived in the outpost of Liverpool. "But I was never . . . you know . . ." Neumann looked at Rossett. "Do you understand?"

"Yes."

"Heidi really went for it, the whole thing. She became a local organizer." Neumann's voice dropped low as he looked off across the bar. "Then party secretary for half of Berlin."

"And you didn't like it."

"It wasn't that I was . . ." Neumann searched for the right words. "Anti-fascist. It was nothing like that. Jesus, I'd be in a cell if it was. I just . . . I just don't get too excited by it all. It isn't in my nature. I'm not the kind of man who enjoys torchlit parades and singing songs."

"Who does?"

"Half of Germany."

"Half of the world since the war," Rossett said quietly.

"We had less time for each other, and more time for our work. I think secretly she sighed with relief when I suggested we get a divorce."

"Is that why you came to England?"

"I was sent here. Not long after she married a senior party member in Berlin. Whether he had something to do with it, I'll never know." Neumann waved his hand at the depressing room. "But here I am."

"Britain isn't that bad."

"Oh, come on, don't get patriotic with me. Would you want to be here if you could help it?" Neumann gestured to the room with the flat of his hand, like he was inviting Rossett to take it from him.

Rossett didn't reply.

"I'm sorry, I didn't mean to be rude," Neumann apologized.

"I could have gone." Rossett looked at Neumann. "During the evacuation, I could have left."

"How?"

"They offered to get me out with the . . ." Rossett looked for the word. "The dignitaries, the king, Churchill, all of them."

"Where to?"

"Canada."

"You didn't go?"

"No."

"Why?"

"My wife, my son. I didn't know where they were, so I stayed behind to try to find them."

"And you got mixed up in the fighting?"

"As always."

Neumann smiled, then paused. "Did you find them . . . before the bomb?"

"No."

"I saw in the file that your son was a baby; did you . . . did you meet him?"

"No."

"Jesus."

"Yes."

"I'm sorry."

"So am I." Rossett took another drag on his cigarette, and they both sat in silence for a while, together, but alone with their memories.

WHAT PASSED FOR the hotel kitchen had made them six cheese sandwiches. The bread was grayer than the wallpaper in the bar. Rossett managed two, then slid the plate across to Neumann with a shake of his head.

"You need to eat more food." Neumann was chewing.

"I'm not sure that is food."

"Today you've had toast, a sandwich on the road, and two here."

"Are you my mother?"

The German shook his head, then also gave up on the sandwiches.

"You want another beer?"

"My round." Rossett pushed himself out of the booth.

"My turn to go the toilet then." Neumann did the same.

THE BARMAN SAW Rossett coming, dropped his newspaper onto the counter, and started to pour the beers. Rossett rested an elbow and spun the paper around to read.

Local news. The kind of stuff that would normally be squeezed in between ads and pictures of prize-winning vegetables. There were no ads or vegetables, just a lead story about how the patriotic workers in the docks had moved more tonnage than at any other time in their history. Under it, another article detailed the heroic efforts of a group of local volunteers, off fighting communist guerrillas in someplace called Yakutsk.

They were in the newest British brigade of the Waffen SS, the Legion of St. George. Rossett stared at the photo. Young men with dirty faces gathered in front of a tank, holding a hammer-and-sickle flag. In the middle of flag was a hole, through which one of the men was holding his hand in the V for Victory salute.

The one that hadn't worked for Churchill.

The kids looked cold and thin. Most of them weren't smiling. Rossett recognized their eyes as the eyes he'd seen a million times in the mirror. He stared so long at the picture, the dots it was printed with seemed to float off the page.

He blinked.

They were too young.

He folded the paper and slid it away from him.

"Here's trouble," said the barman.

Rossett looked at the barman, who flicked his head toward the door without moving his eyes.

Rossett turned to look.

Three SS privates had just walked in.

They were each carrying a long StG 44 assault rifle. One of them placed his rifle on the bar heavily, then called down to the barman.

"Three beers, quick." Halting English accompanied by a rap of knuckles on the counter.

"I'll be right with you." The barman did his best to not make eye contact as he finished pouring Rossett's drinks.

"Now." The German jabbed a finger into the countertop. "Or I'll kick your ass."

The barman placed Rossett's half-filled glasses on the shelf below the pump before selecting three fresh ones for the Germans.

Rossett looked at the SS men.

"He's serving me," Rossett said quietly in German.

"Are you German?"

"English."

The soldier smiled. "Well, fuck you then."

Rossett looked at the barman. "Pour my beer."

The barman didn't look happy as his hand hovered near the pump.

"We're the SS. We get served first, so get at the back of the queue, Englishman." The second soldier lowered his rifle onto the bar, then took off his field cap and placed it carefully next to the gun. He rested his elbow on the counter and pointed at the barman, then at the pump.

"I'm a police officer." Rossett said it quietly.

"I don't give a fuck," the first soldier said loudly, then smiled at his comrades.

"I'm attached to the Kriminalpolizei." Rossett felt the rage rise inside him like a dread chill.

"You'll be attached to my boot in a minute, Englishman." The first soldier pushed off the bar.

Rossett stared at the counter.

He waited to see if the rage was going to subside in the face of a bully. It didn't.

He turned his head and looked at the soldier closest to him. "I'm not going to back down."

"What?"

"I'll not be bullied by you."

The soldier looked at his colleagues, then back at Rossett. "I don't—"

"I'll not be bullied by you. Either you back down, or we fight."

"I'm the SS."

"I don't care. I'll not be bullied. So . . ." Rossett pointed to the barman. "He is going to pour my beer, and when he has done that, he'll serve you. If you disagree, I am going to knock you on your arse." Rossett looked at the other two soldiers. "Then you, and then you will be next." Rossett looked back at the soldier who had done most of the talking and waited for a reply.

It came weakly. "But we are the SS."

"I don't care."

The barman gripped the pump.

The soldier closest to Rossett went for the rifle on the bar.

He didn't reach it.

Rossett slammed a solid right into his solar plexus, then pivoted at the waist as he threw a straight left into the chin of the second German. The second man's StG clattered onto the floor as he stumbled backward into his colleague.

Rossett felt the smooth sole of his left shoe slide, then spin on the beer-stained carpet as he rolled through after the punch and danced a step forward. He paused, his feet spread, the muscles in his legs tensed, ready to reload the whip with a pivot from his toes to the top of his head.

It only took half a beat. It felt like winding up a clock as the tension wound into his body. He weaved his head nine inches to the right, as his fist hovered next to his cheek. The last SS man turned and reached for his rifle on the counter. Rossett slammed the flat of his left hand onto the muzzle, pinning it to the bar.

The German looked at him, then raised his hand.

Rossett uncoiled and the whip crack rattled up his body in an explosion of power, a right cross that knocked the German to the floor.

Silence.

Rossett looked down at the three men on the floor, then at the barman.

"Pour," Rossett said, with a flick of his head to the pump.

The barman started pouring.

Neumann emerged from the toilet at the end of the bar and stopped. "What the . . . ?"

"They tried to push in." Rossett was already starting to regret what had happened. He looked at the barman, who placed a pint on the bar with a nervous rattle of glass on wood.

"It's the SS," Neumann said. The first soldier was now groaning as he clutched his stomach and rolled onto his side.

Rossett looked at the men on the floor, then frowned. "Yes . . . it is, isn't it."

"We need to—" Neumann broke off as four more SS soldiers, followed by a huge staff sergeant, came through the doors of the bar.

They all stopped, took in the scene, then raised their weapons toward Rossett, who took a moment before lifting his hands.

"It's not what it looks like." Rossett forced a smile.

The big staff sergeant pushed through his men, all the while keeping his submachine gun pointed at Rossett. "Back up."

The German's voice rumbled low like distant thunder.

Rossett considered his options, then did as he was told. "I'm a police officer."

"He's with me," Neumann said, but his explanation drew the aim of two gun barrels at his chest.

He lifted his hands.

The sergeant glanced at the men on the floor and nudged one of them with his toe. "Get up."

Only one of them was able to immediately comply. The other two rolled onto their backs and stared up at the ceiling, still unsure of what was going on.

"He attacked us." The first soldier was still rubbing his stomach as he reached for his weapon on the bar.

"I told them what was going to happen," Rossett said calmly in German to the staff sergeant, who didn't reply.

"We are police officers," Neumann said from over by the toilet. "I have identification in my pocket."

"I know who you are." The sergeant didn't look around at Neumann. "Take your beer, and go and sit down."

EVERY CUSTOMER WHO wasn't involved in the fight had been cleared out of the bar. All that was left was a terrified-looking barman wringing a dishrag in his hands, and Rossett and Neumann with two pints of beer.

They were back sitting in the booth, both of them staring at the Germans, who were tending to the three soldiers Rossett had put on their backsides.

"I go to the toilet for two minutes, and when I come out I discover that you've started another war." Neumann was turning his head slightly so that the other Germans in the bar wouldn't be able to see his lips moving.

"I'm sorry."

"Sorry? You'll be sorry if they put you up against a wall and shoot you."

"What was I supposed to do?"

"You are supposed to let them do what they want." Neumann picked up his pint and tried to avoid eye contact with the staff sergeant, who was standing at the end of the bar staring at Rossett and Neumann.

"Is it always like this?" Neumann shielded his mouth with his pint.

"What?" Rossett stared back blankly, not bothering to hide his words.

"This, the trouble. Does it follow you everywhere?"

Rossett didn't reply for a moment. Instead he leaned forward, picked up his beer, and took another slug. "Stop panicking, it's going to be okay."

"You think?"

"I know." Rossett looked across at the staff sergeant. "If we were in trouble, would he have sent us over here to finish our beer with our pistols in our pockets?"

Neumann had to resist the urge to check his pocket for his gun. What Rossett had said made sense. He nodded, almost to himself, then took a sip of beer.

They both watched as an SS major entered the bar, took a look at the scene, then headed toward Rossett and Neumann.

"Do me a favor." Neumann was back to hissing.

"What?"

"Don't hit anyone else."

The major was at the table's edge before Rossett had a chance to reply.

"Gentlemen, do you mind if my colleague and I join you?" It came out in excellent English.

The big staff sergeant was already dragging two chairs across.

"Please do," Neumann replied.

The major dropped into his chair without bothering to check if it was behind him. He placed two empty glasses down, then produced a quarter bottle of brandy out of his trench coat pocket.

Rossett heard the seal break on the cork. He knew the sound all too well. It was probably the second bottle of the night, judging by the major's slight sway as it opened.

"I didn't want to risk the beer." The major winked at Rossett, then poured two glasses, one for himself and one for his staff sergeant.

He lifted the brandy for a toast.

"Gentlemen, please . . . the Führer." This time he spoke German and left his glass hanging like a challenge in midair, daring them to ignore it.

Rossett and Neumann paused, then lifted their drinks, a little less high and a lot less enthusiastically.

"The Führer," Neumann said softly.

Rossett noticed that the NCO had placed his glass on the table with its contents untouched. Their eyes met. The big man stared back at him. There was no challenge, just two more eyes that had seen too much and were tired of it all.

Neumann and Rossett put down their glasses, but the officer pouted. He reached across with the bottle and sloshed some into Rossett's almost empty pint glass. Neumann quickly pulled his own glass closer to his body, as the officer banged the bottle back onto the tabletop.

The major picked up his glass again.

"Gentlemen." He paused, waiting for Rossett and Neumann to raise theirs. "The king!"

He shouted it in English, and the words seemed to bounce off the far wall and then back to them. The officer drank angrily this time. He slammed the empty glass onto the table like a full stop. Rossett noticed the NCO hadn't even bothered to pick up his drink, but instead had sat staring straight ahead.

"I'm talking about the king in England, not the coward who ran away," the officer stage-whispered, one hand held to the side of his mouth as he smiled at Rossett, who didn't reply. The officer feigned surprise, then looked at Neumann. "Maybe we should toast absent friends? Would that cover Churchill as well?"

Nobody answered, so the officer shrugged and looked at the staff sergeant and gave him a drunken wink.

Neumann broke the silence.

"I am Generalmajor Erhard Neumann of the Kripo, and this is Detective Inspector John Rossett of the Metropolitan Police."

"I know who you are." The major's smile slipped and his head seemed to wobble. "This is Staff Sergeant Becker, and I am Sturmbannführer

Theo Dannecker." Dannecker looked at Rossett. "That means Major," he said, as if he were speaking to a child.

"I know what it means."

"Of course you do, forgive me." Dannecker took a drink, then set the glass back down. "You worked with Ernst Koehler, didn't you?"

Rossett nodded.

"He was SS, wasn't he?" The "SS" slurred on the way out.

Rossett nodded.

"Do you know Major Koehler?" Neumann dipped into the conversation again, trying to pull it away from Rossett and back to himself.

"No." Dannecker was speaking to Neumann but looking at Rossett. "But I'm a soldier, and Koehler . . . he just killed Jews, didn't he?"

Rossett stared back across the table at Dannecker.

Neumann shifted on his chair and gave a little cough before speaking again.

"My colleague and I would like to apologize for the misunderstanding involving your men, Major."

Dannecker looked at him. "What?"

Neumann coughed again.

Rossett thought about banging him on the back.

Neumann spoke. "The, erm . . . the incident, just before you arrived?"

"There was a fight, sir." Staff Sergeant Becker rumbled into life. "Involving the inspector and three of our men."

"The three on the floor?"

"Yes, sir."

"We're sorry." Neumann coughed again.

"I'm not," Rossett chipped in, eyes still on Dannecker.

"I don't care." Dannecker pulled the curtain down on the conversation by holding up his hand. "Conscripts, idiot boys, barely worth the uniforms they are wearing. I really don't care."

Rossett watched Becker blink as his boss dismissed the men under him. The staff sergeant cared; Rossett saw it for just a second.

The big man cared.

Rossett smiled.

Dannecker took another drink, so Neumann tried to fill the silence once again.

"May I ask, Major, how did you know who we were?"

"I came here to speak to you." Dannecker looked at Neumann, then pulled the cork on the bottle again. "Off the record, if you don't mind?" Dannecker held a finger to his lips. It almost missed, and he had to adjust it slightly.

Neumann nodded and gestured that Dannecker should continue.

"Would you prefer I continue in German?" Dannecker asked with a nod of the head toward Rossett.

Rossett resisted the urge to rip the nodding head from its shoulders.

"My colleague speaks excellent German, but I think English would be best," Neumann replied in English.

Dannecker smiled as if he were enjoying the tension, glanced at his men sitting patiently on the other side of the bar, then pointed at Rossett's cigarettes.

"May I?"

Rossett slid the pack across the table.

Dannecker lit up, closing his eyes as he took his first drag, then opening them again as he exhaled.

"These things will kill you." He smiled at Rossett.

"So I've heard."

Dannecker smiled again and drew on the cigarette, deeper this time. The smoke from his lungs was darker than the smoke from the cigarette as it snaked up toward the cobwebs. It looked like shadows under clouds, and Dannecker watched it a moment, before returning the conversation.

"I know why you are here." Dannecker used the cigarette to point at Neumann.

Neumann made to speak, but Dannecker held up his hand.

"Please," Dannecker said, his voice husky from the cigarette and the alcohol. "Allow me to finish." He tapped the cigarette on the ashtray. "Evans, the policeman you spoke to today? He called me not long after you had left his office. He told me what you want to do."

"That was nice of him," said Rossett.

Dannecker smiled. "The games Evans has to play are a lot like these cigarettes. They can kill him. They can kill all of us." Dannecker put the cigarette in the corner of his mouth, then reached for the brandy and poured a measure. "He may not be a very good policeman, but the chief superintendent is a great high-wire walker." Dannecker replaced the cork without topping up anyone else's glass.

"He telephoned me because he knew that he had to. He knew that if he didn't, things would go badly for him."

"Same as when he released my prisoner?" Neumann asked.

"Yes." Dannecker paused as he took a sip of the brandy. "Exactly the same as that. This part of the country is a long way from London, and it is even further from Berlin. Here, the muzzle of my gun is a frontier of the Reich. It may not look like it, but it's a battlefield out there, and we are in a trench." He paused, then pointed at Rossett with the cigarette. "The inspector will tell you, when you are on a battlefield, there are no rules. You do what you have to do to stay alive."

Neumann took the opportunity to speak. "I'm afraid, Major, I think you are wrong. The rules do apply. The law applies. It is very simple; I have a mandate from the High Command to deal with matters such as this. I understand that you want to protect your man. I would probably want to do the same if I was in your position. But I have to investigate this incident, the same as I would investigate any other. If the evidence points toward your officer being responsible for the death in question, he'll have to be charged."

Dannecker held up a finger.

"You are wrong." Dannecker shifted slightly on his seat, then leaned forward over the table. "What you don't understand is that Liverpool is a rat's nest. And I am king rat. I am the highest-ranking officer for over one hundred miles in any direction you care to point. I'm the king of all I survey." He seemed to sway a little on his stool before putting the cigarette back into his mouth and taking another pull. He took the cigarette out, studied it, and then looked back at Neumann. "Don't make me an enemy. I mean it. This city is a dangerous place, people disappear, lives end, worlds end . . . you need me, you need my protection. So don't fuck up, really . . . just don't do it. It isn't worth it, because you'll need me, and when you do, you'll want me to come running."

"This man killed an American and must be dealt with accordingly."

"This man?" Dannecker jabbed a finger into the tabletop, then lifted his eyes to stare into Neumann's. "Do you know who 'this man' is?"

"No," Neumann said quietly.

"He is the Bear." Dannecker said it in such a way that Rossett and Neumann looked at each other, each thinking the other should understand the significance.

"The Bear is a hero of the Reich. Do you understand?"

Neumann nodded.

"He has an Iron Cross with Oak Leaves and he earned it the hard way. He has fought nonstop for eight years for you." Dannecker leaned in over the ashtray. "So don't you fucking forget that."

Becker coughed behind his boss, who straightened slightly in his seat.

"I have a job to do . . ." Neumann trailed off as Dannecker wiped his mouth and then gestured a halfhearted apology.

"I understand you have a job to do. All I am asking is that we try to find a way to deal with this quietly, and that we take our time. Captain Bauer . . ."

"Bauer?" Rossett this time.

"Captain Bauer, the Bear. He . . . he has been under a lot of pressure. He is worn out by this war, by what he has to do. I suggest we give him a few days to recover?"

"We don't have a few days, Major. We have to expedite this matter quickly." Neumann softened a little as he tried to explain. "Due to the nature of what is alleged, plus the American involvement, it means I am under considerable pressure. I am sympathetic, and I will be fair, but I have orders and a mandate. There is no other way."

Dannecker stared at them both, then nodded. He stood, collected the brandy, and tossed his still-lit cigarette onto the table without bothering to aim for the ashtray. He turned on his heel and left the bar so quickly, the enlisted men struggled to catch up with him as he charged through the exit doors.

Staff Sergeant Becker remained seated opposite Rossett and Neumann for a moment, then finally pushed himself up to his feet.

"Nothing more will be said about the assault here tonight." Becker pulled a field cap out of his pocket and put it on. "Captain Bauer will be available at the city garrison tomorrow."

"It'll be an official interview. I don't know how long it will take."

Becker nodded, then picked up his MP40 machine pistol off the floor next to his chair and turned to leave.

He stopped, paused, then looked back at Neumann and Rossett.

"Things are complicated here. I want you to understand that Major Dannecker is under a lot of pressure at the moment."

"We understand," replied Neumann.

"No, you don't," Becker replied before walking away.

CHAPTER 6

THERE WAS A girl with a wooden cart blocking their way down the narrow side street. Rossett's hand hovered over the horn, and he glanced at Neumann, who had a map open on his lap.

Neumann looked up through the sweeping windscreen wipers. "We're lost."

Rossett sighed, yanked on the hand brake, and got out of the car.

"Hey!" Rossett shouted, but she didn't seem to hear him.

She kept on walking ever so slowly, hands on the cart handles, eyes on the ground. Rossett could see that one wheel of the cart was loose. It was barely clinging on to the cart, much like the girl pushing it.

Rossett called again. "Hey!"

She stopped, paused with her back to him, and set the handles down. She turned, only slightly faster than the rickety wheel had been doing, and looked at him. Rossett saw she was in her early thirties. The rain that had been falling all morning had plastered her fine blond hair to her scalp and was dripping off her forehead into her eyes.

"The SS barracks, do you know them?" Rossett pulled up his coat collar in an attempt to keep the rain out.

Her hands hung down at her sides. She was holding them so that Rossett could see her palms. Doing her best to be as unthreatening as possible.

Rossett looked past her to the barrow. It was half full of bits and bobs of collected litter, metal, and the odd scrap of broken timber.

Her mouth moved, and her eyes seemed to roll a little in her head. She was soaked, and where the rain had run down her face it had cleared lines in the dirt, almost like tears in mascara.

"Do you understand me?" Rossett tried again, more gently this time.

The rain was thundering down now, slapping noisily onto the pavement. Rossett had to blink a drop out of his eyelashes as he waited for her to answer.

Her jaw flexed, and she nodded in several rapid jerks that shook some water off her hair. Her mouth seemed to clamp tight. Her left hand slowly twisted, as if some unseen force were bearing against it.

"'S-'s-'sup there . . ." She finally lifted her left hand and just about managed to point to the end of the side street. "L-l-l-left." Her arm jerked as she stuttered.

Rossett saw her wrist was as thin as an old dog's bone. Every sinew was visible in her neck as the words squeezed out through her mouth.

"Where?"

"Th-th-there." She pointed again.

Rossett looked back at the Jaguar purring behind him, then at the specimen standing in front of him.

"G-g-got any change, m-m-mister?" She ducked her head on the last word, relieved at finally getting it out.

The car made him feel guilty, so Rossett dug in his pocket. "What are you doing here?" He nodded at the barrow.

"L-loo-l . . ." She paused and sighed, then took a run at it again. "Looking for stuff to t-trade."

"Scrap metal?"

She nodded in short staccato snaps of the head. Her left hand folded into her side once more, then flexed, then grabbed the seam of her tattered trousers and held on tight.

"What's your name?"

"I-I-I . . ."

She broke off for so long, Rossett thought she might have forgotten the answer to the question. She gulped a breath, ducked her head, then came back up and tried again.

"Iris."

"Iris?"

She nodded, causing a few flecks of rainwater to flick off her head before she sucked in another breath.

"W-what's . . . what's y-yours?"

"Rossett," he answered, then felt bad about replying with a surname so tried again. "John."

"J-John."

"Do you make much money?" Rossett took a few steps toward the barrow and saw it was basically just garbage off the street.

Slung shit, worthless.

"F-f-foooooood."

"You get money for food?"

"No." Sharp shakes of the head this time as she gripped the seam of her trousers and sank the other reluctant hand into her pocket. "Foo-food."

She pulled out a potato.

It was small, covered in dirt, and there was a chunk chewed out of one end. Behind the bite marks it was gray and rotten. She smudged the dirt with her thumb as she rubbed the chewed end and held it higher for Rossett to see.

Rossett had once eaten that kind of potato.

He looked back at the Jaguar again and saw Neumann raise his hands: What's taking so long?

Rossett took some change out of his pocket. She took a tiny step closer, drawn by the sound of the clinking money. She stopped in front of him, so close that she cast a shadow across his palm.

The rain seemed to take a breath and lighten for a second or two before another drift wafted by on the breeze that was blowing in from the River Mersey, a quarter mile to the west.

Rossett looked up at the girl and realized she had looked younger than she really was. He adjusted her age to late thirties, then dropped all the change he was holding into her hand.

"Top of the street on the left?"

She nodded.

"Thank you, Iris." Rossett turned away and started to walk back to the car.

"Mm-mmm-mi . . ."

Rossett looked back at her over his shoulder.

Her head flexed on her neck again, and Rossett saw both fists were clenched tight as they rolled on her bony wrists.

"J-John, are you s-sure you w-want to go there?"

"What?"

She looked frustrated at being interrupted while she was on a roll, but she battled on anyway.

"It-it's dangerous."

"I have to go."

She squirmed, then managed to lift her right hand to wave good-bye.

The effort it took made Rossett feel tired from watching it.

The car was suddenly too hot when he got back inside. Rossett cracked the window to let some air in and some condensation out.

"What took you so long?" Neumann asked as they were waiting for Iris to manhandle the barrow up onto the narrow curb and out of their way.

"She had something wrong with her."

"What?"

"A stammer, maybe something else, I don't know." Rossett slipped the car into gear and they started to crawl forward. "She seems a bit . . . wrong. You know?"

"She's a mental?" Neumann smudged the side window with the back of his hand to take a closer look as they squeezed past.

"I don't know."

Iris was standing with one hand on the barrow, the other up at the side of her head in flaky salute.

Rossett didn't look at her.

"We got rid of them years ago," Neumann said quietly as he watched her. "There's no point to them."

Rossett glanced at his boss, who had begun to fold the map in his lap. Neumann looked back at him.

"What?"

"Nothing."

"Do we have far to go?"

"Yes," replied Rossett, even though the garrison was only around the corner.

"THEY ARE COMING to speak to you." Dannecker rolled his head a little on his shoulders, in an attempt to ease the pressure of the hangover that made it feel top-heavy. "We don't have much time, so please tell me what I need to know."

"Are you scared?" the Bear replied.

"You've had your fun, Bauer, and made your point, so please . . . tell me."

"You're scared." Bauer smiled. "You should have tortured me last night when you had the chance."

"It wouldn't have worked."

"It might have made you feel better." Bauer sounded like he was almost feeling sorry for Dannecker.

"I should just put a bullet in your head."

"But you need me. Ever since I found your gold and then moved it, you need me."

Dannecker made to speak, but instead paused to watch as the Bear lifted a hand off the table and moved it slowly through the air. It cut like an oar through an unseen sea, then stopped and hovered. Dannecker stared at it for so long, he felt like he was slipping under, hypnotized, almost drifting through waves.

The Bear was watching his own hand, as if he were unsure of what it was going to do next. One second, two seconds, three seconds, then the hand drifted slowly down to the tabletop, like the last leaf to fall in a winter forest.

Once it settled, the Bear looked at the man who was supposed to be his boss.

"I'm enjoying this." He smiled.

"You enjoy being stuck in a cell?"

"I'm not stuck here, and if you think I am, you're a bigger idiot than I thought. I'm as free as the air my hand just moved through."

"You're in my cell."

The Bear placed one fingertip against his right temple. "I can go anywhere I want. When I want. You can't stop me; nobody can stop me."

"They are coming to talk to you. They've come from London. If you don't play their game, they'll take you back there under arrest, and if they get you back to London, you are out of my protection. I won't be able to help you, Bauer."

"Protection?"

"Yes."

"You want to protect me?"

"I am protecting you."

"From what?" The Bear tilted his head.

"From the SS, from our organization, and from the law."

"Why?"

"Because you are not well, and you made a mistake."

"In hiding what you want?"

"You are tired. You need support."

"You said I'm not well?"

"Your mind is tired, and that is making it unwell."

"Are you are saying I'm mad?"

"No."

"I'm not mad, Major, I'm bored, so I'm playing a game with you."

Dannecker thought for a moment, staring at at his hands, until finally he looked up and replied.

"I don't have time for your games. I want to help you. You know what you have to do to get me to help you, so do it. If you tell me where the gold is, I'll sort this all out."

"They'll execute me for the murder of the American."

Dannecker linked his hands on the table and rubbed one thumb against the other.

"I won't let that happen."

The Bear smiled, a thin smile that didn't reach his eyes. It disappeared almost before it had time to get comfortable on his face.

"You're finished, Major. Your dreams will all be gone in a puff of gun smoke when they take me to London."

"You're going nowhere."

"What if I tell them about your gold?"

"You are going nowhere."

The Bear smiled. "You think you're in control."

"Karl, please . . ."

"The minute I found it, that was the minute it all went away from you."

"I really am worried about you; I can help you."

"When they realize what has happened, they'll execute you, too."

"We can work this out, Karl. We can work it out before the resistance have a chance to find—"

"Will you ask for a blindfold?"

"Please, Karl, be serious."

"When it is your time, will you want to see it coming?" The Bear pointed at Dannecker, then cocked his thumb as if he were a kid playing Cowboys. "Pow."

"You're not listening to me."

"Pow."

"Bauer, this isn't—"

"Pow," the Bear interrupted again.

They stared at each other. Dannecker waited. He was expecting more to come, but it didn't. The silence seemed to leach out of the cell's concrete walls as he stared into the eyes of the Bear.

"You don't know what you have done," Dannecker finally said.

"I've killed you, Major. You're dead."

Dannecker could hear his own pulse.

"We have one chance of making them go away, Karl. One chance of tying this matter up and making things good." Dannecker looked over his shoulder at the door, then back at the Bear. "The clock is ticking; you have to tell me. Where is the gold?"

The silence returned for a few seconds, then the Bear blinked. His eyes weakened, his brow slid a millimeter or two, and there was a glimpse of the man who might have been.

"It's too late for you, and it is too late for me."

Dannecker looked at the door and back at the Bear. His hand dropped to his holster. He pulled open the stud and lifted the flap.

The Bear watched him, shook his head, and smiled sadly.

"It's too late, Major."

Dannecker's pistol slid an inch out of his holster.

"I can't let them take you, Karl . . ."

"You can't kill me." It was said as a matter of fact, without fear. Bauer sounded so certain, the pistol grip seemed to get hot in Dannecker's hand.

The knock at the cell door was so loud that Dannecker jumped as the pistol slammed back into the holster. He realized he was breathing heavily through his nose, one hand still on the gun, his lips pursed tight, other hand flat on the tabletop.

They just stared at each other. As if they were waiting to get out of a rocking rowboat to the safety of the shore. Neither wanting to move first, for fear of tipping them both into the water.

There was another knock, louder this time.

"Too late." The Bear smiled, then nodded his head toward the door. "They're here. You should always take the shot when you get the chance."

ROSSETT AND NEUMANN sat shoulder to shoulder across the table from the Bear with their backs to the door.

The cell was cramped. There was a bed with a mattress thinner than a slice of bread, covered by a sheet folded so perfectly, it looked like it could give you a paper cut.

Dannecker and the Bear had been sitting at the table when Rossett and Neumann were shown in by the young SS private. Dannecker had left the room without speaking, which had caused both Rossett and Neumann to raise an eyebrow each. The young private had been tasked with waiting outside.

If it hadn't been for the pulse in the kid's lean neck, he could have been a convincing waxwork. Instead, he was an unconvincing human being. The kind who clicked heels and held his hands stiff and straight when he walked.

The Bear, meanwhile, was all dead eyes and dead silence.

Neumann placed a leather folder on the tabletop, opened it, and held a writing pad out toward Rossett.

"Do you mind?"

Rossett did mind, but took the pad anyway.

He waved away the offer of the fountain pen from Neumann and took out a stub of pencil that looked too small for his hand to hold. Rossett was aware that his jacket collar was damp from the rain outside, and he gave a little shiver because of it.

The Bear looked at him, catching the movement but not commenting on it.

Neumann gathered a breath and some thoughts, then began.

"I am Generalmajor Erhard Neumann, and this is Detective Inspector John Rossett. We have come from London to investigate the shooting of—"

"Rossett?" the Bear interrupted.

"Yes," Rossett replied.

"*The* Rossett? The hero?" The Bear perked up a little. "The one they called the . . ." He looked at the ceiling. As though he was hoping the words he was searching for were going to be written on it.

"The British Lion." Neumann supplied what he was searching for.

"Thanks for that." Rossett looked at Neumann.

"*The* British Lion." The Bear lifted his hands out of his lap and placed them on the table. He leaned forward a few inches, bending at the waist and elbows so that his palms remained flat. The skin stretched on the back of his hands, so that his nails turned white except for the half-moon ridges of dirt at their tips. "I've read all about you."

Neumann tried again.

"We are here to investigate the—"

"You were the hero of the British people, and then you turned your back on them." The Bear eased forward another inch or two. "I read all about you in the newspapers and kids' comics. You won the Victoria Cross, you met Churchill, the king . . . and then you joined us when we won."

Rossett didn't reply.

Neumann gave it another try. "We are here to investigate—"

"Does it bother you?" The Bear said it quietly, using English for the first time since they had arrived. His eyes seemed to glisten, as if they were lit from behind. "Being a traitor?"

Neumann looked at Rossett to see if he was going to react.

He didn't.

Rossett simply stared at the Bear.

Neumann coughed, a clearing of the throat before speaking. "We need to work our way through this interview, Captain Bauer."

"Make him answer me and then I'll talk." The Bear was talking to Neumann but looking at Rossett.

"No," Rossett answered before Neumann had the chance to veto. "It doesn't bother me."

The Bear considered Rossett's answer, then nodded to himself before speaking again.

"You're a liar. It does, I can feel it. You hate yourself."

Rossett didn't reply.

Neumann glanced at him, waited a second, then started again.

"We are here to—"

"You stink of anger." The Bear said it as if Neumann weren't even there in the room with them. "You stink of pain. Shame. I can smell it. You're in agony."

Rossett stared at him across the table.

Bauer leaned forward a little more, his chin dropping closer to the table, so it was only an inch or two above his hands. He looked like a cat about to pounce, and Rossett felt the muscles tensing in his own stomach in preparation for an attack.

"You're a repentant killer, you hear the souls calling. I can see it in your eyes." Bauer looked up to the ceiling, then back at Rossett. "You hear them just the same as I do."

Neumann cleared his throat.

"We are here to—"

"They come to you in your dreams, the same as they come to me." The Bear closed his eyes and shook his head. "We share that, Lion, we share them. Maybe we see the same faces, hear the same voices . . . What do you think, Lion? Do we have mutual enemies?"

Rossett started to turn the pencil stub between his index finger and thumb.

The Bear tilted his head. The bare white light pooled on his pupils and seemed to swirl like oil in water.

"Do they reach out to you in your dreams the way they do to me in mine? Their hands muddy and mucky, with skin falling off? Pushing through the soil, grabbing and scratching at your ankles with dirty nails as you try to run away?" The Bear paused. His eyes flicked to Neumann and back to Rossett.

"No."

The Bear smiled, then leaned back and shook his head.

"They do, I know it." The Bear pointed at Neumann. "He doesn't understand, he isn't a reaper, but we are . . . me and you." He tapped a loose fist against his chest as he stared at Rossett. "We're reapers. We understand, I know we do. We understand. We are brothers, the Bear and the Lion, bound with the blood of brothers, and the blood of others."

"No, really." Rossett shook his head. "Honestly, we're not."

The Bear smiled at Rossett as if he had just told a joke. He folded his arms, his mood appearing to brighten as the shadows from the light above slid off his face.

"It's good to meet an equal at last. It's been too long since I had someone who could look me in the eye."

Neumann broke up the party.

"We are here to investigate the shooting of Franklin Hawthorn, the United States consul in Liverpool, two nights ago. In addition to this, the shooting of three other local men. You were arrested near to the scene with the weapon believed used to kill Hawthorn in your possession. You refused to account for your presence upon arrest, nor make any statement to arresting officers." Neumann paused, watching Bauer, checking to see if he understood what was being said to him before continuing. "Detective Inspector Rossett and I are here to ascertain what took place on the night in question. We want only the truth. We have no opinions. We don't want to trip you up or treat you badly. We are sympathetic to your service to the Reich, and we only wish to get to the bottom of what took place. Do you understand?"

The Bear looked at Neumann.

"I understand."

"Good." Neumann smiled and nodded encouragingly. "Can you tell me why you were there?"

"No."

Rossett rolled his eyes.

"Excuse me?" Neumann rested his elbows on the table.

"You are excused."

"What?"

"What?" The Bear tilted his head.

"I'm trying to give you an opportunity to explain yourself."

"I know."

"So explain yourself."

"No."

Neumann sat back from the table, looked at Rossett, and then back at the Bear.

"I'm trying to help you, Captain. If this shooting was resistance related it changes the whole—"

"I don't want your help."

"This is your opportunity; we are sympathetic to you."

"He isn't." The Bear pointed at Rossett. "He doesn't like me, I can tell."

"I am." Neumann chose not to argue after taking a look at Rossett's stony face. "I want to help you."

The Bear leaned forward and stage-whispered to Neumann, "I don't want your help, you fucking idiot."

"You will end up in prison if you don't speak to us."

"I won't, but thank you all the same."

Neumann looked down at the blank pad in front of Rossett, then up at Rossett himself. He flicked his head when Rossett met his gaze.

You have a go.

Rossett sighed, and then put down the pencil.

"Did you kill Franklin Hawthorn?"

"Yes." The Bear leaned forward an inch.

"Did you have orders to kill him?"

"No."

"Why did you kill him?"

The Bear paused for a moment and nodded to the pad and pencil.

Rossett obliged him by picking up the pencil and pulling the writing pad closer.

"Yes?"

"I'm not telling you."

Rossett put the pencil back down and folded his arms.

"Why not?" Neumann this time.

"Because there is no fun to be had if I do."

"Fun?"

"Yes. Fun."

A wide smile filled the Bear's face before fading to nothing almost as quickly as it had appeared.

Rossett picked up the pencil and wrote one word on the pad, then slid it toward Neumann.

Lunatic.

Neumann laid his hand across the pad to hide what was written, then looked at the Bear.

"Why don't you want us to help you?"

"Because I finally have what I have been looking for."

"Which is?"

"A challenge."

"Which is?"

The Bear pointed at Rossett.

"Him."

ROSSETT SENT THE young soldier who was waiting outside into the cell to wait with the Bear. Neumann folded his arms as Rossett took a cigarette from a battered pack.

Neumann leaned against the wall opposite the open cell door.

Rossett pulled out a matchbox, and what sounded like the last match gave a lonely rattle in its cardboard coffin.

"Shut the door." The cigarette bobbed in the corner of Rossett's mouth.

Neumann swung the heavy steel door shut and watched Rossett as he lit up.

The cellblock corridor had eight identical blue steel doors running down both sides. It was basically a white concrete tube with bright white lights spaced equidistantly along its ceiling. All the other doors were locked and identical, and despite the occasional dark patch of damp in the concrete, the block was as warm as a hospital.

Rossett flicked the spent match onto the concrete floor of the corridor and wandered over to the other side to drop the hatch on the cell door opposite the Bear's to check that nobody was inside listening.

They weren't. Inside it was exactly the same as the one they had just been in, except it was empty and there were no sheets on the bed.

Rossett took a drag, blew the smoke through the hatch, shut it, and looked back at Neumann.

"It's pointless spending all afternoon asking him questions. He's as mad as a March hare."

"We need to ascertain exactly what took place." Neumann's voice was clipped as he wafted away smoke.

"It's pointless, we're just going to go around in circles with a madman. He's told us he did it, and he's told us he had no orders. The blame lies with him; it is a straight cough."

"A straight cough?"

"An admission of guilt. There is no gray area, we've nothing else to explore. I can't see the point in wasting any more time with him."

"There may be possible defenses he'll bring up later."

"You basically told him he can walk if he says the shooting was tied to the resistance. If he wanted to talk his way out, he would have done it already."

"We could look bad if it gets to court and we . . ."

Rossett took another drag, then dropped the cigarette onto the floor and slid it around under his foot.

"There is no chance on earth, none whatsoever, that he will take the stand in a courtroom." Rossett leaned in so close, Neumann could smell the cigarette on his breath. "He's an embarrassment to the SS. He'll look crazy, and he'll make the Reich look weak. We're wasting our time. I say we take him to London, drop him off at a military hospital with a note tied to his neck saying he is nuts."

"He's murdered a diplomat."

"Not our problem."

"It is our problem. It is our job; it's why we were sent here."

"We've done our job. Pat on the back all around, let's go home."

"What about witnesses?" Neumann tried again.

"Nobody saw the trigger being pulled. We've already got the arresting officers' statements in the file. There is nothing left to do here. Trust me."

"What about the Englishmen he killed?"

"What?"

"You don't want to question him about the three Englishmen who died?"

Rossett flushed.

"Yes, of course . . . I'm sorry, we should."

"Yes." Neumann stepped back and gestured that Rossett should lead the way back into the cell. "Maybe we should."

———

"YOU SHOT SOME Englishmen."

"Hmm?" Bauer dragged his eyes away from Rossett and looked at Neumann.

"You shot some Englishmen," Neumann repeated.

"What about it?"

"Why did you shoot them?"

"Why?"

"Why?"

Bauer looked at Rossett, then back at Neumann before beckoning him closer. "I want to tell you a secret."

Neumann nodded encouragement. "Go on?"

Rossett folded his arms.

"This secret is a very dangerous thing."

"Please, tell me." Neumann wafted a hand.

"I know where there is a lot of gold."

"Gold?" Neumann leaned forward, but Rossett didn't move.

"Gold."

"What kind of gold?" Neumann again.

"How many kinds are there?" The Bear tilted his head.

"Two," said Rossett flatly.

"Two?" The Bear looked at him.

"The real kind, and the bullshit kind. And I know which one you are talking about."

The Bear smiled. "That's funny."

Rossett didn't reply.

The Bear looked at Neumann. "He's funny."

"What gold?" Neumann tried to steer the Bear back on track.

The Bear was still smiling when he replied. "Enough gold to make everyone in this garrison rich ten times over."

"Everyone?"

"Everyone. The Englishmen who died, they'd hidden it, but I found it and moved it."

"You found it?"

"Then I moved it."

"Where is it?" Neumann tried to sound calm.

"If you are good enough, you'll find out."

"And if I'm not?"

The Bear shrugged.

"You'll be dead."

CHAPTER 7

NEUMANN GLANCED AT his wristwatch, then linked his fingers and started to tap his thumbs together. The clock on the wall ticked toward 2 P.M., and he considered getting up and walking out of the office. He called over to the admin corporal, who was in the middle of loading a piece of paper into a typewriter that almost hid him from view.

"Corporal?"

"Yes, sir?" The corporal almost had to stand up to be seen.

"You're sure the major knows I am waiting?"

"He does, sir."

"Can you tell him we need to get back to London tonight?"

"I already have done, sir."

"Then tell him I'm here merely as a courtesy. I can take Captain Bauer without his permission if I wish."

The corporal wearily got to his feet, crossed the room, knocked on Dannecker's office door, and entered.

One minute later, he came out and smiled at Neumann.

"The major will see you now, sir."

Neumann stalked past him and into Dannecker's office.

It was drabber than he had expected. Dannecker was seated behind a plain wooden desk that looked like the sort of thing a teacher would use in a run-down school. There was a map of the city on one wall, while on another a large-scale map of the northwest of England was pinned next to the obligatory portrait of Hitler. Under the portrait was Staff

Sergeant Becker, seated in a leather armchair, his chin in his hand as he stared at Neumann.

On Dannecker's desk, next to a pile of files, was a bottle of brandy and a half-full glass. Behind the glass, Dannecker stared at Neumann through watery red eyes that looked like they had just watched a late night slide by slowly.

"Generalmajor." Dannecker pointed to a wooden chair against the far wall. "Please, take a seat."

"I'm not stopping."

"Drink?"

"I'm not stopping," Neumann said again.

"You've spoken to Captain Bauer?"

"I have, and he is now in my custody."

Dannecker nodded and pulled the cork on the bottle.

"Isn't it a little late to be driving back to London?" Dannecker topped up his glass, but didn't replace the stopper.

"I prefer to expedite the captain's transfer as quickly as possible."

Dannecker looked at Becker and repeated one word. "Expedite."

Becker didn't reply.

Neumann continued, "I trust you'll be able to spare us a prisoner escort?"

"I'm afraid not."

"I must insist."

"We don't have the spare men." Dannecker picked up the brandy glass and shrugged. "I'm sorry."

Neumann glanced at Becker and back at Dannecker.

"If we may have a moment in private, Major?"

"The staff sergeant runs this place, Generalmajor. If it has to be said, it's best said where he can hear it." Dannecker leaned back until his chair creaked.

Neumann stared at the floor for a moment before speaking.

"During the interview, Captain Bauer mentioned gold."

"Gold?"

"A lot of gold. I understand that it is probably just an attempt to distract me, but . . . well . . . it would be remiss of me not to ask you if you have heard anything about it."

Dannecker looked at Becker. "Have you heard anything about gold, Staff Sergeant?"

"No, sir."

"Neither have I." Dannecker looked back at Neumann. "Did Captain Bauer say where this gold was?"

"He did not."

"How much there was?"

"Other than to say that there was a lot, no."

"Where it came from?"

"No."

"That's unfortunate. I could always do with some gold." Dannecker smiled at Neumann, who managed a weak smile in return.

"Couldn't we all."

Dannecker took a sip of the brandy, swallowed, and leaned forward with another creak.

"I'm sorry, Generalmajor. Captain Bauer has been under a great deal of stress of late. His work is difficult in the extreme. He operates alone, living among the English, pretending to be English, basically being English. He hears loose talk, rumors, information, anything anti-German or anti-fascist, and then he targets the people who are subversive."

"And?"

"He kills them." Dannecker took another drink.

"Many of them?"

"Unfortunately—or fortunately, depending on your point of view—yes. He kills them by the dozen. He's the best of the best, but unfortunately he's been out there for a long time now, and it has taken its toll." Dannecker touched his left temple with his index finger, then shrugged.

"So the gold?"

"The rambling of a madman?" Dannecker glanced at Becker and then back at Neumann.

"Whatever it is, I'll have to report it to London when I get back."

"Of course."

"There may be further enquiries to be made down the line."

"I understand."

"I'd best get going, Major."

"Are you sure you won't leave tomorrow?"

"The sooner we are back on home ground, the better."

"I'll drink to that." Dannecker lifted his glass.

Neumann managed another half smile and an informal salute. Dannecker returned it with the glass.

BECKER AND DANNECKER sat in silence for a few moments before Dannecker addressed his staff sergeant.

"If they make it to London with Bauer, we are totally fucked."

"So?"

"Make sure we aren't by making sure they don't."

THEY WERE STUCK in traffic on a one-way street.

Rossett sighed, looked out the back window, then grabbed the seat in front of him and leaned forward so he could see out the windscreen.

"What's the holdup?"

Neumann smoothed his hands across the top of the Jaguar's steering wheel.

"Looks like an accident. I think a truck or something is blocking the road."

They had barely traveled one hundred yards from the garrison in the last fifteen minutes. The pavements on either side were dotted with pedestrians, while ahead of them a line of cars snaked their way toward the truck that was blocking the narrow road. People were blaring on horns, and Rossett could see a couple of drivers leaning out of windows shouting.

He glanced at the Bear, who was staring straight ahead at the back of Neumann's head.

The wipers juddered across the window, so Neumann flicked them off, then looked at Rossett. "The road isn't wide enough to turn around in this thing."

"We should have brought the Austin."

"No we shouldn't," replied Neumann flatly.

Rossett glanced out the back window again, at the van and driver stuck tight up behind them.

The Bear moved for the first time since he had been placed in the back of the Jaguar. He looked at Rossett.

"It's a trap."

"What?"

"An ambush, insurgents, resistance. It is a classic trap. I knew they wouldn't let me leave."

"Quiet." Rossett looked over his shoulder at the van again.

"We are in a bottleneck; they knew we were coming."

Rossett turned back to the front just as the car ahead rolled forward a couple of feet. He noticed Neumann's eyes watching him in the mirror.

"It's a trap," the Bear said softly, eyes still on Rossett.

Rossett pulled out his Webley, thumbed the hammer, and checked over his shoulder once more.

The girl from earlier, the one with the barrow.

Iris.

She was limping down the narrow pavement toward them on the passenger side of the car. She was moving slowly, and he could see the wooden wheel of her barrow was still rhythmically wobbling with each quarter turn.

"What do we do?" Neumann in the mirror again.

"Let the gap open in front of us as the cars edge forward. Hold the foot brake, keep your eyes open, and if you see anything strange ram the car in front to move it. Just keep your head down and keep driving if I tell you. A moving target is harder to hit."

"Mount the curb and reverse away from the blockade. Don't worry about the pedestrians." The Bear sounded bored.

Neumann looked at Rossett in the mirror again. "Should I?"

"Curb's blocked. Give it a minute, let's see how this plays out."

"Head back to the garrison." The Bear again.

Rossett saw Neumann chew his bottom lip and stroke the steering wheel again.

"Give me the cuffs." Rossett placed the Webley under his leg, then took hold of the Bear's wrist. The Bear didn't resist as Rossett unlocked the cuff from one wrist and reached across to attach it to the leather strap on the door of the Jaguar. Rossett closed the cuff back up, then leaned forward to place a reassuring hand on Neumann's shoulder.

"He's secure. I'm going to move some of these cars out of the way. Have you got your pistol?"

Neumann held up his Walther.

Rossett clamped his hand tighter. "If he moves an inch, shoot him."

Neumann adjusted the mirror so it was pointed at the Bear.

"Okay."

"This is a trap. You should stay in the car and we should force our way back to the garrison." The Bear's head was leaning to one side as he stared out the window next to it, like a bored child on a long journey.

Rossett nodded to Neumann, opened the door, and stepped out of the car.

The change in temperature made him shiver; they'd been in the vehicle for longer than he'd realized. He checked on the barrow girl again. She was thirty feet away, limping along in the same short awkward steps that sounded of studs in old boots being dragged on cobbles. Nobody, other than Rossett, seemed to notice her edging along the pavement, eyes downcast, scanning the ground for scraps.

Rossett took a few paces and then stood with his back to the Jaguar. He checked the street ahead. Neumann had been right; the truck was causing the delay. Rossett could see two men standing by the front wheel, which looked like it had come loose and folded up under the weight of its load.

One of the men started to argue with a taxi driver.

Nobody was going anywhere for a while.

Rossett stepped farther away and then up onto the curb so that he could see past the van behind the Jaguar. There were cars stretching back to the gates of the garrison and beyond. Pedestrians were picking their way through exhaust fumes and smog, too wrapped up in their own existence to notice the car horns and the gridlock.

The barrow girl was getting closer, limping along at a pace that could barely be described as a walk. Rossett edged back toward the Jaguar's passenger window, leaned down, and gestured that Neumann should lower it.

The heat from the car warmed his face.

"Well?" Neumann was leaning right over, and Rossett could see that he had his finger on the trigger of the Walther.

"I'll get the cars in front to roll forward as much as I can. There is a girl with a barrow, the one from before, coming down toward us. As soon as she's passed, pull forward onto the curb and use the extra space to turn around. We'll head back to the garrison."

The Bear said something in the back that made Neumann glance at him before he looked back at Rossett.

"Is there no way past the truck? I wanted to get home tonight."

Rossett checked on the barrow girl's progress, then looked back at Neumann.

"We should just wait until this road is clear; we're too exposed here."

"There must be another—"

Rossett held up his hand and cut Neumann off.

He'd heard a shout, something different from frustration that he couldn't quite put his finger on.

Rossett leaned back from the window, then looked toward the truck ahead.

The men who had been inspecting the wheel were gone.

His Webley emerged from the folds of his coat. He looked toward the van driver behind the Jaguar, who stared back at him, hands still on the wheel. Rossett checked the truck again, and noticed for the first time that the three cars closest to it were empty.

He took a few paces along the pavement toward them. He checked over his shoulder at the barrow girl, then ducked his head to check the drivers of the cars just in front of the Jaguar. They looked just as impatient as Neumann to get going.

Rossett noticed movement on the other side of the truck up ahead.

Pedestrians were still all around, carrying on with their lives, pushing past, unaware of Rossett's heart rate rising. He tapped the windscreen of the car nearest to him with the Webley.

"Move forward so that you are touching the bumper of the car in front." Rossett showed his police warrant card and, more important, the Webley, to the driver.

He looked back toward the truck as the engine next to him revved.

The car moved, then Rossett noticed the van behind the Jaguar was now empty.

Its driver was gone.

Rossett took a half step back to the Jaguar, and that was when the explosion blew him off his feet.

ROSSETT'S EARS WERE ringing and his face was in the gutter.

He had the dull sense that he was seeing the world through a dusty tunnel.

He tried to get up, but barely managed to move more than a few inches before a great weight stopped him and pushed him back to the ground. There was water in the gutter. It was cold on his cheek. He rolled his head and discovered the water tasted of soil.

Soil and blood.

He tried to get up again, but the weight pushed him down again.

He thought about staying on the ground, shutting his eyes, resting a while.

This time the water was edging past his left temple. It felt good. The whistling in his ears rolled like a radio scrolling through the long waves, then it popped.

Gunfire.

Somewhere around him, on the edges of his reluctant senses, coming into focus, like a vague memory of a bad dream.

Rossett tried to get up out of the gutter again, and this time realized the great weight was the bottom of the car he had been half blown under.

He edged backward on his elbows so that he was clear, then it struck him his hands were empty.

He didn't have his gun. He squinted into the shadows and the smoke as the gunfire grew louder. He couldn't figure out if his hearing was coming back or if the shooting was getting closer.

He felt drunk, even though he knew he wasn't.

He saw the Webley, a few feet ahead of him, lying under the car like a dead rat.

Rossett crawled forward on his elbows and reached for the gun. He could hear screaming over the gunfire.

High pitched, maybe a woman? Maybe a man? Rossett had heard men scream under fire; screaming was universal when you were scared.

Rossett didn't have time to be scared.

He picked up the gun and felt a little sick as he edged back out from under the car. He felt weak, spat some blood out of his mouth, and realized he had bitten his tongue when he had fallen over.

He rolled out onto the pavement and tried to sit up.

He couldn't, so he settled for resting on one elbow.

The gunfire had eased a little, but there was still the sound of screaming.

The Webley felt too heavy to lift.

Rossett fought off the urge to lie down again. He scanned the pavement and through the smoke saw a woman staring at him. Rossett could see blood pooling in her lap. She said something to him, but he couldn't hear the words.

He wanted to help her. He wanted to stand.

He couldn't, so he lay back and closed his eyes.

The pavement felt cruel against the back of his head.

He blinked as gray smoke drifted across lighter clouds. Far away, up above him, the clouds slowly faded away as he drifted back into unconsciousness.

THE BEAR HAD seen it coming.

These policemen were idiots.

Even the Englishman, the one they all talked about, the so-called Lion. Even he had been too slow. The Bear had to give Rossett a little credit for sniffing something wasn't right, but not much. He'd been slow to react, slow to read the situation properly.

Not like the Bear.

They should have moved the car when they had the chance. They should have mounted the curb and pushed their way through. Either forward or back would have done.

Anything to keep moving, anything to stay alive.

But the Lion had been slow. He'd been worried about the people on the pavement instead of looking after himself. That had made the Bear a little sad as he dipped his head as low as he could get it.

A second before the bomb went off.

He'd seen the barrow the girl had been pushing toward the car, and he had realized what it was long before the Lion and the dumb German he was working with had even noticed it. The Bear had recognized the girl and realized he should have killed her months earlier. She was always hanging around the garrison, always begging for scraps, always looking pathetic and pointless.

All that, and one more thing: she was always watching.

She was resistance. He knew it now.

But she hadn't killed him.

The car had rolled a little. The Bear guessed the wheels had lifted a few inches on the passenger side as the explosives had detonated. It hadn't been a big bomb. He guessed it was probably less than a few grams of plastic, maybe a few feet from the Jaguar when it went off. The charge definitely wasn't underneath the car, nor was it shaped to cause maximum damage, with nearly all the explosive energy being wasted.

English amateurs.

Or maybe they hadn't wanted to kill him?

Maybe they wanted what he knew? Maybe they wanted him alive?

Either way, as good as he was, now wasn't the time to think about it.

His ears were still ringing as he reached over the seat toward Neumann, who was slumped against the steering wheel, and took his gun. The Bear was dazed by the shock wave, covered in glass, and a little deaf, but he had two things that Neumann didn't.

Combat experience, and the policeman's Walther PPK.

He dropped back into his seat, worked the slide on the Walther and released the safety, then noticed the door opening next to his head.

He fired once.

Combat experience.

Ready your weapon before you do anything else.

He hit the man who had opened the door just below the throat, around the second button of his shirt.

The man dropped.

The Bear saw a Browning pistol slip out of the man's hand as he reached up to grab at the wound. The Bear angled his Walther and fired a shot into the leather strap his cuffs were fastened to. It split halfway across. He jerked against the strap, couldn't rip through it, so fired another shot and finally broke free.

He slipped out of the car like smoke off a stage, his body twisting and sliding like a snake as he landed on the wet cobbles next to what was now a corpse. The Bear lay flat for a second or two, then lifted his head a few inches and saw figures running toward him through the smoke.

His mind did the calculations almost as he pulled the trigger.

Nobody runs toward a bomb blast. Not since the resistance learned that a secondary bomb was often more effective than the first.

These people were coming to either kill or capture, and the Bear didn't want to be either of those two things.

So he shot them.

Three fast rounds. The pistol popping in his hand like a tiny barking dog. The figures ducked behind the van that had been parked behind the Jaguar. The Bear grabbed the Browning and was up and running so fast he was almost away before the echo of the shots had the chance to bounce back off the buildings around him.

Away from the Jaguar, away from the garrison, and away from the SS.

What was it the English said?

The game was afoot.

CHAPTER 8

NEUMANN WAS NAKED and scared.

It had been hours.

Wherever they had put him was freezing cold and soaking wet. Twisting and pulling against the ropes around his wrists had stripped off the skin, and now it was agony to move them at all.

They'd tied a sack that smelled of rotten vegetables over his head. As he breathed it sucked in and out of his mouth, like a lover's lips.

He was wheezing now. Short, gaspy, raspy breaths. The bad chest that had kept him out of the army scraped against his ribs like he had swallowed barbed wire.

He stopped struggling.

He needed to slow down.

The bag worked against him and he had to concentrate, push away the panic, take his time, make every breath count.

He tried to remember what had happened.

They had come from nowhere.

One minute he had been watching Rossett, thirty feet from their car. The next minute he was being dragged out the driver's door and onto the pavement.

He closed his eyes.

Take another breath.

Try to fill in the gaps.

He saw Rossett again, concerned, one hand just inside his coat, glancing at him through the windscreen, then looking ahead at the line of traffic. Neumann remembered Bauer saying something behind him. He squeezed his eyes shut tighter as another wheeze threatened to distract him.

What had Bauer said?

He squeezed his eyes closed, the memory seemed so far away.

"A bear trap."

Neumann opened his eyes, then heard his voice repeat the memory out loud.

"A bear trap."

He rolled onto his side and tried again with the ropes. He was weak now; his efforts were pathetic. He gave up, rested his head on the floor, and felt the ache of the concrete through the sack.

He remembered a flash. There hadn't been any noise—well, none that he could recall. He remembered glass, lots of glass, fine sprinkles and large pieces swirling like a shaken snow globe.

His head ached.

Not that it mattered. He was alive, for now.

There was shooting.

He could remember it.

Or was his mind playing tricks?

He could definitely recall the sound of shooting. There wasn't much, but what there had been had seemed very close.

Neumann wondered if it had been Rossett. Was he shooting at the men who had dragged him out of the car? He considered it, then dismissed it. Rossett would have been too close to the bomb. He wouldn't have had the protection of the car to save him.

Rossett was probably dead.

Neumann was on his own.

He started to pull at the ropes again.

CHAPTER 9

THE PILLOW FELT soft, and its case was clean and smelled of carbolic soap. Rossett inhaled the freshness, enjoyed it, then opened his eyes and remembered where he was.

He sat up.

His head ached and he felt a little sick.

The room was small, maybe ten feet square, as white as the pillow his head had been on and just as clean. He was in bed, but he already knew that much. He was wearing a green gown, the type that fastened at the back and showed your arse to anyone behind you.

He lay back and remembered waking up in the ambulance. A bell had been ringing, and he had been confused, unsure if the sound had been in his head or not. The medic had pushed him back down onto the stretcher. Rossett had noticed an SS private sitting on the other side of the ambulance as he had drifted off back into unconsciousness.

He'd come around again when he was in the hospital. He'd been confused, then surprised to find himself sitting up on the edge of a trolley. He'd been talking to the nurse, who was running her fingers through his hair looking for signs of obvious damage.

She was answering a question he couldn't remember asking, and his head had hung low as he enjoyed her gentle touch.

He'd known he was concussed, and he had fought back halfheartedly when they told him he needed to stay the night in the hospital. He was tired, half deaf, in pain, and certain that Neumann had been killed in the attack.

He'd asked about Neumann. They had just told him not to worry, everything was all right, just lie back down on the trolley, rest, it'll be okay.

It didn't feel okay.

Rossett didn't have his watch, but the sky he could see through the window was lightening, so it was morning.

Or maybe it was darkening?

Maybe it was evening?

He rubbed his eyes.

It must be morning.

He listened for clues and heard a far-off crash of a trolley in a corridor.

It sounded like china and cutlery.

Breakfast?

It must be morning.

He'd been asleep all night. He swung his legs out from under the covers and felt the chill of the tiles on his bare feet. There wasn't a mirror on the low bedside cabinet, so he checked his face and head for injuries with gentle prods of his fingers.

Aside from a lump behind his right ear and an inch-wide dressing on his forehead, he came back clean. He stood up, slow, one hand on the bed just in case his legs hadn't got the message. He straightened, feeling the ache from some bruises picked up in the explosion, but otherwise okay.

He moved toward the door. It was half frosted glass with dazzling white, smooth paint and a silver handle.

Rossett rested an ear against it and listened.

Silence.

He took hold of the back of the gown with one hand and turned the handle slowly with the other.

The corridor was empty. He looked both ways and saw the same white paint that looked so clean, it made him feel dirty. It was way too clean to be an English hospital. Those places were barely surviving on the meager dregs of what a hostile government handed down to them. They didn't have money for paint—they barely had money for bandages. This place was too good to be wasted on normal people; it was either military or private.

His head ached. He blinked off the pain and focused on what he could see. Eight doors, including his own, running down either side of the long corridor. The corridor finished at a pair of double doors, the kind that swung back and forth a few times after you had passed through them. He guessed they were the exit and looked back into his room again, in case he'd missed his clothes the first time he had looked around.

He hadn't.

With his bare feet slapping, he moved fast toward the exit. He stopped at the double doors. He could hear a phone ringing, far off, like it was at the edge of his dream. A woman's heels, brisk, rat-a-tat, in a hurry but not running, maybe heading away.

He pictured a nurse, then pressed against one of the doors lightly. It moved easily, so he pushed it forward an inch or two until he could see through the gap.

He was at a T junction with another corridor which was longer, and slightly darker. Doors led off on either side, and an empty patient trolley was sitting against one wall about forty feet away. At the end of the corridor was a lime-green wrought-iron staircase, and next to the staircase someone had painted a perfect number 5 in gloss black on white paint.

Rossett made a mental note not to jump out of any windows if he had to try to escape.

He let the door fall back and leaned against the other one so he could check the corridor in the other direction.

A nurse at a dark wooden desk looked up from the paperwork she was reading, then smiled at him. Rossett felt like a child caught by his parents after getting out of bed.

"Good morning, sir. I didn't know you were awake."

English, well spoken but with the upward intonation of the Liverpool accent chasing each word. She was pretty in a smooth, starched way that reminded Rossett of the pillowcase back in his room. The nurse rose from the desk as Rossett made note of the "sir" and felt foolish for peeking through the gaps in the door. He pushed it open a few more inches, then realized his mouth was dry when his first attempt at speaking ended in a croak.

"Whe—" He paused, swallowed, drummed up some saliva, and tried again. "Where am I?"

"You're in the Liverpool Royal Military Hospital, sir, and you should be in bed."

It was the voice.

Rossett thought of his wife.

He'd forgotten her voice, and yet here it was, all these years later, coming at him from a stranger.

"Are you feeling all right, sir?"

Rossett hadn't realized he'd forgotten his wife's voice. All those years of thinking about her, dreaming about her, and it had taken someone he didn't know to remind him of how she sounded.

She didn't speak in his dreams anymore, she was fading away.

"Sir?" The nurse tilted her head.

Rossett felt a lump in his throat and had to croak his way past it. "How long have I been here?"

He eased the door slightly wider and noticed a young army private sitting behind another desk at the very end of the corridor. The private looked up at the sound of voices, checked who was speaking, and closed the book he was reading. He nodded a greeting to Rossett, politeness personified, then picked up the heavy black receiver of the telephone on the desk. Rossett couldn't hear what he said because the nurse started speaking again.

"The explosion—do you remember?"

"Yes."

"How do you feel?"

She was walking toward him now, so Rossett took a step back and held the door open for her. He couldn't help himself from staring into her eyes as she approached. Even her eyes reminded him of his wife. He touched the side of his head.

"I've a bump on my head, but other than that . . . I . . . my clothes?" He ran out of things to say.

She stopped in front of him and placed a hand lightly on the door.

"Are you sure you are okay?"

"You remind me of someone."

She smiled, like she already knew. Rossett felt confused and wondered if he was still concussed.

"You should be in bed." She said it so gently, Rossett thought he might cry and didn't know why.

"My clothes."

"We sent them to be laundered." The nurse gestured that Rossett should lead the way back to his room.

"Am I under arrest?"

Another smile, like a mother fending off a silly question.

"Concussion can be dangerous, so we decided it was best that you stayed here for twenty-four hours so we—"

"I've been hit on the head before."

She gestured that he should start walking again. "Then you'll understand the best place for you is in bed."

"My colleague, the German policeman, do you know what happened to him?"

"I'm afraid not, sir. Now please." She gestured again. "Bed."

Rossett started to walk, then remembered his arse and gripped the back of the gown again. He glanced at the nurse, who ignored it, like she had seen it all before.

"Generalmajor Neumann, can you check if he was admitted?" Rossett tried again.

"I'll let the doctor know you're awake."

"I need to know what happened to him."

"I understand, sir."

"Can you get me a phone?"

"After the doctor has spoken to you." The nurse reached around and opened the door to Rossett's room for him.

"Your voice." Rossett paused at the threshold of the room. "You reminded me of my wife."

"I hope that's a good thing," she joked, then seemed to regret it.

"It is," Rossett said softly.

The double doors at the end of the corridor swung open. Rossett felt a buzz of nausea as he turned his head a little too quickly to see who was coming through them.

Dannecker and Becker. All boots and black leather, striding along, dirtying up the corridor.

"You're up," Dannecker said in German, a statement, not a question.

"Where's Neumann?" Rossett didn't have to look to know that the nurse had taken a couple of steps away from him.

"Gone."

"Dead?"

Dannecker shrugged and then looked at the nurse. "Does he have clothes?"

"Yes, sir," she answered in perfect German. "In the laundry."

Rossett looked at her. German had swept away the Liverpool accent, and with it the scent of his wife. He felt a strange sadness as he watched the warmth sucked out of her by the darkness of the SS.

"Get them." Staff Sergeant Becker didn't even bother to look at her.

"The doctor will be—"

"Go get his clothes."

Rossett felt the draft as the nurse hurried past him toward the doors. She almost hugged the wall as she squeezed past Becker, who had his arm hooked through the sling of an MP40 machine gun. The shoulder stock was folded, and the weapon looked tiny as he rested his hand across the top of it. His coat was open, and Rossett could see a holster on his hip and an additional pistol hanging in a shoulder rig. Dannecker also had an MP40. He was holding it casually down at his side by the grip next to the trigger.

They stared at Rossett, as Dannecker's MP40's muzzle tapped lightly against his boot.

"Are you injured?" asked Dannecker.

"Concussion."

"You were lucky."

"What happened?"

"Bomb." Dannecker sounded bored as he looked casually around the corridor. "It was only a small thing, just enough to cause confusion and kill a few pedestrians. You were blown off your feet and you banged your head."

"They took Neumann?"

"Must have. We didn't find a body." Dannecker shifted his weight so that the MP40 stopped tapping against his boot. Instead it hung lazily, the strap like a vine hanging low and brushing the floor.

"Are you looking for him?" Rossett tried again.

Becker answered for his boss. "We're making enquiries."

"Who with?" Rossett felt the conversation sticking like mud on his boots. Short answer following short answer. He reached up and touched the dressing on his forehead.

"You." Dannecker this time.

"Me?"

"It was lucky that you climbed out of the car just before the bomb went off," said Becker.

"Very lucky." Dannecker this time.

The double doors behind them opened and the nurse appeared with Rossett's clothes. Neither Becker nor Dannecker looked around as she took a few steps toward them.

She coughed.

"I'm a suspect?" Rossett said, ignoring her.

She spoke. "Mr. Rossett's clothes."

Becker finally flicked his head, indicating that she should hand the clothes to Rossett. She edged past, holding the clothes across her chest as a shield.

The nurse almost curtsied as she gave them to Rossett. "They're a little wet."

"I've a feeling that's going to be the least of my problems."

DANNECKER LED THE way down the cast-iron staircase that ran through the hospital like a spine. Each floor looked as immaculate as the one on which Rossett had been recovering, and he noticed that the lower they got, the more uniformed guards there seemed to be. By the time they reached the first floor he counted at least twenty men milling around and trying to look busy as they dodged doctors and nurses going about their work. For every German, there were two British Home Defense Troops in their royal blue dress uniforms and Sam Brown belts.

As Dannecker stalked past, smartly presented salutes snapped up.

He ignored them all.

Rossett realized he'd been stowed away from the other patients. He wondered if that was because he was English, or because he wasn't military. Either way, he was cold and his shirt, trousers, and coat were still wet and stank of smoke.

The lower they went, the quicker Dannecker and Becker seemed to walk. It was as if gravity were pulling them down. They hit the ground floor at almost a run. A fifteen-foot-high portrait of Prime Minister Mosley hung at one end of the entrance hall to the hospital. The reception desk sat opposite the revolving entrance doors, and behind it a huge Union Jack mural filled the wall. Up the other end of the hall, a portrait of Hitler glared down determinedly at six German army privates. They were hunkered behind a row of sandbags, on top of which three heavy machine guns stuck out like oars on a longboat.

The soldiers looked a lot less confident than their leader behind them.

"What's with all the guns?" Rossett asked Becker as they headed for the exit.

"Resistance assault a few months ago. They made it inside and shot up the ground floor."

"They made it inside?"

"Ten of them. There wasn't much security back then, it being a hospital."

"What happened?"

"They killed thirty-four people, a mix of doctors, soldiers, and a few patients. Then they set a fire before fighting their way out again."

"I didn't hear anything about it." Rossett looked around the foyer and realized the fire was the reason for the fresh paint everywhere.

"It isn't the sort of thing they stick in the papers." Becker flipped a hand and the revolving door started to spin. He stepped back as Dannecker exited first without having to break step or touch the door.

Rossett stopped and looked at the Union Jack mural. He could see slight shadows dotted across the wall. He stared at them and saw they were cast by ceiling lamps falling across fresh plaster. The dots traced an arc, left by a spray of machine gun fire.

"Did they catch them?" Rossett looked at Becker, then touched the lump on his head lightly again.

"Who?"

"The people who attacked the hospital." The lump behind his ear ached a little as he turned his head again.

"Some dead, some got away." Becker glanced at the dressing over Rossett's eye. "We rounded up a few locals, killed them outside, then left the bodies there for a few days."

"What?"

"A lesson."

"How many?"

"Seventy." Becker shrugged. "I think."

Rossett tested the dressing with a fingertip for blood. He felt weak and useless in the face of casual violence. When he looked up again, the door was spinning and Becker was gone.

IT WAS GRAY and cold outside. A thick cloud that felt like it was only inches above his head pushed down on Rossett as a slight drizzle carried on the wind. Dannecker was standing at the top of the steps that led down to the street, where his staff car waited, boxed in by an armored half-track at either end.

Rossett could see a roadblock at one end of the street, topped off with coiled barbed wire, like iron icing on a concrete cake.

Sandbag emplacements were everywhere. He started to button his coat as he waited for Dannecker to finish lighting a cigarette. Becker took one step down so that he was a little below eye level with Rossett. Everyone seemed to be waiting for Dannecker to make a move.

Dannecker sucked on his cigarette as he stared at the roadblock. He exhaled smoke, then turned to look at Rossett.

"Understand this." Dannecker used the cigarette to point at Rossett. "I don't like you, and all the hero British Lion bullshit doesn't wash with me either. So do as you're told, and don't fuck me about. Yes?"

Rossett didn't reply.

Dannecker tilted his head as he slipped his lighter into his coat pocket. "Yes?"

"So I'm not a suspect?" Rossett replied to the question with one of his own.

"London says you aren't. And that you're to help in finding Neumann and Bauer."

"Help?"

"That's what they said."

"So what do you want me to do?"

"I'd like you to fuck off, but I've a feeling that isn't going to happen, so you can shadow Becker. Take notes or something, offer suggestions, I don't care. I just don't want to see you."

Rossett looked at Becker, who stared back at him with the sort of look people had when they were waiting for a bus to turn up.

"It'll be a pleasure," Rossett lied.

Dannecker took a few steps toward his car, then stopped and looked back at Rossett.

"Just remember, this isn't London, with its ring of steel and solid security. This is Liverpool, so do as you are told."

"I always do."

Dannecker's coat was spattered with rain, and the black leather seemed to glitter. He set off down the steps toward his staff car. Rossett watched as his SS protection squad started to move closer to the half-tracks.

"Is he always so cheerful?" Rossett asked Becker.

"He is under a lot of pressure."

"If you can't stand the heat . . ."

"Burn down the kitchen." Becker started off down the steps.

THE SUN WAS still sulking behind the clouds by the time Rossett, Dannecker, and Becker reached the SS garrison. The rain had come and gone and then come back again as what was left of Liverpool slid past on the journey from the hospital. Dannecker had made Rossett sit with the enlisted men in the lead half-track. It had been a snub, and Rossett knew it was meant to sting, but it didn't. He was happier with the enlisted men, even as he wiped rain off his face and shivered in the cold wind.

Rossett spent the journey taking in Liverpool.

It wasn't a pretty sight.

Buildings stared back at him like charred skulls. Big granite blocks looked like crumple-creased charcoal drawings. Many were bomb damaged. Rubble piles and half-collapsed walls stuck up out of the ground like carcasses. Picked clean, rotting, and forgotten as time slipped by.

The brick piles showed that at some point streets had been cleared and reconstruction had begun. Reconstruction seemed long forgotten now, though. Money and motivation had wandered off forgetfully to head down south to London. Rossett had a feeling the ruins would be there as reminders for generations not yet born.

The dereliction wasn't the worst thing, though. The worst thing was the people. Pathetic stick figures. Dirty and gray, like listless bruises smudged on the landscape. Hollow eyed, blue lipped, dead but not realizing it, as the convoy snaked through the slums.

Children sat in doorways, limp like half-stuffed sacks. Little bruised legs with bare feet and black grazes stretched out and lifeless. Just bones wrapped in paper skin.

Here and there huge bloodred flags hung from buildings like shrouds. Swastikas.

Curtains in a crematorium, the decoration of death.

Rossett noticed there weren't many Union Jacks on show. Nor were there many pictures of Mosley or King Edward at street level. Hitler still had the nerve to hang around, though. Shameless, high up on billboards, furrowed brow looking down disappointedly on the edge of his empire.

He spotted the odd crude painting of the hammer and sickle on boards and walls. Some looked like they had been there for some time, which surprised him. Down in London graffiti didn't last long, but in Liverpool it just seemed to be ignored and left to fade like a memory of freedom long lost.

It wasn't all dereliction.

He caught sight of a few cars, some battered, some in decent shape. Occasionally the odd smartly dressed person picked their way through the detritus. Like some sort of diversity quota, put in place to protect a propaganda picture of normality in the despair.

One thing that struck him was the lack of troops on the streets. He'd gotten used to seeing squads of men, sometimes individual soldiers, strolling around London and taking in the sights. In Liverpool the only troops he saw were the ones he was traveling with.

Rossett looked around the half-track.

Steel helmets wet from the drizzle, rubber ponchos pooled with rain. Faces set, wary eyes flicking here and there, weapons clutched in pink, cold hands dotted with white knuckles.

Tired, wanting to go home.

Rossett knew the look; he'd had it himself once upon a time. It came from fighting too long and living on the edge of a blade that could cut you in two if you relaxed for one second.

He wondered how much longer they could hold on. The Germans here seemed desperate. Like they were tilling barren soil long after it had nothing left to give. Knee-deep in dust, looking for something to crush, without the energy to do it.

London was different.

Down there things seemed stronger, brighter, better for the powers that be. Liverpool made Rossett wonder if all that was an illusion.

Gossamer, waiting to be blown away on the wind.

He wiped his face again, then elbowed the young private sitting next to him on the bench.

"Cigarette?" Rossett held his fingers to his lips as he spoke, just in case the German couldn't hear him over the roar of the diesel engine.

The soldier shook his head and went back to watching the passing rooftops. Rossett followed his gaze and realized they were in bandit country. He remembered he had lost his Webley. He started to watch the rooftops himself.

Eventually, the half-track slowed a little, then swung a right. Rossett found himself back on the street where he had been blown up. The truck that had blocked the road was still there, but this time he was heading back toward the garrison instead of away.

About half of the cars were gone, with just the ones too damaged to be moved remaining. Rossett saw that there were two new sandbagged machine gun emplacements by the truck, which had been shunted aside just enough to allow the half-track to squeeze past.

Rossett looked over his shoulder and saw Dannecker's car tucked in behind them. Becker was in the front passenger seat, almost filling the windscreen, which was reflecting gray clouds as the wipers swept the glass.

Rossett couldn't see Becker's eyes, but he had a feeling they were staring back at him.

He leaned forward and clapped a hand on the driver's shoulder.

"Stop!"

The driver looked around, unsure, the revs dying slightly as he lifted his foot.

"I want to get off."

The vehicle clattered to a stuttering halt.

Rossett dropped down and waved to the driver to get moving. He didn't need much encouragement. The half-track lurched, then rumbled away toward the garrison in a cloud of burnt oil, rattles, and squeaks.

Rossett tried to wave the staff car through, but instead it stopped and Becker unfolded out of the passenger seat. He straightened up, then slapped a hand the size of a dinner plate on the roof.

The car moved off and Rossett caught a glimpse of Dannecker sitting in the back. He had one elbow on the window frame, while the palm of his hand shielded his eyes, perhaps trying to keep the nightmare out.

The second half-track passed between Rossett and Becker, and then the two men faced each other across the road as the rain and the silence fell around them.

"I want to look at the car." Rossett could still taste diesel fumes.

Becker shrugged, then started walking along the line of vehicles snaking back toward the garrison.

Rossett fell into step about five feet behind and slightly to the right, closer to the cars. They were all empty. A few driver's doors were hanging open, and the rain was drifting in and soaking their seats and carpets.

"You've not moved anything?"

"We've not had time." Becker didn't bother looking over his shoulder as he answered. "And now we've closed the road off, there isn't much point. Besides, they are good for slowing down truck bombs."

"Truck bombs?"

Becker looked at him. "Trucks filled with bombs; the clue is in the name. They're a resistance favorite."

Rossett didn't reply. They walked for a while, Rossett making a cursory inspection of each car they passed.

"Have you interviewed the drivers of these vehicles?"

"No." Becker kept on walking.

"Do you know who they were?"

"They are at the garrison."

"All of them?"

"The ones still alive, yes."

Rossett stopped and looked into the interior of a Rover saloon. In the passenger footwell there was what looked like a doctor's bag. It was brown leather, open, and its contents were tipped out on the wet carpet.

He leaned in and lifted the bag so he could see what had fallen out. There was a stethoscope, dressings, a few bottles of pills, and a prescription pad.

The pad was stained with blood.

Rossett frowned, dropped the bag onto the passenger seat, and saw that the carpet was saturated with blood, then wiped his hand on the seat.

Becker had stopped and was watching him.

"What are you doing?"

"Looking for evidence."

"This car is fifty feet from where the bomb went off."

"Which is why I'm surprised there is blood in it."

"What does it matter?"

"I'm a detective. Spilled blood matters, wherever it is."

"That blood"—Becker nodded his head to the Rover—"doesn't matter."

"What happened after the bomb went off?"

"You were here."

"I'd just been blown up."

"Blown over, you were blown over."

"Either way, I was out of the game." Rossett resisted reaching up to touch the lump on his head again.

Becker sighed, looked over his shoulder toward the garrison, and then back at Rossett. They stared at each other for a few seconds until Becker removed his field cap, looked up at the gray sky, and then finally spoke.

"The bomb went off. The sentries sounded the alarm at the garrison, even though everyone had probably already heard the explosion." Becker glanced at the garrison as he continued. "The men on the gate were experienced enough to know that it can be suicide to rush toward a bomb site."

"In case it is a trap?"

Becker nodded and hooked his thumb through the strap of his MP40. "Oldest trick in the book. A small bomb followed by a big bomb. You know how the resistance play."

Rossett knew how the resistance played only too well. He looked at the palm of his hand to check that he'd gotten all the blood off it.

"Go on."

"Our standard drill is to wait, let the dust settle, and then slowly approach the site of the explosion."

"And that's what you did?"

"No."

"Why not?"

"You."

"Me?"

"We knew Captain Bauer was out there, and Neumann . . . and you."

"So you came out?"

"Major Dannecker led out the reaction squad."

"The major?"

Becker nodded.

"It took maybe three minutes before they were out the gate."

"And?"

Becker started to walk alongside Rossett. "There was a firefight. A few resistance pinned them down for a few minutes before they forced their way out."

"Neumann and Bauer, was there any sign of them?"

"A vehicle fled the scene as our men made it onto the street, and we think they were in it."

"What vehicle?"

"A van."

Rossett thought about the van that had been parked behind them in the jam, then wondered if he would recognize the driver if he saw him again.

They stopped at the Jaguar. The windows were shattered and both the driver's-side doors were hanging open, but Rossett was relieved to see that aside from a lot of broken glass, the interior didn't look too bad.

"There's no blood inside. Hopefully Neumann was uninjured." He looked more closely at the driver's seat.

"Neumann would have been better off dying in the explosion." Becker looked around at the empty buildings, then back at Rossett. "You don't want to be caught by these English bastards . . . no offense."

"None taken." Rossett stepped back from the car and pointed to the inside of the back door. There were holes in the red leather. "Two holes."

"What?"

"Two holes."

"So?"

"The metal is punched through from the inside out." Rossett crouched down and inspected the broken glass on the ground. "There is blood here."

"There was a body, shot in the chest." Becker pointed to just under his throat with a finger it would take a lumberjack to break.

Rossett picked up a shell casing from under the front seat of the Jaguar. "Bauer had Neumann's gun." He looked at the inner door again, then straightened up. "Bauer shot through the strap I used to secure him, killed the man here, and then . . ." He looked around the scene, then back at Becker. "Who knows?"

Becker nodded to himself.

"If Captain Bauer had a gun and was able to get out of the car, there is no way the resistance would have taken him alive."

"You sure?"

"I know Captain Bauer. He's the best."

"So he ran?"

Becker looked around, then back at Rossett. "I wouldn't put it like that, but he would make sure he got away. Captain Bauer would be a real prize for the resistance."

Becker shifted the MP40 a little on his shoulder, took a step closer to Rossett, and lowered his voice.

"Liverpool has been difficult to control of late. We've done things that some might consider to be heavy-handed. Even by our standards. Do you understand?"

Rossett frowned. "Like the hospital?"

"Like the hospital."

Becker slapped his cap against his leg, then continued. "The Bear, Captain Bauer, he's been at the forefront of those efforts. The resistance know that, so they wouldn't treat him well if they caught him."

"Even by their standards?"

"Even by their standards."

"So he ran." Rossett looked off toward the garrison.

"Wouldn't you?"

"I wouldn't have done what he did."

Becker snorted and shook his head.

"What?" Rossett turned to him.

"I know about you, Rossett. I know you've been working with us to get rid of the Jews. You know you haven't been sending them on a picnic, so don't start pretending you can look down from where you are standing."

Rossett touched his head again. His hair was wet, and even though he was cold, the lump behind his ear felt warm to the touch. He stared at Becker for a moment, considering a reply, but instead of speaking he walked around the Jaguar to inspect the side that had taken the brunt of the explosion.

The doors were buckled, and the roof had creased a little. The paint had lost its shine and seemed a little crazed where it had taken the heat from the bomb. The surface of the street seemed unmarked.

A row of two-story brown brick buildings ran along the gentle arc of the street, all the way from the garrison to the gun emplacements.

They were all empty, and most were boarded up.

"The people who lived here?" Rossett looked at Becker.

"We moved them out when we took over the garrison."

"All of them?"

"We like our privacy."

Rossett chewed his lip, then turned back to the two buildings nearest to him. They were boarded-up shops, with what looked like residences above. The boards on the shop windows had held up to the blast, but the glass in one of the doors was gone, along with the windows of the upper levels. Rossett looked down at the pavement on this side of the street.

There was blood on the pavement, amid the broken glass.

A lot of blood, so much the rain hadn't been able to wash it all away. He remembered the face of the lonely woman with blood in her lap, staring at him as she died.

He turned to Becker, who was standing by the back of the Jaguar watching him.

"How many were killed in the blast?"

"Five in the bomb blast, eleven in the firefight. All Brits, assuming Bauer and Neumann made it away alive."

"How many prisoners?"

"Fifty-odd, back at the garrison."

"Have you interviewed them?"

"We don't normally bother."

"Two Germans are missing."

"Resistance don't allow themselves to be captured alive anymore."

"So then why are you holding people if you aren't going to interview them?"

"Like I said, sometimes we need to be a little heavy-handed."

Rossett took another look at the broken windows above him, shook his head, then headed for the garrison.

THE BEAR SMILED.

The wait had been worth his while.

The Lion was alive.

Maybe he was better than he looked after all?

It had started to rain again, fat drops this time.

The Bear stepped back from the shattered glass as a few spots of rain landed on the windowsill and pooled in the dirt. He touched the water, lifted his finger to his tongue, and tasted it.

"Dust to dust," he said to nobody but himself. He was on his own again, doing what he did best.

CHAPTER 10

MICHAEL O'KANE COUGHED politely on the other side of the desk. "If you'll forgive me for saying so, Major Dannecker, and please, take this as an observation and not a criticism, some people would suggest that you are drinking with your mouth a little too close to the bottle."

Dannecker looked up from the brandy he was pouring and frowned at O'Kane.

"What?"

O'Kane shrugged his shoulders and smiled.

"It's just an observation, Major, no more than that."

"If I was worried I was drinking too much, the last person I'd ask for an opinion would be an Irishman."

"I'm a teetotaler myself. I took the pledge in 1930, and haven't touched a drop since. I found it was getting in the way of my work, and I couldn't afford for that to happen. So it went, before I did."

Dannecker went back to pouring, and once the glass was three-quarters full, set the bottle down gently on the desk.

Dannecker leaned back in his chair and asked the question he'd been avoiding since O'Kane had turned up at the garrison, unannounced, fifteen minutes earlier.

"What do you want?"

"I've been sent to see what the problem is."

"There isn't a problem. I have this under control, so there isn't a problem."

"There is a problem, Major, and it appears to be a fucking big one."

"I'm telling you, there—"

O'Kane held up a hand, waited to see if Dannecker was going to remain quiet, and then spoke so softly the German had to lean forward to make out the words.

"A month or so ago, my organization came to you with an opportunity. We explained that this was an opportunity we needed your help to exploit, but that it was an opportunity for both parties, just the same. With that in mind, you agreed to help us sort out some issues, so that we could all end up better off. Do you remember that?"

Dannecker scratched at his temple but didn't reply.

"And now, another man who was also helping us in this matter, U.S. Consul Hawthorn, is dead. On top of this, we also have two detectives from London sniffing around and opening boxes we don't want opened." O'Kane leaned back from the desk and held out his hands palm up. "Now, some people would say that is a big problem, but not me." He waggled his left index finger, dropped it into the palm of his right hand, and closed his fist around it. "For me, and this is only a personal opinion, the biggest problem we have is that we, and by 'we' I mean 'you'"—the index finger popped out again and pointed at Dannecker—"have gone and lost our gold bullion."

O'Kane dropped his hands onto his lap.

"Now, Major, I'm sure, whichever way you look at it, that is one big fucking problem." He flicked his head to the glass on the table. "Now would probably be a good time to take a drink."

Dannecker went for the glass, slowed when he realized how desperate he looked, then speeded up when he saw O'Kane had noticed the hesitation.

"There isn't a problem." Dannecker took a sip of the brandy.

O'Kane stared at Dannecker with sullen flat eyes that showed nothing but the green of the ocean.

He was a big man, not as big as Becker, but big all the same. His suit was brown flecked wool, expensive, good quality. Handmade, Harris Tweed, the best. Fitting where it was supposed to and relaxing where it wasn't. His skin was the same, taut on wide cheekbones, but easy around lips that looked like they were used to laughing.

O'Kane's hands were the only things the suit didn't seem to fit. They were wide, with fat fingers that looked like they would fold into useful fists thrown by the big biceps that smudged the suit's sleeves, like sharks swimming just under the surface.

O'Kane's soft Irish accent sparked up again.

"My people are concerned, and, in fairness to them, I think they have a right to be when you consider what it is at stake. This isn't a few crates of guns that you are selling out the back door to pay for your prostitutes and bar bill. This is gold. Bullion worth millions of dollars." O'Kane let the words hang, then repeated them like an echo to drive their weight home. "Millions of U.S. dollars. Now, that gold was in this city last week. And as we speak, a U.S. Navy ship is waiting to collect it. A U.S. Navy ship that I have gone to a lot, and I mean an awful lot, of trouble to get to help us. So my people want their gold, Major, and you"—O'Kane pointed across the table—"have gone and fucking lost the lot of it." O'Kane folded the finger back into his fist. "So what are you going to do about it?"

"It's under control."

O'Kane blinked, watched Dannecker take another drink, and then spoke again.

"Do you know my name?"

"O'Kane."

"My full name?"

Dannecker searched his desktop for a memory, then looked up again. "Michael O'Kane."

"No. Do you know my name?"

Dannecker stared back at O'Kane in silence.

"Michael Mad Dog O'Kane," O'Kane said.

"Mad Dog?"

"Mad Dog." O'Kane scratched an ear, then shifted a little. "Of course, my mother never christened me 'Mad Dog.' There was no way the priest would have allowed it. And besides, the Mad Dog bit didn't come along until I was growing up, finding my way in the world, fighting my way through the world, battling battles, battling men, right up until I ended up here, in this office, right now. Do you understand?"

"Yes."

"I earned it, the name, the hard way. First off, by fighting in the old country of Ireland, and then, fighting the G-men in the new country."

Dannecker nodded that he understood, so O'Kane continued.

"What I'm telling you, in case you haven't already got it, is that I'm a killer. Initially for the love of Ireland, and then, God forgive me, for the love of money. I do it for the money, and for the people I work for, who are like my family. Do you understand?"

"Yes."

"I can do it close up with a brick just as well as I can do it from afar with a bomb. Either way doesn't bother me." O'Kane leaned forward a few inches conspiratorially. "Some fellas don't like the close-up bit, they don't like to see the eyes. But sure, if you've done it once you can do it a thousand times. It isn't as hard as some folk make out."

O'Kane leaned back.

"Now, I know you've done a bit of the topping yourself. I can see that from all the medals, and your red eyes, and the rattle of the bottle and the glass. But I can also see it from the respect that your men have for you. Sure, that big fella, the sergeant outside, what's his name?"

"Becker."

"Becker," O'Kane repeated. "I can see that he'd walk through fire for you." He smiled again. "Anyway, what I am saying to you is that I'm a killer. A proper killer, and a very good one at that. Now, this is the point that I'm getting to: I've been sent over here to kill someone."

"Who?"

"Whoever is the problem." O'Kane rested his hands in his lap and tapped his thumbs together like a bank manager as the words sank in. "So, when I asked you a minute ago what the problem was, and you replied there wasn't one, well, that makes me wonder if you're the problem I've got to fix, and you just haven't realized it yet."

Dannecker put the glass back carefully on the desk.

"Are you threatening me?"

"I would say that was a fair summation of the situation."

Dead eyes stared back across the desk.

"You're in my garrison, surrounded by my men, and you are threatening me?"

"I am that, yes." O'Kane smiled, pushed himself up the chair a little, and adjusted his right shirt cuff, so that it was hanging out of his sleeve by just the right amount, before continuing.

"I know you could pull a gun on me and have me dead in a ditch inside of ten minutes, Major. You're the fucking SS, it's what you fellas do for a living." O'Kane lifted his hands. "Sure as hell, you're good at it. If there is one nation better than the Irish at digging ditches and filling them up again, it is you Germans." His hands dropped back onto the arms of his chair. "Which is why, when I was asked to come and speak to you today, I put certain guarantees in place. You see, Ireland is a small country, but your High Command value our position with the Americans, and the Americans value our proximity to Europe. So the Irish government, and my family on the East Coast of America and back in Dublin, we are like the little cogs spinning in a big fucking gearbox."

O'Kane held up the fingers of both hands, then meshed them together to make his point.

"Now, I'm not a government man. What I am is a shadow, a man who is connected on both sides of the water to people you don't ever want to meet. Now, a lot of people on both sides are invested in this gold." O'Kane dropped his voice again, then glanced theatrically over his shoulder at the door behind him before turning back to Dannecker. "Including a few who wear the same uniform as you do, but of a significantly higher rank."

Dannecker wasn't used to certain matters being spoken of so loudly. He shifted his feet under the desk but didn't speak.

"Now, a lot of folk will know that if I'm not back in my hotel room tonight, with a full belly and a warm cup of cocoa on the bedside table, you've been a bad boy. If they want to keep making money for their pension funds, they will come looking for you, and they'll make sure you're lying in that fucking ditch next to me come dawn."

O'Kane leaned back in the chair and smiled again.

"So when I threaten you, boy"—the big broad index finger rose up and pointed squarely into Dannecker's face—"you are well and truly fucking threatened. Do you understand me now?"

"Yes."

"Good." The finger dropped and O'Kane smiled. "So, I'll ask you again, who is the problem here, so I can get on and kill them, and then get back to home to a bed without bugs?"

Dannecker stared back across the table.

O'Kane sat silent; he knew when a man was best left alone to make a decision.

It didn't take long.

"The Bear. Captain Bauer. He killed the men who know where the gold is."

"Why?"

"It's what he does. His job is to operate independently in bandit country. He keeps the resistance's heads down. He disrupts them, hunts them, kills them, kills their associates, and generally ties them up so they can't focus on us, the regular troops."

"He terrorizers the terrorists?"

"I suppose so."

"So he killed these men thinking they were terrorists."

"Well, technically, they were, but I don't think that was the reason."

O'Kane gestured that Dannecker should elaborate, so he did.

"I think he killed them for fun."

"Fun? Why?"

"To cause me, or rather us, trouble. Captain Bauer has been a little unstable of late."

"Unstable?"

"Mad. I think he found about the gold, about what was happening, and then took matters into his own hands for the fun of it."

"How did he find out? Did you tell him?"

"It's his job. He interrogates people. If Bauer found someone who knew about the gold, Bauer would know about the gold not long afterward. But how he found it doesn't matter. The fact that he found it, then moved it, is what counts."

"Has he told London about it?"

"No."

"You know this how?"

"Because if he had, they'd be here by now and I'd probably be dead."

"So only he knows where it is?"

Dannecker shrugged. "He says so, and the fact that you are sitting here rather proves him right."

O'Kane pondered this information, then looked up.

"You were approached by my organization because we needed you to turn a blind eye."

"I'm aware of that."

"Well, you'd better get that eye open and find this fucking gold quick. I've a ship waiting, and it can't wait for long, do you understand me?"

"I know about your ship. It was I who let it dock, and it is I who wants to sail out on it."

"Have you still got communication channels with the British resistance?"

"Not since the shooting. Our contact died with the consul, and as I'm sure you can imagine, we don't have a telephone number for them. I take it the resistance are out looking for the gold themselves?"

"They will be."

"I've enough men. If we search the docks and find it before them, I'm sure we can cut them out of the deal and increase our margins."

O'Kane shook his head.

"There are seven miles of docks in this city. It would take a year, and that is based on the assumption he hid it in the docks." O'Kane steepled his fingertips and rested his forehead on them. "We need to find this Bear character. He's the only one who can lead us to it before my ship has to sail."

"The problem with the Bear, Mr. O'Kane, is that he has a habit of finding you first."

CHAPTER 11

ROSSETT COULD HEAR them screaming long before he could see them.

They weren't being held in the cellblock where the Bear had been held. There was no brushed floor, no folded sharp sheets, and no fresh paint for the poor souls swept off the street after the explosion.

It was also a different jailer who led the way down the steps into the darkness. This one was a Brit in a too-tight uniform and boots that creaked like coffin lids as they made their way along a corridor that reminded Rossett of a drain.

"You'll have to shout." The jailer smelled of rotten teeth. "The minute we open the flap they all start barkin' like dogs in a kennel."

Rossett didn't reply.

"You wait till they get a bit of fresh air." The jailer laughed, then stopped next to a metal-framed wall light in which a bulb was flickering reluctantly. He banged it with his fist and the flickering stopped as the bulb blew, adding to the gloom. He tried the fist again, and when it didn't work, turned back to Rossett. "Shithole, this place, absolute shithole."

Rossett didn't argue. The jailer started walking again and Rossett followed.

The walls were running with water, and as the two men went farther along the corridor, their feet began to splash across the uneven floor.

"Why is it so wet?" Rossett ran a finger down the wall while he waited for the jailer to find another key, for another door, on their journey to the depths.

"We're belowground, and the sewers overflow when it rains."

Rossett sniffed his finger then wiped it on his leg.

"If that isn't bad enough," the jailer continued, "a river runs underneath us on its way down to the Mersey. They built this place on top of it, and whenever it rains the basements flood." The key rattled into the lock, and he pulled on the rusty door. "Sometimes the electrics fuse. You should 'ear these fuckers scream when it goes dark."

The jailer smiled at Rossett, who caught sight of the reason for the smell of rotten teeth.

The shouting died down a little as the splash of their footsteps gave their approach away as they made their way along a row of cells. They stopped at the end one. The jailer winked at Rossett, and flicked his head toward the door.

"'Ere, watch this." The jailer dropped the flap in the door, and the screaming and shouting started up again, louder than before.

Rossett took a step backward.

Arms, hands, fingers fired through the eighteen-inch slot and reached toward them. Through tiny gaps Rossett caught sight of teeth and eyes, the odd flash of hair, a snatch of colored cloth, all crushed into a space so small it seemed to squeeze the sound through the hatch like toothpaste out of a tube.

The arms were like flames out of a furnace.

Rossett took another step away.

The jailer pulled a short wooden truncheon and started to beat the prisoners back through the slot. He hacked and slashed like he was cutting bamboo, but it still took a minute to clear the desperation.

He nodded his head, indicating that Rossett could move closer to inspect the contents of the cell again. As Rossett moved, the shouting and screaming seemed to fill his head and push against his skull.

One hand snaked out, but the jailer flicked it away with a solid swipe that probably broke a few fingers. "Take a look. If they grab you I'll knock 'em off, don't worry."

Rossett placed a hand on the cold steel door and leaned in closer.

The sound was nearly swamped by the smell.

Humanity.

Its basest form.

Stinking, sweating, screaming, slammed into a space too small.

Faces swirled in the gloom like they were circling a drain. Rossett saw his past. He heard the Jews, their screams, the smell of fear and desperation washing over him and knotting his stomach so tight, it seemed to pull his knees up to his chest.

He put a hand on the wall to steady himself against the guilt.

He couldn't look through hell's gate; he didn't want to see his future; he didn't want to see his past.

He turned, and then started walking back to the light.

BECKER WAS WAITING in the sergeant's mess.

Two enamel mugs of black coffee were sitting on a bald wooden bench. There was a metal plate with a little cheese, three inches of dried sausage, and a chunk of black bread that looked like it had been ripped out of a bowling ball.

Rossett sat down heavily across the table from Becker, who slid a coffee toward him.

Neither of them spoke.

It took Rossett two minutes to pick up the mug and take a drink. He stared at the food, his hands still wrapped around the mug.

Becker broke the silence. "I got you some food. You should eat."

Rossett looked up. "Do you have a cigarette?"

Becker took out a tobacco pouch and papers. "I can roll you one."

"Please."

Rossett watched as Becker's ham hands produced a cigarette that looked like a toothpick, passed it across, and lit a match.

Rossett took a drag, then took hold of his coffee mug again. He held on to the smoke awhile, then finally let it go as he started to speak.

"Have you been down there?"

Becker was busy rolling himself a cigarette, so he just nodded without looking up. Rossett took another drag and looked around the mess hall. It was all bare walls and benches. The kind of place that might host a Bavarian beer festival, but without the beer.

Hitler was there, same as usual. This time in a plain frame that made it look like he was peering through a window. Down at the other end of the hall was Himmler, in a slightly smaller frame. Rossett stared at him for a minute, wondering how someone who looked like a librarian could climb to the top of the Third Reich.

Another match flared. Rossett looked up and saw that Becker was lighting his own cigarette, while pulling at the top button of his tunic to free his tree-trunk neck.

"It's wrong."

"The people in the cell?" Becker settled again, then flicked the cigarette to the corner of his mouth with his tongue as he answered.

"Yes."

"Hmm." Becker squinted through the smoke.

"It's inhuman."

"It's no worse than what you did with the Jews."

"I never did that."

Becker took a pull on his cigarette. "How much elbow room do you think those Jews had by the time they made it to Poland?"

"When I saw them off from London, they—" Rossett knew he was losing the argument before it had even begun, and he hated himself for trying to justify his crimes. Embarrassment broke off his sentence like a snapped stick.

Becker filled the silence.

"You need stop thinking about them as people. Don't listen to their voices, don't for a minute ever think they are like you. You work for us now. You have a job to do, same as I do. If you can keep them at arm's length and see them as being totally different from you, well . . . I think it is easier." Becker shifted on the bench and tapped the cigarette against the tin ashtray at his elbow.

"You don't care about them?"

"I don't even think about them."

"Those people down there have families."

"Not like ours."

"I'm English, same as them."

"You're a Nazi, or at the very least you work for us, so therefore you are different. Besides, you're from London, this is Liverpool. These people aren't really British. Most of them are immigrants, Irish, Welsh. There were even some Gypsies, blacks, and Chinese here when we arrived."

"They are human beings."

Becker tapped a finger against his right temple. "Just accept it, they aren't like us." He took another drag on his cigarette and picked a piece of tobacco off his tongue. "Anyway, does it really matter if a few more die?"

"It matters to them."

"On a grand scale, though, does it matter? How many in Europe have died in these last few years?"

Rossett didn't answer Becker's question as he ripped off a hunk of bread.

"A million?" Becker conjured a figure. "Five? Ten? Fucking hell, it could be twenty in Russia alone for all we know. I saw the bodies piled as high as houses when I was out east, thousands of them. When they were burned they stank of pork, and you could smell it for ten miles around. They had to dig ditches to trap the fat that was running out of the fire . . . fucking ditches." Becker looked off into the distance and shook his head. "Ditches."

Rossett dropped the hunk of bread back onto the plate uneaten.

"All I'm saying is, those people down there"—Becker pointed with his cigarette to the floor—"they don't matter. Same as the Jews, same as the Russians, the Poles, the French . . . even the Germans. None of it, none of them, and none of us matter. If I die today, who cares? I'll be gone and that will be that. You should realize, we are alive only for this moment. Accept that they are already dead, accept that you're dead, Neumann is dead, I'm dead, fucking humanity is dead. Trust me, it's easier that way."

Becker turned on the bench, then stood up. He pinched the end of the cigarette between his finger and thumb, and fastened the top button of his tunic again.

Rossett watched, and then spoke. "I need to speak to my headquarters, down in London. Do you have a telephone?"

Becker picked up his field cap off the bench and looked at his wristwatch. "The lines to London are down, so you'll have to wait."

Rossett nodded. Problems with communication between London and the rest of the country were common. Phone cables were easy to cut, and radio time was often at a premium.

"I'll still need to speak to the people in the cell, but I can't do it down there."

"They're being transported shortly; the major had already suggested you should come with us, and it's only a short journey. You can speak to them as they are assembled off the trucks. If you find someone who can help you with your enquiries, I'll pull them out of the line so you can interview them at length later. Okay?"

"Thank you."

The German rechecked his top button, and walked to the door.

"Becker?"

Becker turned.

"How do you do it?"

Becker smiled, opened the door, and stepped halfway through before pausing, then looking back at Rossett.

"You of all people should know, it's easier than it looks."

BECKER HAD BEEN right; the journey hadn't taken long.

Rossett was standing next to the staff car, squinting into drizzle and staring out across a windswept River Mersey. Waves were flecked with froth, and the tide was heading back out to sea, like it was attempting to get away from what was about to take place on its bank.

Across the river, Rossett could see thick black smoke rising from what looked like a tire fire in the far docklands. The wind was pushing the smoke low for the first few hundred yards. It scraped across slate-roofed warehouses, then finally up and away in a column that fattened at the top into a dark smudge on the sky. At the smoke's source Rossett caught glimpses of angry orange, as the flames bubbled their way toward what little oxygen seemed left in the world.

Rossett turned away from the river and rested an elbow on the roof of the car. He was standing on a square plaza at the foot of three tall buildings. The buildings had once been famous. They'd once stood sentinel proudly over Liverpool's riverbank flank.

Not anymore.

It had taken a while, long after he had been driven to the plaza, for Rossett to finally recognize the Royal Liver Building and its neighbors. He'd once watched a cinema newsreel, back before the war, about the Mersey ferries that had docked at the Pier Head, where he was now standing.

The ferries were long gone. And the floating landing stage they had used was now half submerged in the quickening Mersey. The crowds of commuters were replaced by sour-looking troops, drenched by the falling rain and misery.

All that was left from the newsreel was the occasional shell-shocked pigeon, limping around with glassy eyes and cold-looking salmon-colored feet.

Rossett looked up at the remains of the three buildings in front of him. In the newsreel they had looked like they would last forever, but now they barely clung onto existence. Where there had once been windows, smoke-smudged cavities dotted the walls. There were more holes blasted by artillery, and piles of rubble where gravity and indifference had dumped falling stonework and masonry.

The city's famous Liver birds looked down sadly at the scene below them.

The plaza was cordoned off with a twelve-foot barbed-wire blockade fence. It had the look of something that was intended to be temporary but had ended up becoming permanent. The gates Rossett had just been driven through hung on hinges that seemed more rust than metal. The plaza itself was maybe two football fields wide. There was no grass, just concrete, and the wind whipped through the fence, sweeping the place clean.

A truckful of miserable Waffen SS soldiers were jumping down into the rain and forming up into awkward ranks that had to be jostled into some sort of shape by shouting NCOs.

It struck Rossett that the men were green, untested, and lacking in discipline. They were chatting among themselves, shifting from foot to foot as they casually ignored orders.

They were different from the soldiers he saw in London. These were the dregs, wasting away their service in a distant outpost hoping not to get shot.

Rossett looked around for the driver who had brought him to hell. The car was there, but the man himself had melted into the gray mass of uniforms that was getting bigger by the minute. There were three trucks now, and two old half-tracks had also rumbled into the compound. Machine gun nests were being set up with several heavy MG42s, their crews keeping their heads bowed to the wind that was gusting into their faces.

The circus had come to town.

Rossett needed another cigarette.

He started to walk toward the nearest troop carrier.

"Cigarette?" he asked a fresh-faced corporal, who produced a packet of German Ecksteins and a lighter.

Rossett cupped his hands over the flame, nodded thanks, and then turned as two BMW motorcycle outriders led a canvas-backed Opel Blitz truck through the compound gates. It sounded like one of the motorcycles had a defective muffler. It was popping and roaring, and its echo bounced back off the buildings and out onto the river.

The truck lurched as it bounced up onto a low curb, closely followed by two beetle-black cars, with men crammed into them like sardines. Rossett watched to see if Dannecker's staff car was going to follow them through the gates.

It didn't.

He turned back to the newly arrived vehicles and saw Becker climbing out of one of them. The German put on his cap and took an StG 44 assault rifle from one of the men who had got out behind him.

Becker held up a hand to someone Rossett couldn't see in the back of the truck, then scanned the scene for a few seconds until his eyes met Rossett's. He gestured that Rossett should approach, so Rossett walked across the plaza like an actor on an empty stage. He felt the tickle of the gunsights on the heavy machine guns as he passed between them and the three derelict buildings that flanked him on his right.

He dropped the cigarette as he joined Becker near the back of the truck.

The canvas was flapping and whipping, but as he stepped into the lee between the truck and buildings, the wind dropped to become cold, still air.

He could hear voices in the truck to his left. He strained, tilting his head as he approached Becker, trying to catch words he could make out. The German worked the bolt on the StG 44 and nodded to one of the troops standing near the back of the truck.

Rossett glanced over his shoulder and saw that the soldier was untying a frayed rope that was holding down the canvas flap. Rossett turned back to Becker, who pointed at the truck.

"You can speak to them as they climb down, but make it quick, just one question. If they have something interesting to say, or if they saw anything, I'll pull them out and you can have them for a few minutes. Understand?"

Rossett nodded that he understood, even though he wasn't sure that he did.

"Don't waste my time by dragging half of them to one side, though. I haven't got all day."

Rossett wished he hadn't thrown away his cigarette. He took up station near the back of the truck, then had to step away again as two soldiers lowered the tailgate to allow the people inside to jump down.

Three tumbled out all at once into the arms of the waiting guards.

"One at a time!" Becker shouted, and in turn the guards held up their hands and gestured that the people on the back of the truck should wait until they were summoned.

Rossett leaned in, so that he could see under the canvas flap that was now hanging free.

It was crowded full of shifting shadows and blinking eyes.

He looked at Becker, who gestured that he should speak to the people who had climbed down. They looked nervous; one had his hands folded across his stomach, as if he had just eaten a heavy meal. His head hung low, his eyes hidden behind a loose fringe of hair.

Rossett glanced back at Becker and noticed for the first time that there was a soldier carrying a small movie camera. He was filming the scene, walking behind Becker and the other men, capturing a tracking shot of the unloading of the prisoners.

Becker nodded and pointed at the prisoner standing closest to Rossett. Ask him.

Rossett didn't know what to say.

The words were lost.

Two British Home Defense troopers pushed the first prisoner even closer to Rossett, who realized he hadn't noticed the HDT arriving. He stared at them, then at the prisoner.

"I've got a family," the prisoner said quietly, without panic. "I don't deserve this."

Rossett didn't reply.

The prisoner tried again. "I was just on my way home for lunch. I don't know anything about the resistance. I just want to go home."

Rossett looked at the cameraman and then back at the prisoner.

"I can't help you," Rossett said.

"They took the pictures of my kids." He finally looked up at Rossett. "Can you get them for me? I want to see them again."

One of the soldiers lightly jabbed a rifle butt toward the man, who took a step forward and then looked back at Rossett. "They'll be worried about me."

"I'm sorry."

"I don't want them to be worried, that's all . . ." This time the rifle hit home slightly harder, and the man took the hint and walked away.

Rossett watched the man walking, then turned back to the truck and found another man in front of him waiting. He was shorter than Rossett, confused, another one with lowered eyes, too scared to look up. Rossett had to lean forward so that he could catch the prisoner's attention. He was crying. Rossett took a step back. The HDT standing next to the man paused, unsure, then led the prisoner away.

Another prisoner was brought forward.

This one was calm, his suit jacket bunched up around his shoulders because an HDT trooper was holding his arm too tightly. His tie and spectacles were askew. He waited for Rossett to play his part. The man glanced at the HDT, and then back at Rossett, unsure whether he was supposed to speak first.

Rossett filled the silence.

"Did you see anything?"

It was all he could think of to say. It sounded stupid, and embarrassed him a little.

"When?" The man looked confused.

The HDT trooper looked at Becker, who signaled that he should hurry the prisoner away.

The trooper did as he was told.

Rossett turned to look at Becker.

"How am I supposed to interrogate them here? Like this?"

Becker shrugged. "You had your chance in the jail."

"I need time . . . to prepare . . . I . . ." Rossett looked back up into the truck, and the next prisoner waiting to drop down.

They stared at each other, and it struck him that this prisoner wasn't scared.

Rossett realized *he* was scared.

An emotion he'd forgotten all about had just woken up in the pit of his stomach, for the first time in years.

This was wrong. Where he was was wrong. What he was about to witness was wrong.

He was scared.

He didn't know what to do.

He wanted to stop it, but he wanted no part of it.

He was scared.

The prisoner dropped down off the truck.

"Proud of yourself?" the prisoner said flatly.

Rossett looked at Becker again.

"We don't have all day," Becker said in German. "It isn't fair to make them wait."

Rossett swallowed and shook his head. "Fair?"

Becker sighed, then waved to the soldiers and the queue of HDT at the back of the truck. "Get them off and line them up. Let's get this over with."

IT BEGAN.

Tumbling death.

Almost silent.

Everyone knew their part and carried it out to perfection.

People jumped down.

Dropping into the arms of their executioners, who were waiting to catch them. Some jogged, some couldn't, but all of them moved toward the plaza and its guns. Quietly, mostly confused, going toward their end like children answering a bell in a school yard.

Rossett turned away and walked out of the lee of the wind so that he could feel it bite.

He looked at them.

They were lining up in front of the emplacements.

Shivering.

The wind blew, and the only movement was the cracking of skirts and coats against the legs of the doomed.

There was a child.

Rossett hadn't seen the boy at first. Amid the shuffling confusion, the kid had been lost in the legs and shadows.

"There is a child." Rossett said it quietly, almost to himself.

He pointed at the kid.

"There is a child."

This time louder. He looked around, and then back at the boy.

The corporal who had given Rossett the cigarette stood between him and the prisoners, one hand on his hip, the other tapping a pistol lazily against his thigh.

"Hey!" Rossett shouted at the corporal. "There is a kid there!"

The wind whipped at the words and sucked them inland.

Rossett took a few steps toward the corporal, who turned away. Rossett could see the smoke of the corporal's cigarette. It all seemed so normal, so relaxed.

"There is a kid!"

The camera moved over to Rossett's left, scanning the huddled prisoners, who were being hectored into a line. The camera panned around, capturing Rossett before drifting back to the prisoners.

Rossett looked at Becker with his finger still pointing at the boy.

"There is a kid in the line! A child! Be careful!"

An SS private was watching Rossett from over by one of the machine guns, and their eyes met.

"He's only a boy!"

The private stared back, not understanding or not caring.

Rossett felt like he was in a nightmare.

Nobody seemed able to see him.

Nobody seemed able to hear him.

He caught hold of a passing sleeve but it shook itself loose.

He looked at the boy.

The kid was crying. Looking for someone to hold his hand.

The boy looked at Rossett and held out the hand that needed holding.

"It's okay, it'll be okay, I'll get someone." Rossett tried to soothe the kid from sixty feet away.

The camera moved in between them, blocking the boy and pointing at Rossett again as its operator smiled and gave him a thumbs-up.

Rossett realized he was captured in a crime. Forever on film. Damned by anyone who dared to watch through their fingers in future times.

He was ashamed and felt his heart thudding. He saw Becker, who in turn glanced up to the once-great clock in the tower of the Royal Liver Building above them. It was broken, frozen, its tick and its tock long forgotten.

Rossett started to walk toward Becker, still pointing toward the kid.

"He's just a kid!" Over the wind this time, shouted with all his strength. "You can't . . ."

Becker lifted a hand, then pointed.

Rossett followed the direction over his shoulder and saw the corporal behind him.

The corporal nodded, looked at Rossett, and smiled.

Two Germans, one on either side, with hands like vises, took Rossett's arms and propelled him forward. He kicked, his heels caught a curb, and then his knees folded as they rushed him on toward the huddled group who were waiting to die.

Out of the corner of his eye he saw the camera panning around again, capturing the struggle as its operator moved so that he was walking backward a few feet in front of Rossett.

Rossett twisted at the waist and managed to shake one hand free. He drove up with his elbow into the face of the soldier on his right, catching him on the tip of his nose and breaking it. His fist was already folded and sweeping across to hit the man on the left when someone else grabbed his free arm, and two more swept his feet up off the ground.

He heard a pistol slide being pulled.

Rossett bucked like a bronco. Arching his back and gritting his teeth, he pulled the men and forced them to stagger from side to side. Finally, they closed in above him. The man holding his left foot slipped and let go. Rossett didn't hesitate; he flicked his leg and swept with a scissor kick into the face of the man holding his right leg.

Another one down.

Three of them left.

Two more took their place, then another one, then another.

They held him down this time, pushing him onto the ground as they struggled to control him. Rossett spat and snarled like a caged cat. He twisted, grabbing and scratching, fighting for his life, an animal struggle against superior numbers.

There were too many.

Rossett saw Becker through the gaps, circling the crowd of people holding him down. One of the HDT gripped Rossett's head and pushed it onto the wet cobbles. Rossett sank his teeth into two fingers and tasted blood.

The HDT screamed and let go.

There were more of them.

So many they felt like soil on a coffin lid.

Rossett tried his best, but it wasn't enough.

He screamed and tried with all his might, but they wouldn't let go.

He saw Becker again.

Their eyes met.

Rossett wanted to call out, but someone clamped his mouth with a rough hand that smelled of diesel.

Becker was holding a Walther pistol, high, next to his cheek, pointing at the sky. He leaned in, pulling one of the men holding Rossett to one side so that he had a clear shot.

"Hold him still."

Becker didn't shout. He was calm, as if he were putting an animal out of its misery.

Rossett was going to die.

He stopped, just a fraction of a second, watching the black eye of the muzzle come toward him through the arms of the troopers, like a snake through long gray grass.

Finally, it was time.

Rossett realized he was relieved.

BLOOD.

Sticky, wet, hot blood.

Splashing across Rossett and the men holding him down.

He saw brain matter spattered on the uniform of one of them, then felt the pressure holding him down ease a little.

Someone fell across him.

Rossett felt his arms come free as the people holding him realized they suddenly had greater priorities. He twisted, rolling a little and then pushing against the body on top of him until a horizon of light formed that he could see out of.

There was panic on the plaza. People were running, soldiers were lying flat on their stomachs, and four bodies lay around and on top of Rossett.

There was a lot of blood and a little brain, but none of it was Rossett's. He rolled out from under, then crouched down low as he heard a shot behind him. It had come from the Royal Liver Building. There was another shot. Rossett scanned the black sockets that used to be windows. He counted off at least ten floors with ten windows each.

Another shot.

He started to run in a crouch toward the building. Experience told him that moving away from a sniper across open ground got you shot, especially if the shooter was high up in a building. If you headed toward them and managed to cover the ground quickly, once you were below them, you always had the advantage.

To his left the German machine gun nests opened up on what was left of the British prisoners who hadn't had the sense to start running themselves.

Bodies were dropping.

Chaos.

Rossett kept moving.

He could see the bee-sting flecks of dust on the building. He knew people were shooting at him from behind.

He kept running. Head low. As fast as he could. Dipping shoulders, weaving like a rugby player, throwing off whoever was behind trying to line up their sights. He was five feet from a hole in the wall when he finally jumped into the black shadows and safety of the other side.

Touchdown.

BECKER DIVED FOR cover as whoever was sniping at them took out the man next to him. Being six foot four was never an advantage whenever there was a sniper around, especially one as good as the one who was shooting at him at that moment.

Another soldier spun and dropped. Becker scuttled across the cobbles and slid in close to the fresh corpse so quickly it barely had time to bounce. He looked around for Rossett and saw him running toward the bombed-out buildings that flanked the landward side of the plaza. Becker fired two shots at Rossett, and missed as another round came in from the sniper.

Shit.

Dannecker had wanted Rossett dead.

"He can't contact London if he is dead, so make him dead!"

Becker had been reluctant, but orders were orders. Dannecker wanted Rossett dead, but Becker had been making sure it happened in such a way that if things went wrong, he would come out of it clean. Hence the camera to record the Englishman's futile attempts to stop a legal execution of some civilians.

It should have been easy.

It would have been easy.

If someone hadn't decided to start shooting at him.

Becker scanned around at his men, then started shouting at them to catch Rossett. Becker needed a dead body to show his boss; otherwise his boss might decide that Becker's body would do instead.

ROSSETT HIT HARD, landing on a rubble pile and bashing his elbows and knees. He rolled, down into what had once been a basement, but now, due to most of the ceiling above being blown away, was the ground floor. The space was filled with more rubble, and he was spitting dust as he hit the bottom of the pile. It stung his eyes and he blinked as he scrambled deeper into the building, away from the sound of the guns outside, into the darkness.

Rossett didn't stop. He knew it wouldn't take long for the Germans to sort themselves out. It appeared that most of the men on the plaza had never been under any sort of sustained fire. They'd panicked, and like sheep sticking together for safety, they'd been caught in the open and mostly stayed there, blasting away at shadows and rumors.

Rossett's mouth was dry from the plaster and brick dust. He spat again, then started moving. He could hear shouting behind him. Germans, on the hunt for him now, creeping through the building, not knowing where he was and probably not wanting to be the one to find him.

The rattle of distant machine gun fire stopped, but Rossett didn't. He finally made it to the front of the building, the farthest side from the plaza. He climbed up a fallen steel girder, heading for street level and light.

He was trapped. The front of the building was almost as damaged as the back. The only difference was that here there were wooden boards nailed where windows had once been. Thin shafts of light leaked through holes in the timber, tiny spotlights that made it easier for him to see the state of what was all around him.

Someone had attempted some sort of cleanup. The rubble was piled in a more uniform manner, and here and there a marble floor and remnants of carpet could be seen in the quarter light. Dust drifted in the beams as Rossett moved through the high-ceilinged lobby searching for a way out.

They were coming after him. The sound of their shouts and boots was louder.

Rossett tested some of the boards across the windows. Solid. He wondered if the Germans had installed them to stop people from making their way through to the killing field that was the plaza behind the building?

He moved on through a dark doorway that led to a high atrium. He guessed it had once been the main entrance hall. A set of dusty brass and broken glass revolving doors was at one end, but the outside of them was also covered in wood, blocking the way out.

Rossett started off across the atrium. The sound of German voices now seemed to be on his right, as well as behind, getting closer. They were outflanking him, moving quickly.

He speeded up, jumping across the occasional hole in the floor and past the rubble piles that gave him cover to check over his shoulder.

He heard the Germans entering the atrium just as he was leaving it.

They opened fire.

Plaster and dust kicked up around Rossett as he ran. He dived head-long into a long corridor that ran along the right-hand side of the front of the building, scrambled to his feet, then sprinted down the corridor. Along one wall were frosted glass doors that backed onto the atrium.

They exploded around him as he ran. Someone was tracing a line of bullets inches behind his sprinting shadow on the glass. The noise, dust, and flying glass chased him until he barged through the swinging double doors at the end of the corridor.

He felt like a fox barely ahead of the hounds, heading deeper into the gloom of the warren he was trapped in. He ran along another corridor, then through some adjoining offices, all the while trying to catch his breath.

There was an explosion behind him.

They were using grenades to clear rooms.

Another explosion.

Gunfire.

Some shouting, then more shooting.

He was opening a gap as the SS took their time. They'd lost sight of him and seemed worried that they would pass him by, or maybe that he would ambush them if they moved too quickly. They had the luxury of a trapped quarry to hunt, and they were going to enjoy it.

Rossett turned a corner, jogged along another corridor, then skidded to a halt and ran back to look into one of the offices.

A wide shaft of light. One of the window boards had been removed. Rossett ran toward it. He slammed into the wall next to the chest-high open window, paused for a quarter second, then bobbed his head so that he could look out. There were some tall warehouses. He ducked back to check the corridor.

There was another explosion, and this time Rossett felt the percussion through his feet. Some plaster dropped down from the ceiling above him and settled on his shoulders. They were getting closer. He looked back through the window toward the warehouses. He couldn't see any people, but some of the tall timber doors were pulled open, and a few handcarts and horse-drawn carts looked like they had been abandoned outside them.

There was a raised steel train line between him and the warehouses. Liverpool's famous Overhead Railway. Parts of the track had been cut and twisted by explosions during the city's siege and hung down like vines in a jungle. They offered Rossett a little cover on the open ground between where he was and the warehouses.

It was enough; he had no choice. Rossett grabbed the window frame and pulled himself up.

Another explosion behind him, this one close enough to ruffle his clothes as he climbed up and through. He slithered out, catching on the frame and the remnants of broken glass in the bottom of it. He saw the board that had once been in the window some eight feet below him. Six-inch nails were sticking up out of it. He slipped the last few inches through the gap and felt his coat catch and rip as he went.

The Germans entered the room behind him and started shooting.

Rossett dropped and missed the nails more by luck than design. He was too far from cover to start running, so he rolled and looked up to the window to see if he would be able to grab any weapon that was likely to point through it.

He wouldn't.

He leaned back against the wall, looking left and right for something to hide behind.

There was nothing.

He looked up.

A German looked down, disappeared, and then reappeared, this time clumsily trying to angle an StG 44 through the gap and down toward Rossett.

A shot rang out.

Blood spattered the wall next to the German soldier's head. He disappeared back through the window and his StG 44 fell toward Rossett, who caught the gun and then looked toward the warehouses on the other side of the Overhead Railway. Searching for his sniper friend.

He couldn't see him.

Rossett started to run. There was another shot from over by the warehouses.

Rossett kept on running.

Fifty yards.

Another shot over his head.

Thirty yards away and blowing hard.

Then the guns opened up behind him.

Bullets skittered off the cobblestones, then came back off the twisted steel girders of the Overhead Railway toward him. Rossett flinched, lifting one arm to cover his face as he ran.

He got lucky. Nothing hit him. He grabbed a girder and spun so that he could take cover behind the narrow steel shield. This time there was no sniper to protect him. This time he closed his eyes and ducked his head as sparks arced off the metal all around him.

This time he lived again.

He guessed there were several people shooting at him from the building now. The rate of fire was erratic, but heavy enough to make sure he was pinned down.

He flinched again as another round flicked sparks and cut the air. He leaned in tighter to the girder and forced open his eyes to try to work out a route to the warehouses behind him.

Rossett could see the horses by the warehouse doors, skittish and pulling against the wooden chocks placed under their cart wheels. One of them was already down on the ground, rolling, trapped by the yoke around its neck, blood on its flank as it brayed and frothed with pain and panic.

Rossett crouched, checked that the StG 44 was cocked, and fired blindly around the girder back toward the building.

The gun danced in his hands.

He had to run.

Not moving was suicide.

They'd be coming for him soon. Not just the soldiers in the building, but the ones with vehicles in the compound. A burst of gunfire sounded and rounds rang like tossed gravel off the steel girders holding up the railway. Rossett looked over at the warehouses, took a deep breath, and made ready to run.

The gunfire stopped.

Rossett rested his back against the girder. He waited, unsure, and then risked a look at where he'd just escaped from.

There was a hole, low in the wall, near the window he had climbed out of, but closer to the plaza. He could see some of the British prisoners from earlier stumbling out as they made their escape. The soldiers in the building were shouting and pointing at them. It didn't take them too long to get organized and react.

They started shooting at the fleeing prisoners.

Rossett wanted to draw their fire. He lifted his StG 44 and pulled the trigger.

Empty.

He tossed the gun and ran.

An occasional shot followed him, but he moved quickly, with short breaths and high knees.

He made it to a warehouse and through an open wooden door. It was dark inside, but he could just about see a few men with dirty faces huddled behind some cubic cotton bales. Rossett ran through to the back of the building without stopping.

It took him two or three attempts to find the rear exit, but finally, he burst out of a door and onto a street full of abandoned horses, carts, trucks, and cars. It was like time was standing still except for his heaving chest. More empty buildings stood on the far side of the wide street. Towering office buildings, more modern than the warehouse he had just run through.

Rossett listened to the sound of the distant gunfire behind him as he caught his breath. He looked around, trying to get his bearings. The river was at his rear. He was at the boundary of Liverpool city center, and hopefully some form of safety.

He set off at a jog. Moving quickly, dodging low between the carts and trucks. As he stopped and took another look around, a big cart horse shivered and snorted when he rested a hand on its warm flank. It started to rain again, heavy fat drops that slapped on the cobbles and hissed and spat at him.

He needed to get to cover.

The shooting had stopped. He could hear sirens now. It sounded like police cars, but he doubted they were.

He felt hunted.

He ripped off the dirty dressing on his forehead and started moving again, the heavy rain falling faster. Soaking him, dragging him down, and causing his head to steam from the heat of his exertion. He found a cap and a heavy peacoat in the cab of a truck, ditched his ripped overcoat, and put them on. He considered taking the truck but decided moving on foot would allow him to evade roadblocks more easily. He hit the city center building line at a run, and then slipped into a narrow alleyway to keep off the main road.

As he moved along the alley he took off his tie and undid two buttons on his shirt. The peacoat was tight over his suit jacket, but the dust and dirt on his face helped him look like a docker and made him feel a little safer as his feet splashed through the puddles that formed on the uneven paving stones.

He hit the end of the alleyway at a fast walk and was relieved to see that there were crowds of pedestrians. The kind of crowds into which he could disappear from view. People seemed oblivious to the recent sound of gunfire. They had a curious calm, the kind of calm people adopted when they didn't want to look as scared as they really were. There was a mix of office workers, shop workers, some beggars; and the odd car or two was parked at curbside or drifting down the street.

It was almost normal.

Rossett dug his hands into his pockets and started to cross the road, head down, moving fast but not too fast. Going nowhere, but heading somewhere, anywhere far away from where he was.

He needed time.

Maybe he could call London? Get some help? He found a telephone box, entered, lifted the receiver, and tapped the cradle.

Dead.

He looked out the window as an army truck thundered past through the rain, its canvas covering whipping in the wind.

Rossett slammed down the phone and left the box.

He kept walking.

Deeper into the city. He felt like a rock in a river as he elbowed and edged his way through the lunchtime crowd. Rossett guessed he was maybe half a mile from the Pier Head, moving farther away as the downpour eased. He realized he stood out in his dirty clothes and thought about ditching his docker's peacoat, then realized he'd thrown away his tie and would look strange without one.

He stepped into a doorway to take stock of his situation. A tram rattled past, sparks bouncing off its roof, then dropping down onto the wet street. Pure bright white, too bright to look at. Honest, white, clean, out of place in a city gone to the devil and the darkness.

He had no ID, no money, no weapon, and he was a long way from home.

He needed help.

There was a café on the other side of the street. It looked busy, full of lunchtime rush and cigarette smoke. There was a phone number painted on the sign over the door, which meant there was a telephone he could use inside.

He set off, dodging traffic and splashes as he crossed the street. There was a bell over the door, but he hardly heard it over the clatter and bang of conversation and the crashing of dishes. He squeezed through the few tables and pushed his way to the head of a grumbling queue at the counter.

"I need to use your phone." He interrupted the man serving at the counter.

"Pardon?"

"Do you have a phone?" Someone behind was tutting loudly, and he had to resist the urge to turn around to see who it was.

"Business use only, there's a call box over the street."

"Police emergency."

The man looked at Rossett's dirty face, and then down at the old peacoat.

"What emergency?"

"There's going to be a murder if you don't let me use your fucking phone."

The man took a step back.

"Please?" Rossett held up a hand of apology and tried again. "I need the phone quickly."

The man paused, then lifted the flap on the counter.

"Through that door." He nodded his head toward an open doorway at the back of the shop. "And don't touch anything else, you're filthy."

Rossett nodded thanks, edged past the flap, and headed for the door. It led into a steaming kitchen where a woman was sweating into the pan of soup she was stirring, while another washed dishes in a sink.

They both looked up him as he entered. He pointed to the squat black telephone on a shelf to his right. The woman stirring the soup frowned, while the one washing dishes turned back around and carried on with her cacophony.

The humidity in the kitchen was intense. Steam billowed like marsh gas from some pans on an unattended cooker in the corner, while the stirrer stood guard over three pots of broth on another range.

Rossett was sweating. His clothes felt soaked from both sides as he picked up the telephone and tapped the cradle.

"Operator?"

"Operator." She sounded faint, like the line was barely connecting.

"Police emergency."

"Putting you through, sir."

Rossett listened to a click and crackle, then noticed that kitchen had gone quiet behind him. He looked around and saw that the man from the counter had joined the women and that all three were staring at him intently.

Rossett held an imaginary cup to his lips.

"Tea?"

"Free phone, free tea? He must be a copper." The man gestured that the soup stirrer should take a break by making Rossett a drink.

"Liverpool City Police, what's your emergency?" the voice came back on a noisy line. Rossett had to shove a finger in his free ear to hear it.

"My name is Detective Inspector John Rossett, and I need . . ."

"Putting you through, sir."

"What?"

"Putting you through."

The line clicked again.

Rossett mopped his brow with his sleeve.

"Where the hell are you?" The line crackled in his ear.

"Hello?" Rossett jabbed his finger back in his ear and turned closer to the wall.

"Where are you?"

"Who is this?"

"Chief Superintendent Evans."

Rossett breathed out. "I'm in a café . . ."

"This isn't the time to be having a meal."

A teacup and saucer rattled onto the shelf next to the phone, and Rossett nodded thanks to the soup stirrer.

"I need someone to come and get me."

"Someone will be coming to get you, all right. Where are you?"

Rossett looked at the soup stirrer.

"Where am I?"

"In the kitchen," she replied flatly.

"Where?"

"Capaldi's Café."

"Capaldi's?"

"I know it," Evans crackled. "I'll send a radio car."

"Dannecker tried to kill me."

"I'm not surprised."

"What?"

"You're wanted for murder."

"What?" Rossett knocked the teacup with his elbow, and a little spilled into the saucer. He looked over his shoulder and saw that the staff were still watching him, so he waved them away with a flick of the hand before leaning in closer to the wall. "Who said I am wanted for murder?"

"I've only just put the phone down on Dannecker. He says you've escaped from their custody and he's issued a warrant for your arrest." Evans's voice dropped so low, Rossett could hardly hear it over the interference on the line. "I warned you, I told you to be—"

"Who am I supposed to have killed?"

"Neumann. Plus you tried to stop a civilian punishment execution by attacking his guards."

"Neumann is dead?"

"According to Dannecker he is."

"I haven't killed anybody." Rossett paused, then tried again. "Well, I have, lots of people, but nobody today, and definitely not Neumann."

"Just come in, we can sort this out."

"Have you spoken to London?"

"Not yet, and I'm not expecting to, either. Most of the lines out of the city are down again."

As if on cue the line crackled and popped in Rossett's ear as the lighting in the kitchen flickered for a moment. Everyone looked up at the bulb and waited to see if it would hold out.

It did.

The woman at the sink started to crash pots and pans again, as a trickle of sweat ran down the side of Rossett's face. He swiped it away as the man shouted a food order through the doorway behind him.

"Evans?" Rossett turned back to the wall.

"Yes?"

"They'll kill me."

"My men are on their way; we can sort this out when they get you back here. Just sit tight, we can sort it out."

"If Dannecker gets hold of me I'll be dead before the night is out."

"Two scouse!" The soup stirrer called out a completed food order behind Rossett.

The phone line popped again. "We can sort it out, Inspector. Sit tight—"

The line died.

Rossett tapped the cradle a couple of times. "Hello?"

Nothing.

He tried again. "Operator?"

Nothing.

"Hello?"

Nothing.

Rossett put the phone down and rested his head against the wall above the shelf. Even the white tiles were hot. He lifted his forehead and looked at the man who had come to collect the soups.

"The phone's dead."

"It does that."

"Is there another one?"

"Where d'you think you are? The Savoy?"

"Will it come back on?"

"Probably, but God knows when." The man picked up the two bowls, and Rossett saw one of his thumbs dip down into the scouse.

He was right, Rossett wasn't in the Savoy. The man waited a second or two to see if Rossett was going to ask another question, and when he didn't, took the soups out into the café.

Rossett turned back to the phone and tapped the cradle again.

Still dead.

"Drink your tea, love."

He looked up at the soup stirrer. She smiled at him. "Sometimes it goes off for days. You might as well just drink your tea and relax."

Rossett looked at the receiver in his hand, then set it down in its cradle.

"Are they coming for you?" She was still smiling when Rossett looked over, but instead of stirring she was now adding what looked like pepper into the mix.

"Who?"

"Your friends?"

"Who?"

"The police." She put down the pepper, used the spoon to taste with, and then set to stirring again.

"I think so."

"Are you a local policeman?"

Rossett saw the pot washer glance over, waiting for his reply.

"No." He put her out of her misery, and she went back to scrubbing. "I'm from London."

"Ooh, lovely." The stirrer looked at her colleague, but she was too busy washing to reply. "I always wanted to go to London."

Rossett picked up his teacup and sat on the low stool next to the telephone shelf. "You should go, you'd like it."

The stirrer chuckled and picked up the pepper again. "Don't be daft, how am I going to get a pass to go to London?"

Rossett nodded. "Yes, of course."

"The local police won't give out travel warrants without you paying them off, and I haven't got the money for that sort of thing."

"A bribe?"

"Yes." She shook the pepper again. "Right thieving sods they are around here."

The pot washer glanced at her, but the stirrer waved her away. "This one doesn't mind me saying it, he's from London. I bet the police are different down there . . . aren't they, love?"

Rossett sipped his tea and didn't reply.

"Do you want a bowl of this?"

"No, thank you." Rossett forced a smile and held up a hand.

"No charge, we won't tell him out there." She nodded toward the door.

"No, honestly, thanks."

Her turn to smile, and then continue to speak over the sound of a fresh load of crockery in the sink. "This police force up here are a terrible lot. My poor Ronnie, my youngest lad, was dragged off the street by the local police about six months ago and given a terrible beating. Honestly, it were shocking, he could hardly walk when the Germans released him."

"Who beat him?"

"The police. They beat lads black and blue and then hand them over to the Germans. It is a disgrace."

"They hand prisoners over?"

"All the time! When there is punishment, after there's been some graffiti and vandalism, the Germans nearly always get the police to do their dirty work. It's a disgrace."

"They're not all bad," the pot washer chimed in for the first time, with a nod of her head toward Rossett.

"No." The stirrer tilted her head. "No, there are a few decent ones, that's true."

Rossett took another sip of tea. "Your boy, what had he done?"

"Bugger all." For the first time since Rossett had arrived, she stepped away from the stove and walked over to him. She leaned in so close, he could smell the soup on her face and feel the heat off her overalls. "You want my advice, you don't trust these locals. They've done some terrible things. Terrible, terrible things." She nodded, almost as if she was agreeing with herself, and then went back to her stirring.

Rossett looked at the phone. It took him half a minute to make the decision, then stand up.

"Thank you."

The stirrer smiled at him, and gave him a wink. "Sure you don't want some scouse? It'll put hairs on yer chest."

Rossett smiled, then turned and left the kitchen.

The crowd of diners had thinned a little as the lunchtime rush sub-sided. Rossett moved from behind the counter and headed for the exit. A woman was putting on her coat, blocking the gap between the tables as she finished a conversation with her still-sitting friend.

Rossett was stuck. He scanned the room for a quicker way to the door, then saw two uniformed police constables entering the café.

The first copper's eyes met Rossett's, and he half drew his truncheon slowly from his pocket.

The sound of the café faded into the background. The young copper lifted his left hand and indicated that Rossett should remain calm by wafting it slightly, as if he were gently patting a horse.

Rossett wasn't a horse.

He was a lion.

And you should never pat a lion.

Rossett grabbed a bowl of scouse from under the chin of a man sit-ting next to him and shoved the woman who was still blocking his way. She sprawled across another table, knocking food and drink onto the floor at the feet of the copper with the truncheon.

Instinct made the copper reach for the woman as she fell, and as he leaned forward, eyes still on Rossett, he got the bowl of scouse into the side of his head.

A chopping right hand followed the food, and the copper landed hard on top of the woman, who started screaming the place down. Rossett moved quickly across the café, dodging between the cowering diners, eyes on the second policeman. The copper took a step back and to the side as he lifted his truncheon and held out one hand.

Rossett feinted, twisted, slipped the swipe of the truncheon, and then punched the copper in the solar plexus.

The copper went down in a heap.

Rossett was at the door almost before he heard the policeman's trun-cheon hit the floor.

He stepped out onto the curb and saw a police car half blocking the road outside the café. The driver's door was open, and the driver himself was talking into a police radiotelephone, one foot on the curb as he sat on the red leather seat.

He looked at Rossett.

Rossett kicked the door shut against his leg, then grabbed the frame, opened the door a few inches, grabbed the copper by the hair, and slammed the door against his head twice.

The driver fell back into the car, as the café door opened behind Rossett. The first copper emerged, food down his tunic, blood down his face. He came at Rossett fast, head down, an angry bull, shouting with anger, intent on driving Rossett into the side of the car.

Rossett stepped left and rolled the copper past him, then halfway across the hood of the car. He hit hard, turned, and then tried to grab at Rossett's coat. Rossett sidestepped again, pushed away the copper's hand, and hooked his right hand just behind the copper's ear.

The policeman sprawled onto the hood, then slid to the ground. He wasn't out cold, but he was out of the fight. He held up a hand to shield the side of his head and scrabbled away a few inches.

Rossett started to run.

High stepping, puddle splashing, sprinting through the crowds sort of running. He could hear sirens in the distance. They sounded like they were coming from everywhere as they bounced off the tall buildings on either side of him. He turned a corner, knocked a man to the ground but didn't bother to stop. He could see a tram up ahead, threading its way through the traffic on silver rails that glinted in the cold, wet blackness of the road.

Rossett dodged between two parked cars into the street, aiming for the open platform at the back of the tram.

He didn't care where it was going, he just wanted to be on it.

He glanced over his shoulder and saw an Opel Blitz truck behind him, juddering to a stop by the café.

SS.

Either they were monitoring the police radio or Evans had tipped them off.

Fuck.

Rossett pushed harder for the tram, head down, doing his best to catch it before it picked up too much speed. His fingers pointed as the run became a sprint, then a tumble, then a roll, and then finally, a sprawl onto the floor.

A car door had clipped him on the left leg. He was stunned, but still managed to scrabble up onto all fours. He looked at the car that had hit him. It was maybe fifteen feet ahead. A battered old Rover saloon, green matte paint with scratches of rust on the rear fenders.

Both front doors were open, as a hint of blue exhaust smoke made his nose crinkle. Rossett made to get to his feet, then froze as he felt a pistol push hard into the right side of his neck.

"Need a lift, Lion?" The Bear grabbed a handful of his coat and dragged him up off the ground. "I think I'm heading your way."

CHAPTER 12

TIME HAD LONG left Neumann. Hours and minutes had drifted away to become nothing but meaningless words bouncing around his brain. He was cold. Incredibly cold. Shivering didn't seem enough. His jaw ached from being clenched for so long.

He rolled onto his stomach. Whatever kind of box they had locked him in was rough and dragged at his skin.

Was it wood?

A coffin?

He couldn't remember.

He could only manage to hold the position for a few seconds before he had to roll again, this time onto his other shoulder.

It ached.

He shifted, trying to find a spot that wasn't tender. He couldn't. He started to shiver again and fought the urge to scream. The sack on his head was making his scalp itch. He scrubbed against it by moving his head and felt the string at the bottom dig into his neck.

"Maybe I can hang myself?"

Neumann wondered if he had spoken out loud.

"Hello?" This time he spoke clearly, testing the sound, comparing it to what he thought he had heard.

"Jesus," he whispered. "I've only been here a few hours and I am going mad."

He rolled back again, banging his head. He ignored the dig of the handcuffs and pressed against the bottom of the box as hard as he could. His head hit the top of the box.

"Fuck." Loud this time, the top of his voice. "Just kill me!"

Nothing.

Nothing but the rasp of his lungs.

No reply, nobody was there, he was alone.

He was going to die.

He started to shake again.

This wasn't how it was meant to be. He wasn't a bad man. Sure, he was part of the occupation, but he wasn't a Nazi. He just did his job. He was a policeman, and the law was the law.

He didn't make it.

He just enforced it.

Neumann lightly banged his head against the box.

It wasn't fair.

THE SOUND OF footsteps woke Neumann up.

He jerked, hit his head, then rolled over so that he would be lying on his side when they opened the box. He lay still. Someone was rattling a padlock.

Maybe he should lie on his back?

Neumann started to roll over, but the light flooded in and beat him to it. Someone grabbed his naked shoulder and maneuvered him up into a sitting position.

"Please," he said in German, before the confusion cleared and he repeated it in English. "Please . . . no."

They didn't reply.

He knew it was "they" because there were now two of them. One on either side, hands under his armpits, lifting him out of the box. Neumann cried out as the handcuffs dug into his wrists. His legs were numb and couldn't hold him up, so he sank onto the ground in a half-sitting heap.

Someone pulled at the sack. The string caught his chin and cracked his teeth together as it scraped past.

He kept his eyes shut and let his head fall forward.

He was in danger of falling over until one of them gripped his shoulder and straightened him up again with a shake.

"Open your eyes."

His head lolled on loose shoulders, then lifted a few inches to look up.

Neumann blinked. He was in what looked like a workroom. There was a selection of rusty tools hanging on various hooks and a battered bench that went around three of the twelve-foot-long walls. The ceiling was old, cracked, blackened at the edges and showing signs of smoke damage where it met the wood-paneled walls.

Cobwebs filled the corners, and the boards he was sitting on were worn smooth by years of work boots and shuffling.

Neumann looked up at one of the men.

"I need a drink."

"In a minute."

"Are you going to kill me?"

"Quiet."

"I'll be good."

"I'll get you a drink in a minute."

"I'm not a Nazi."

"Quiet."

"Please. I have a family."

The guard slapped the side of Neumann's head so hard the room spun, and he had to squint to push down the pain in his ear. It took him a moment, then he opened his eyes and stared at the floor.

"D-don't hit him." A woman's voice, behind him.

"I only gave him a tap."

"D-don't hit him," the woman said again. "Not yet."

Not yet? Neumann turned his head to look over his shoulder, trying to see the doorway behind him. He couldn't, so he shifted a little and felt the hands on his shoulders tighten and push him down. He looked up at the man who had struck him, then tried to turn again, this time slightly slower.

He didn't have to.

She was coming around. The same limp, but not as bad as it was when he had first seen her with the cart talking to Rossett. Back in the alleyway, when they had been lost and looking for directions.

He felt ashamed, vulnerable. His nakedness weakened him and he tried to shrink before her.

She sat down on a stool Neumann hadn't noticed before. Her chin jutted an inch, twisted, then came under control again as she settled. She stared at him with eyes that were so perfectly blue, they looked out of place on a broken body.

She opened her mouth, a fraction too wide, and spoke.

"Are you scared?"

Neumann nodded.

"You should be. We're the r-resistance." Her chin lifted half an inch and twisted slightly to the left with the stammer.

"Please, I'm just a—"

"Shush. You might not have many w-words left to say, so don't waste them. Understand?"

Neumann nodded.

"J-just answer my questions."

"Yes."

She paused, watching him for a moment, before speaking again. "What do you see w-when you look at me?"

Neumann stared.

"I . . . I don't know. A woman. I don't know."

"What do you see?"

"A woman." Neumann tried to sound a little more confident this time. He failed.

"And?" She spoke softly and economically, as if the breath that carried her words was in short supply.

"I don't know."

"What am I?" she tried to help him.

"Resistance?" Neumann was floundering, not understanding.

"No." She lifted a wavering hand and wafted it down her broken body. "What's wrong with me?"

"I . . . I don't . . ."

"You know it. S-say it. Go on, it's okay."

"I don't know the English word?"

She smiled a crooked smile, looked at the two men holding him, and then placed her fluttering hands between her knees and leaned forward a little on the stool.

"S-spastic." Quietly, a slight stutter on the first *S*. "You say it."

"Spastic."

"Good." She smiled again. "You say it better than me. Now, d-do you think my body makes me weak?"

"No . . . I don't, honestly. I'm not a Nazi. I don't."

"You think I'm w-weak."

"No."

"Say it."

"No." Neumann looked up at the men holding him. "Please, I'm just a policeman . . ."

"D-don't talk to them, talk to me."

Neumann looked at her. "Please, I'm just a policeman."

"Say I'm weak."

"No, I don't—"

"Say it. Go on, please, say it."

"I think you're weak."

"You're right." She leaned back, lifted her right hand, and tried to smooth her short blond hair. She almost missed her head, such was the sudden convulsion of movement that hit her. She held up her hand, studied it herself, and then offered it toward Neumann. "My b-body is weak; you could snap this wrist like a twig. See?" The hand flickered and then turned. They both watched as the frail fingers folded and clenched into a fist.

"I'm strong, though." She pulled the fist to her chest. "Strong inside, deep, w-where you can't see it. I've been fighting since my first breath, and then every breath since. Every step, every stumble, every m-move, every word. I might be frail to your eyes"—she leaned forward again and tapped her fist against her breast—"but I am iron inside. Do you understand me?"

Neumann nodded.

"So do as I say, take me at my w-word, and answer my questions. Yes?"

Neumann nodded.

"So, tell me Generalmajor N-Neumann, where is the gold?"

CHAPTER 13

AREN'T YOU GOING to ask how I found you?"

"What does it matter?"

The Bear nodded. "You're right, I'm showing off. It isn't important."

"If you're going to kill me, just do it. I really can't be arsed sitting here listening to speeches."

They were sitting in a derelict warehouse, just the two of them, the Lion and the Bear, a few miles away from the city center. To Rossett's left a hole had been blasted in the thick brick wall. Through it he could see the River Mersey. Dusk had settled, and a thin blanket of mist was putting the dirty old river to bed for the night.

A few lights blinked on the far bank, maybe a half mile away. The cold air blowing through the hole smelled of dead seagulls, smoke, and spilled oil. Rossett's skin felt like it was coated damp with the salt of the sea beyond Liverpool Bay. He wanted to wipe the sheen from his face, but the handcuffs holding his arms behind his back meant the best he could do was swipe a cheek against a shoulder.

The Bear had lit a fire in an old oil drum. It popped as some damp timber cracked.

"I'm not going to kill you." The fire lit the Bear's face from below. "I just saved your life. What would be the point?"

"So what do you want?"

"I wanted to speak to you, to get to know you. See if you are what they say you are, and if so, make you an offer."

"With a gun in your hand?"

The Bear looked at the Mauser and then slipped it into his pocket. "I apologize, that was rude of me. Like I told you at the garrison during the interview, I've read all about you. The newspapers, the stuff in the comics they make for the kids, all of it. I've read *everything* about you. So what I need to know is: Is it true?"

Rossett shook his head, then heard the scratch and scuffle of a rat foraging behind him. He was sitting on a low pile of bricks, and the rodent sounded close. He turned and looked into the dancing shadows being thrown by the fire, but the rat remained invisible.

He looked back at the Bear.

"Aren't you worried someone will see the flame?"

"Why should I be?"

"They might come looking for the idiot who lit it."

"When you are at the top of the food chain, you don't worry about being found. You see people hunting you as prey, saving *you* the hunt. You should know that."

The rat scuttled again. This time it sounded closer, and Rossett worried about his cold fingertips, and turned to look again.

"Do rats bother you?" the Bear asked.

"Their teeth do."

"People hate them." The Bear was sitting on a low milking stool on the other side of the fire. He peered into the gloom beyond Rossett, taking his turn to scour the shadows for the rat. "I don't. I admire them. They are survivors." Smoke drifted past the Bear's face as he looked at Rossett. "Just like you and me."

"They aren't top of the food chain."

"You see any cats around here?"

Rossett shifted on the rubble pile. "So you're a rat?"

"I'm a bear, and you are a lion." Bauer smiled. "It's exciting, isn't it? Together at last, the bear and the lion."

Rossett didn't reply.

The Bear frowned. "I'm sorry," he said. "How's the head?"

"Fine."

"When I was watching you, down at the Pier Head, just before the shooting started, you kept touching it. Did they x-ray for fractures?"

"That was you at the Pier Head?"

"I was looking after you."

"You knew I'd be there?"

"I knew they would kill the people they had rounded up, and I knew they would want to kill you as well. It's what they do."

"So you knew I would be there."

"I told you about the gold, therefore Dannecker wants you dead, and that was the perfect way to arrange it."

Rossett didn't reply, so the Bear continued.

"I saw the cameraman. Dannecker is clever; now he has footage of you trying to stop the execution. Even though he didn't kill you, he now has the means to make you look like a traitor."

"I've been a traitor for a long time."

"Yes, but this time, you are a traitor to the Germans, and that's a much more dangerous proposition."

"Thanks for reminding me."

The Bear smiled and pointed to his head again.

"Did they x-ray it?"

"No."

"Would you like me to take a look?"

"No."

"I have medical supplies. An aspirin, maybe?"

"Shove it up your arse."

The Bear laughed as the fire popped again, and the smoke made Rossett want a drink. He stared through the flames at the Bear, who apparently read his mind: he reached down and produced a quarter bottle of what looked like Scotch from the floor by his feet.

"Medicinal?" The Bear waggled the bottle.

Rossett didn't reply, so the Bear put the bottle back on the floor unopened. He held out his hands to the fire and warmed them before speaking again. "I wanted to see how you reacted."

"To what?"

"All that killing. The buildup, and then the prisoners being shot. I wanted to watch how you handled it."

"I've seen people being shot before."

"Yes, but not like that."

"You think so? I was in France, after the collapse, and during the mopping up of what was left of the Expeditionary Force."

"Ah. Of course. I was there also. We didn't have much time for prisoners." The Bear sounded a little embarrassed. "I'm sorry about that."

Rossett didn't reply.

"So you didn't like what we did, or what we do now?"

"Of course I don't."

"And yet you still work for us? What you do with the Jews?"

"Did." Rossett looked into the fire.

"Do you think you should be punished for what you did?"

"I do, and I will be, one day." Rossett looked back at the Bear.

"A death sentence?"

"Maybe."

"I could carry it out for you now."

"If I am to be punished, it'll be by better men than you."

The Bear nodded in the shadows. "I've just learned something about you."

"What?"

"You like grand statements, but deep down, you're a survivor. Just like the rat, and just like me."

"I'm a coward, hiding in the rubble left after the invasion. Too scared to stand in the light, and too scared to die." Rossett's face was sharp with shadow, his eyes black in deep sockets.

The Bear's face dipped into the weak pool of light, giving both men a better view of each other. They stared, sizing each other up, before the Bear sat back once more. Returning to the night, not giving too much away.

"Would you like a cigarette?" He produced a packet of cigarettes from his coat.

"I don't want a cigarette."

The Bear placed the packet carefully on the ground next to the bottle.

The Bear straightened his legs and crossed his left foot over his right. He was wearing civilian clothes under his overcoat. A suit, not sharp, but not shabby either. Just enough to go unnoticed. He flicked at the fabric near his knee, then nodded, like he was agreeing with someone Rossett couldn't hear, before finally speaking again.

"We're told that you people don't matter. If you aren't German, politicians, newspapers, film, radio, they all keep telling us that you are not worth our pity. Every day, over and over, they ram home the point that you're there to fuel the Reich and to make Greater Germany greater still. We Germans, we're in our rightful place, looking down, as you lift us up even higher." He wiped a finger under his nose and looked out through the hole in the wall toward the river. "If Germans see refugees dying, crying, or going hungry, they see them on the screen. There is distance." He held out his hands as if holding a box. "They are at arm's length, just a by-product of how the world works. Somebody has to be shit on by the system. Someone has always been shit on by the system, and someone always will be shit on by the system." The Bear stared into the fire. "It's just the way it is."

Both men remained silent for a while. A pigeon shuffled about in the eaves of the warehouse, and Rossett watched as a gray feather dropped down, changed color to warm orange as it neared the fire, then rose and drifted on the hot air before disappearing back into the shadows.

The Bear broke the silence.

"What the people back home don't see is the children with lines on their faces like old men. They don't see the beggars with ribs so close to their skin they look they are on the outside." The Bear shielded his eyes a moment with his left hand. The pause went on for nearly half a minute until finally, like a magician lowering a handkerchief, his hand slid down and dropped into his lap. When he finally found the words to continue, his voice was low, like the taste of death was choking it off in his throat.

"If a mother loses a child, Lion, surely it hurts the same, no matter where you were born?"

Rossett nodded.

"I'm tired of it all, so tired I can barely think." The Bear said it so quietly the crackle of the fire almost drowned him out. "I'm broken by it."

"Why don't you stop doing it?"

"What I do or want, it doesn't matter. You can't be saved, I can't be saved, they can't be saved." The Bear lifted his chin as he searched for his next words. It took him a moment.

"Hell is empty; all the devils are here. Do you know who said that?"

"You."

"Shakespeare." The Bear rose off the stool and moved around the fire so that he could get in close to Rossett, who remained seated on the rubble. The Bear dropped to all fours, then edged closer still, only stopping when he was inches from Rossett.

"I can't stop. I try, but . . . it is so hard." The Bear was whispering. He tapped his temple as he stared closely into Rossett's eyes. "I need the game, the excitement, the killing . . . I can't stop. Are we really the same, Lion? Tell me you understand what I am saying."

"No."

The Bear nodded. The intensity faded, his eyes softened, and he stood again and moved back to his stool.

"So, Lion, that's it. We are going to duel and I'm going to try to kill you." The flames found fresh timber in the fire and snaked out of the drum between them. "Not here, but soon. Do you understand?"

Rossett stared back at him through the heat haze.

"You understand what I am saying to you?" said the Bear.

"I'll not play your game."

"You want to protect people?"

"I'm a policeman."

"Good. Well, look at it this way. I'm offering you the chance to kill a murderer."

"I'd sooner catch one."

The Bear raised a finger. "The only option is kill. I'll not be taken alive."

"If I set out to kill you, I'll be as bad as you."

"Not if you are saving lives, lots of lives, tens of them, maybe hundreds."

Rossett sighed. "Look, Bauer, if you want me to kill you, just say it. My arse is aching sitting here, and I can think of better places to be."

The Bear frowned and pointed to the hole in the wall.

"Out there, that will be our battleground. There are lots of people who want us dead, so there will be plenty hunting us. But, and this is the fun bit, we will have to concentrate on each other, or else we will die. How does that sound?"

"It sounds like the rambling of a madman."

"It is; we've already established that."

"What about the gold?"

The Bear waved a dismissive hand. "Gold doesn't matter to people like you and me."

"You're the one who stole it."

"I took it for the thrill of the game, not for the thrill of the gain."

Rossett gave in and took the bait. "When I kill you, what do I get out of it?"

"I like your confidence, Lion. Let's just say that if you kill me, the gold will buy your freedom." The Bear reached into his pocket and produced a small brown envelope. "The location of the gold is written on this paper. When, or rather if, you manage to take it from me, you can retrieve the gold and either use it to make your way out of the country or, if you are stupid, you can hand it to the authorities here, prove your loyalty, and discredit Dannecker."

"What if I don't want to play your game?"

"I'll kill you, and the gold will go to whoever kills me or finds it before I die. Imagine how much damage the resistance could do with that gold, Lion. Imagine how many other families like yours would be blown apart by the bombs it could buy."

Rossett lifted his chin at the reference to his wife and son.

The Bear held out a hand.

"You and I, Lion, we are warriors lost in a forest and we can't find the battle. We can hear it." The Bear tapped his ear and lowered his voice to a whisper. "It is so close, but we can't find it for the trees and the confusion. I need you, Lion, and you need me, so we can lead each other to Valhalla."

"You need me to lead you to the psychiatrist."

The Bear sat back, suddenly indignant, hands on his knees, a frown on his face.

The fire popped.

The Bear stood up, checked his watch in the glow cast by the oil drum, then looked at Rossett.

"It's time. We've already started."

"I've not started anything."

"You have, you just don't know it yet." The Bear took Rossett's Webley out of his coat pocket. "Your old friend was pining for you like a dog left in the rain. I picked it up and brought it along, so it could find its master."

Rossett eyed the pistol, then pulled at the handcuffs and rocked up onto his knees.

The Bear held out a calming hand and placed the Webley on the floor next to the fire. He checked his watch again and tipped his head in farewell.

"Some friends are coming for you. Good luck with them. If you survive, keep an eye open for me, and don't forget our challenge."

"I'll not play your game, Bear."

"You already are."

The Bear set off toward the far corner of the room, where a rickety wooden staircase waited in the darkness. Rossett watched him head down it and strained to pull his wrist halfway out of one of the cuffs. The heel of his thumb was jammed tight against the metal. He shifted, bending double as he pulled at the cuffs, head dipped as he tried to drag his hand through the opening.

Too tight.

He was going to break his thumb.

He sat down again and drew his feet in close, then rocked backward as he forced them through the loop of his arms so that his hands were finally to his front.

He picked up the Webley and checked the load.

Empty.

He turned full circle, then started to head toward the stairs himself. He stopped as he heard the sound of footsteps coming up fast in the darkness. He looked around the warehouse for shelter but saw nothing but shadows. They'd be useful, but they wouldn't stand up to scrutiny. Rossett walked quickly to the hole in the wall.

There was a fifty-foot drop, and with his hands cuffed, there was no way he could even attempt to climb down.

He turned to look at the staircase.

A head bobbed, dipped, then came back into sight again.

Rossett stood stock-still, a little off to the side of the fire, using its light to show he wasn't a threat.

A Thompson trained on him as another two heads came into view, quickly followed by a couple of nervous-looking MP40s.

Rossett was aware that every gun in the place was pointed at him.

This was becoming a habit.

He dropped the Webley.

The first man ran up the last few stairs and started shouting conflicting commands. He was rattling them off as his heart raced and his eyes darted around.

"Get down! Turn around! Don't move!"

Rossett didn't like people who had guns and were panicking, so he stared at the man and complied with the final order and didn't move.

Rossett had been a copper long enough to know that when times were stressful, it was often the simplest message that got through.

"Don't shoot me," he said in a clear voice, not too loud, not too soft, just enough to get the message across. "I'm not a threat."

"Show me your hands! Show me your fucking hands!"

"I'm cuffed." Rossett lifted his hands up.

"Turn around!"

Two of them were shouting now, adding to the confusion. Rossett looked at the first man, waiting for confirmation of what he was supposed to do.

They were edging toward him, baby steps behind the guns. They hadn't cleared the rest of the room, as all their attention was focused on Rossett. It occurred to him that a single shooter in the corner would have been able to take them down without a problem.

He wondered if that was the Bear's plan, and he cast a glance at the shadows.

"Get on your knees!" The third man was shouting and gesturing with his MP40. A fleck of spittle was on his lips and his eyes were bulging.

Rossett settled on a half turn, then dropped to his knees.

The Thompson guy kicked him between the shoulders and drove him down face-first into the dirt and small chunks of rubble on the ground. Rossett was winded but uninjured. He tried speaking again.

"I'm English."

Nobody replied.

"I'm not a threat."

They remembered to search him. Rossett felt the barrel of a Thompson drive into the back of his head, and someone dug into his pockets, twisting and turning him at the same time.

"I'm not a threat," Rossett said again.

"Oh, come on, Inspector, w-we both know that isn't the c-case."

The barrel lifted off the back of his head, then Rossett was rolled onto his back.

He stared up.

The cripple from the alley stared down.

He tried to remember her name.

"Hello again . . ." was the best he could come up with.

She was in the middle of the men, all brittle bones and paper-pale skin, wrapped up by their brawn.

She smiled.

Somewhere on the docks someone was loading a steel-hulled ship. The bangs and scrapes rang out across the night, like a whale calling for a lost love across the oceans.

Rossett had a feeling he was the only one who had noticed the noise. He turned his head, looked out across the river again, and then back at the woman.

"Iris." Her name came back to him.

She smiled and looked impressed that he had remembered.

"I was a prisoner." He spoke slowly, clearly, careful to get his point across precisely. He looked from one face to the next in the hope of picking up an ally. "The man who was holding me, Captain Karl Bauer, left moments before you came in. He must have heard you coming."

"The B-Bear?"

"Yes," Rossett replied.

Two of the men looked over their shoulders at the stairwell behind them, then at each other.

"He was here?"

"He left a few minutes ago. He could be taking aim at you right now. We aren't safe here." Rossett tried not to sound like he was giving orders.

One of the men pointed his gun back at Rossett, who ignored him and stayed focused on Iris.

"I can help you." His voice was still flat.

"You don't look like you c-can help yourself." Iris was the only one of the resistance who seemed calm.

"I have links to the resistance in London, and in Canada. You need to check them out. There is no reason to kill me." Rossett showed her the cuffs.

The electricity that had been in the room moments before seemed to have been grounded by Iris's demeanor. Her men settled down and watched her like well-trained dogs, waiting for her command.

She was good. Rossett was impressed.

"I h-heard D-Dannecker wanted you dead."

"He does." Rossett nodded.

"So that makes you my enemy's e-enemy?"

"I suppose so."

"So what should I d-do with you?"

"I'd take off these handcuffs and give me a gun."

"I'm s-sorry, Inspector, but that just isn't going to happen, I'm a-afraid."

THE RIDE IN the back of the van had been a long one, and they'd killed the engine two minutes ago.

But they hadn't killed Rossett.

Which he took to be the upside of what was turning out to be a rough day.

He could hear the rain pattering on the thin metal roof. It sounded like tiny taunting fingertips, reminding him that the world went on without him outside.

There was no light, no flicker of match or candle.

Just darkness.

He'd not bothered talking to the men seated to either side of him on the bench seat. In turn, they hadn't roughed him up, but then they'd not been gentle either. Rossett had seen them give their guns to Iris before they climbed in the back with him.

That meant they feared him. Because even though he was cuffed, they were still worried he could overpower them.

They needn't have worried.

His will to fight was wearing thin.

And seeing as all he had left to fight for was to stay alive, he wasn't sure it was a fight worth having.

He thought about his wife and his son, gone, lost forever. He didn't even know where they were buried. He couldn't visit a grave to weep, and it struck him that nobody would ever visit his.

One of the guards shifted his feet on the wooden floor. They sounded gritty, the studs of his heavy boots clotted with dirt.

Rossett felt the van rock again and heard the two cab doors up front slamming shut.

They were coming.

He hung his head.

The doors opened to his left. Rossett turned to look and saw the driver and Iris. Behind them was a long, dark, deserted street, with wet cobbles shining under the few streetlamps.

The rain was still falling hard.

The driver was wearing a flat cap and had lifted the collar of his coat. Over his shoulder was a canvas bag, through which Rossett could make out the shape of guns.

Iris was bareheaded, rain running down her face, and her short hair clinging to her forehead like wet grass on a china cup.

She nodded to Rossett.

He didn't nod back.

"Get out." The driver's deferential tone made it sound less like a command and more like an invitation.

The guard to Rossett's left slid off the bench and stepped down into the street. He gently placed his hand under Rossett's arm and helped him down.

Rossett climbed out and looked around, ignoring the rain.

The street was empty. It was lined with warehouses. A few wooden crates and pallets were lying around, but there was no movement except for a straggly bare bush growing high up out of one wall, waving in the wind like it was seeing off a train.

Rossett could still smell the river, and somewhere in the night a ship's horn blew into the wind.

He looked down at Iris.

She was tiny, frail, a waif washed clean by the rain. Her clothes hung loosely, like they were suspended on nothing but bones.

She wiped the back of her hand across her forehead, pushing away the water that was running into her eyes.

She returned his stare, but she seemed to be looking into him instead of at him. It took a half minute before she spoke to the driver.

"T-take off his cuffs."

Rossett felt calm and didn't know why.

The driver fumbled with a key ring, and then pulled Rossett's cuffs close. They clicked once, then twice, and then Rossett was free of them. He rubbed at the lines on his wrists.

"My gun?"

"Y-you won't need it."

"You might be surprised."

"We're not your enemies."

"Then you won't mind me having it."

Iris turned and walked to the set of limestone steps that led up to the nearest warehouse. The driver followed her closely as she struggled to make her way to the door at the top of the steep steps. One of the guards brought up the rear as the driver produced a key and turned a mortise that sounded like it needed some oil.

The old iron door swung inward on squeaking hinges, and the driver went inside and flicked on a light as Iris and the first guard followed him out of the rain.

The remaining guard stared at Rossett, then sighed and followed the others into the building.

Rossett was alone on the street.

He looked around again, still rubbing at his wrists as another wave of rain blew in on a silver sheet, then passed him by as it headed inland.

Rossett looked up at the warehouse, then climbed up the steps and shut the door behind him.

IT WAS A square room, with a boarded-up window and an empty light fixture hanging from the ceiling. It was dark, but getting slightly brighter as one of the guards went around lighting stubby white candles with a long, thin taper.

The driver was drying Iris's hair with what looked like an old potato sack. The other guard was on his knees struggling to get a fire burning in a dirty hearth set deep in the stone wall, which was streaked with soot from a century's worth of burning coal.

There was a table surrounded by four chairs in the center of the room. The top had more old rings on show than wood, and in its center was the canvas bag that held the guns.

"Do you want a drink?"

Rossett looked at the guard with the taper and nodded his head.

The guard dropped down a few steps, and disappeared down a dark corridor. The driver stopped drying Iris's hair and smoothed it against her skull, gently, with the palm of his hand. She stood silent, small, like a tired child getting ready for school on an early morning. Her head was bowed, hands at her sides, twitching occasionally, then flexing at the wrist.

She looked at Rossett.

"Sit."

Rossett remained standing.

"It'll be warm soon." Her stammer was taking some time off.

Rossett looked at the table, then back at Iris.

"What's going on here?"

"Relax. We can talk w-when we're warm."

"Where is Neumann?"

"He's okay. You'll see him soon."

Rossett looked at the bag of guns, inches from him on the table, and then at the others in the room.

He opened the bag.

The driver looked at Iris, who had moved to stand next to the flickering fire.

She nodded.

The driver reached around to the back of his pants.

"Hey."

Rossett watched as the driver produced his Webley, then walked the four steps across the room toward him.

"Here's your gun." The driver handed Rossett the Webley butt first. "There should be some rounds in the bag. Take as many as you want."

The driver started to dry his own hair over by the fire.

Rossett broke open the pistol, then searched the bag for the rounds. He found a half-full box of shells, loaded the Webley, and emptied the rest into his pocket.

He placed the gun quietly on the table in front of him.

"I have to be careful I don't catch a c-cold." The fire was building behind Iris now as the guard added a little more coal. "Last y-year I caught pn-pneu—" Her face twisted with the effort of the word.

"Pneumonia." The driver filled in the blank.

Iris flapped a hand toward him while looking at Rossett.

"Meet Cavanagh."

Rossett nodded, and Cavanagh nodded back.

"We have to look after Iris, now she's the boss." Cavanagh put down the drying sack on the table and pulled out a chair for her as she crossed the room from the fireplace.

She sat and waited for the questions to come.

Rossett stared at her until, finally, she smiled. "This isn't a t-trick." Her jaw flexed. "Just try to relax."

"Relax?"

"As b-best you can."

"I'm confused."

"I understand."

Rossett breathed through his nose and looked around the room again.

"Please, sit." She smiled at him.

Rossett deflated slightly, considered his options, and took a seat at the table.

"I keep hearing about gold." He placed one elbow on the table and sat side-on, the Webley within reach.

"Y-yes."

"Tell me about it?"

Iris looked across at Cavanagh, so he obliged by doing the talking from where he was standing and steaming with his back to the fire.

"At the start of the war, maybe even before the start, the government realized that if the Germans were to invade they would plunder the country of anything valuable."

"And?"

"And there is nothing more valuable than a country's gold reserves. What made the situation even more dangerous was that the Bank of England vaults are in London. So even if the Germans only managed to secure the southeast of England temporarily with a bridgehead out of the channel, they would secure London long enough to empty the vault."

"So the government hid the gold?" Rossett looked at Iris.

"No. They m-moved it out of the country."

"They moved *most* of it." Cavanagh left his spot by the fire, and came and sat down next to Iris. "It was called Operation Fish. They emptied the vaults bit by bit and sent the contents north to be loaded on ships bound for Canada. On paper it was a great plan. Who is going to invade Canada?"

"I don't know."

"*Nobody* is going to invade Canada," Iris said.

Cavanagh smiled and then continued. "How much gold do you think there was?"

Rossett shrugged. "Tons?"

"Try again."

"Twenty tons?"

"Again."

"Fifty?"

"You're not very good at this, are you?"

Rossett looked at Iris in frustration.

She smiled. "Seven hundred tons."

"Of gold?" Rossett leaned back from the table.

"Of gold, maybe even more than that." Cavanagh smiled. "They had ships, pretty much most of what we had left after the evacuation from Dunkirk. Most of the gold had been moved north prior to the invasion. Some to Scotland, some to Liverpool. It was stored, waiting to go, and then the Germans came."

"F-fast," Iris chipped in again.

"Lightning fast," Cavanagh continued. "Most of it got out on the last few ships, but plenty of them were sunk or intercepted en route to Canada."

"But not all of it left Liverpool." Rossett filled in the details.

Cavanagh nodded. "There were rumors, a lot of them old wives' tales . . ."

"Or old d-dockers' tales." Iris smiled.

"But then about six months ago, one of the men who had been tasked with the original safekeeping of the gold came to us."

"He'd not made contact before?"

"No. He was sworn to secrecy, and he took his oath seriously right up until he started to cough up blood a few weeks before he found us."

"Lung cancer," Iris said quietly.

Cavanagh nodded. "He'd worked for Martins Bank in Liverpool. Their vault had been used by the government to store some of the gold while it was waiting to be loaded onto the ships, and he was one of the senior clerks in charge of maintaining the inventory. During the siege, as the last ships were leaving, the remaining gold was loaded onto trucks and sent down to the docks in a panic. The bombs were falling and the Germans were squeezing the perimeter, so most of the army drivers had to start fighting in the last stand to buy the ships some time. That left it to members of staff at the bank to drive the trucks. Our man's truck was one of the last ones, and he ended up cut off from the docks. Sooner than hand it over to the Germans, he hid it."

"Where?"

"Initially he just parked it in a side street. The load was covered with a tarpaulin, and the streets were quiet for a week or two before people finally started to emerge from the rubble. He eventually moved it to one of the disused railway tunnels down by the docks."

"And it sat there all this time?"

"Yes. He couldn't move it, and even if he could, where was he going to take it? Most of those old tunnels have no use anymore, especially the ones damaged by bombing, so he knew it was safe. He checked on it every now and then, but he had no choice other than to wait it out until the political situation here improved, or he got the opportunity to contact someone who could get it to Canada."

"And then he got cancer," Rossett said quietly.

Cavanagh nodded. "He knew he didn't have long, and he didn't want to pass the responsibility on to his family, so he tried to make contact with us."

"Tried?"

"It isn't as easy as it seems. If you aren't connected to the kind of people who live in the shadows, it can be difficult to see in the dark."

"So he found you, but how did the Bear get involved?"

"He eventually found us, but in doing so, he'd asked a lot of questions. Liverpool is a small city; when an old banker suddenly wants to find the resistance, people talk, rumors start. It was the kind of thing the Bear listens out for. So he came hunting."

Rossett looked at Iris. "So he killed the banker and took your gold?"

"Y-yes," Iris said quietly. "And then he killed my father."

"And the man he'd contacted to help us get it out." Cavanagh looked at Iris, and then back at Rossett.

"The consul?"

Cavanagh nodded.

Rossett leaned back in his seat and shook his head. "If the Bear took the gold, why did he have to kill your father and the consul?"

Cavanagh and Iris looked at each other, then Cavanagh replied.

"When he realized the Bear had the gold, Iris's father reached out to Dannecker."

"He reached out to the SS garrison commanding officer?"

"Yes."

Rossett looked at Iris. "That was a hell of a risk."

"He had no choice."

Rossett turned back to Cavanagh. "What happened?"

"We'd heard Dannecker was unhappy and a little . . ."

"Unstable," Iris helped him out.

Cavanagh continued. "Once Dannecker was sure our offer was genuine, he jumped at the chance."

"What was the offer?"

"Get the Bear to give us the gold, and you can ride out of town a rich man with it."

Rossett didn't say anything, so Iris filled in the silence.

"My father had no choice."

Rossett looked at her. "I'm in no position to judge."

"You're right, you're n-not."

"We think, although we can't be certain," Cavanagh continued, "that the Bear either witnessed or got wind of a meeting between Dannecker and our organization."

"He rumbled your plan?"

"Which meant he knew Dannecker was going to betray him."

"Which meant he wanted to kill Dannecker," Rossett supplied.

"No." Both men looked at Iris. "It m-meant he wanted to destroy Dannecker. Killing him would be too easy."

"My father died moments after the meeting that set all this up, along with the consul and some of our men."

"And that is where you and Neumann came in." Cavanagh looked at Rossett.

"D-Dannecker couldn't kill the Bear b-before he knew the location of the gold, and you and N-Neumann showed up before he could get it."

Rossett leaned back from the table and looked around the room as he processed the information he had been given. It took him a moment to ask the next question.

"The bomb, the attack on me and Neumann?"

"W-we couldn't let you take the Bear out of the city."

"You could have killed us."

Cavanagh lifted a hand and shook his head. "We do this for a living, Inspector. We needed the Bear alive."

"But not me and Neumann."

Cavanagh shrugged. "You're alive, aren't you?"

Rossett stared at him.

"You're n-not our enemy," Iris said quietly.

"And we know he didn't tell you where it is."

"You know?"

"W-we know," Iris again.

Rossett glanced at her, then down at the floor. "The Bear is mad," he said. "I've spoken to him. He's either been in the field too long and it has sent him over the edge, or he was always a killer, and the war gave him the cover he needed. Either way, he is crazy."

"C-crazy, and he has our gold." Iris lifted a hand and smoothed her hair again. Her fingers were tight, overextended, and the arm moved as if held up by wires.

She shifted, struggled to pull the chair closer to the table, and finally settled.

Her left hand folded over her awkward right on the wooden tabletop, like a wrestler trying to subdue an opponent. She looked at them like she was expecting them to surprise her.

"I know you h-have no connection to the resistance. I know also what you have done in the past."

Rossett didn't reply.

"We are your friends, John; w-we aren't a threat."

"Royalist?"

"Yes."

"Who told you where I was tonight?"

"Most probably the B-Bear himself."

"You know him, have contact with him?"

She shook her head.

"But he knows you?"

"He knows how to c-contact us."

"How?"

She shrugged. "He just does. The question is why?"

"He wanted to see if I could fight my way out, if I could survive." Rossett finally turned his chair to face the table.

Iris looked at her hands again, then up at him.

"He thought we were going to kill you."

"I thought you were going to kill me. Why didn't you?"

"B-because unlike you, I don't do w-what the Germans want me to do."

"After what I saw today, I won't be doing what the Germans want me to do either."

"You t-took your time, Inspector, but welcome to the club."

Rossett looked away to the fireplace. "The execution today, down by the river?"

"Yes."

"Some people escaped."

"Th-they did."

"There was a boy, just a kid . . ." Rossett turned back to Iris. "Do you know if . . ."

Iris looked at Cavanagh.

He shrugged.

"Probably not," she said quietly.

Rossett nodded, then ran his hand down his face.

"N-Neumann is here."

Rossett didn't reply.

"Y-you can talk to him, if you'd like to?"

Rossett didn't move.

Iris waited for Rossett to speak as the crackle of the fire kept them company.

Finally, Rossett spoke.

"He was scared." Rossett looked at Iris. "The kid . . . he was scared."

Iris nodded.

"He looked about ten. I don't know where his parents were. He looked at me, I could see he was panicking, but I didn't do anything."

The second guard placed a mug of steaming tea in front of him. Rossett looked up and nodded thanks before wrapping his hands around it and letting the steam wash his face. He was silent for a while, watching some stale milk circle before it finally dipped below the surface and out of sight.

Rossett looked up at Iris. "The poor kid just wanted someone to hold his hand, that's all. He needed someone to hold his hand because he was scared, and I didn't do it."

"There wasn't much anyone could do." Cavanagh said it quietly.

"I'm supposed to be a policeman." Rossett looked at him. "I'm sup-posed to look after people who can't look after themselves. These last few months, I've been pretending that I'm a copper again. But when it came down to it, when I was supposed to do the one thing a policeman is supposed to do, protect the innocent . . . I didn't."

"Drink some tea," Iris said softly. "It'll make you feel better."

IT WAS DARK. The corridor was much longer than Rossett had imag-ined it to be. There were doors running down both sides, and nearly all of them opened onto rooms filled with nothing but damp and dirt.

The wooden floor creaked with every step, while up on the ceiling ghost train cobwebs hung low enough to float in the draft made by the passage of people. Rossett walked maybe sixty feet before they came to a staircase, set at a right angle, which led down to even deeper darkness.

Cavanagh stopped and waited for him.

Somewhere to Rossett's right he could hear water dripping into what sounded like a tin bucket. He looked down the staircase, then at Cavanagh.

"I like what you've done with the place."

Cavanagh smiled.

"We don't normally let people take weapons down there. Will you be careful with yours?"

"I'm always careful with guns."

"So I've heard." Cavanagh leaned out over the top stair and called down. "Norman?"

A second passed, then a voice called back.

"Yeah?"

"Two of us—coming down."

"Yeah."

Cavanagh set off, and Rossett followed.

It got colder.

The kind of cold that you could feel burrowing into you as you moved through it.

A lamp clicked on.

Twenty watts, but bright enough to make Rossett squint and hold up a hand.

Norman was seated behind a cube of sandbags.

He was well wrapped up against the cold, with a fur hat pulled down so far it would have reached his waist if it weren't for the two coats he was wearing. On top of the sandbags was a thermos flask, a mess tin, and a pump-action shotgun, which was pointing at Rossett.

"Is this the copper?" Norman's accent was heavy with phlegm and almost as thick as his coats.

"Yeah," Cavanagh replied.

"Is he going in the cell?"

"Yes." Cavanagh again.

"Is he coming out again?"

"Yes," said Rossett.

Cavanagh nodded confirmation, so Norman shifted the shotgun a few inches and tossed a bunch of keys across to him.

"You take him in, I'm havin' a sarnie."

Rossett looked at Cavanagh.

"A sandwich," Cavanagh said.

Rossett looked back at Norman and saw a thick doorstep of bread and cheese in his hand already heading for his mouth.

Rossett followed Cavanagh. Eventually they were in a low cellar space. Cavanagh stopped at a door. It was studded bare metal, rusted red, but still sounding solid as a fumble and jangle of keys got it unlocked.

Cavanagh looked at Rossett.

"It looks bad, but they are fed, watered, and unharmed."

"Just open the door."

"You have to understand, whatever it seems like, the Germans treat our people much worse."

"You don't have to tell me how the Germans treat people. Just open the door."

Cavanagh did as he was told.

Rossett knew the hinges were going to grind and squeak even before the door started moving. When it was finally open, he stood in the doorway, staring into the bare-bulb half-light.

There were four men in the cell. They were all lying on thin straw mattresses, which in turn lay on military-style cots.

Neumann was lying farthest away from the door.

The bucket in the corner made Rossett's nose wrinkle from twenty feet away.

"You'll have to go in if you want to speak to him. Just knock when you want to come out." Cavanagh sounded apologetic.

"Can't he come out to speak?"

"Rules."

Rossett dipped his head a little as he entered the cell.

The door slammed shut behind him.

Four prisoners on beds.

All eyes on Rossett.

"Are you a new prisoner?" The kid nearest to the door surprised Rossett by being English.

"No."

"Have you come to get us out?"

"No."

Rossett had never been very good at delivering bad news.

The kid lay back on the bed, pulled the thin blankets over his chest, and shielded his eyes with his forearm to shut out the world.

Rossett walked toward Neumann, who was over in the far corner. Neumann held up his wrist, and Rossett saw that he was manacled to the bed frame.

"John."

"You doing okay?"

"I've done better," Neumann said quietly.

Rossett looked at the young man in the bed closest to Neumann, who lifted his own wrist to show that he was also chained down.

"English?" Rossett asked him.

"*Deutsch*," the man replied.

Rossett nodded, then sat down on the end of Neumann's bed. "Have they beaten you?" he said quietly.

"They were rough, but I wouldn't call it a beating."

"Questions? Any interrogation?"

"They wanted to know who I was, and they were asking about the gold Bauer told us about." Neumann dropped his voice down to a whisper. "You know, I think there really is gold. These people are desperate for it."

"What did you tell them?"

"What could I tell them? We don't have a clue where it is. I told them I was just a policeman, and that Bauer had mentioned it to me. That's all."

"Did you tell them about me?"

"Not much. I'll be honest, they didn't seem all that interested in me once they figured out I didn't know where the gold was."

"Who are these lot?" Rossett flicked his head toward the other beds.

"Two German drivers. Apparently they got lost on their way home from a brothel and were lifted off the street a few weeks ago. The English lad won't say why he is here, or how long he has been here, so I'm guessing he is either an informer for us, or an informer for them. How did they catch you?"

Rossett looked back at Neumann.

"They didn't."

"You're not a prisoner?"

"No."

Neumann shifted a little, then leaned in close to whisper. "Are you in the resistance?"

"No."

"John, you know I'm not a Nazi. You know I think all that stuff is bullshit. If you are resistance, I won't judge you, but maybe you can help me? If you get me out, it'll be our secret."

"I'm not in the resistance, Erhard."

Neumann processed the information for a moment.

"So why are you here?"

Rossett then rested his elbows on his knees and hung his head. He stared at the floor for a moment.

"Dannecker tried to have me killed."

"Why?"

"I'm guessing it was because Bauer told us about the gold and he thought I was going to inform London."

"You think Dannecker wants the gold?"

"Wouldn't you?"

"I suppose I would." Neumann shrugged. "How did you get away?"

"Bauer helped me. He gave me cover, sniping at them and holding them off as I made my escape."

"Why?"

"Because he wants me to kill him, or he wants to kill me . . . I think."

Neumann moved a little more to try to get comfortable as the manacle rattled against the frame. "I don't understand."

"Join the club."

"Why would he save you, just so that he can kill you?"

"Because he is mad."

"Mad?"

Rossett shifted on the bed and tried to explain. "When I joined the army, we had this old sergeant major who'd been in since the '14–'18 war. He told us about one of the lads he'd served with, who fought nearly all the way through. Proper fighting, lots of action. You understand?"

"Yes."

"This bloke . . . well, the sergeant said this bloke was strange. He didn't mix with the other lads, kept himself to himself, and he . . . he enjoyed killing. He said this fella got a kick out of it . . . the killing."

"He was killing his enemy."

"Yes, but this guy enjoyed it more than just that." Rossett looked at the others in the room, then leaned in closer to Neumann. "He had things that he did."

"Rituals?"

"Sort of. He got excited by it, he'd talk about it to himself. Draw pictures, write letters he never sent. He even hung about with the bodies in the trenches, talked to them . . . he was crazy."

"Why didn't they pull him off the line?"

"Because he was the best they had."

"Like the Bear," Neumann said quietly.

"Exactly like the Bear." Rossett shifted a little on the flimsy bed. "My old sarge thought that this bloke used the war. It gave him a chance to kill without having to worry about being stopped or being arrested. If you are crazy and enjoy killing, what better place is there to be than in the madness of war?"

"I understand."

"Apparently as time went on, this fella got worse. The sarge said he got reckless. It escalated. He started to do crazy things like going into no-man's-land of a night on his own looking for German patrols. Some nights he would come back with bits of people . . . ears, noses, that sort of thing. It ended up most of the lads in his squad were more scared of him than they were of the Germans," Rossett said. "One night, he went over the top and never came back, and that was that."

"So the war drove him crazy?"

"Maybe, or maybe he just liked killing. Either way, the longer it went on, the worse he got. He felt invincible, and he wanted to be tested, so he could prove to himself he was the best."

"Or maybe be put out of his misery."

"Either way, he had to meet someone better than him, or else he was just going to keep going."

"And the Bear thinks you are the one who is better than him."

"I'm his final test."

Neumann nodded. "So what are we going to do?"

"It isn't 'we.'"

Neumann rocked back. "You're not getting me out of here?"

Rossett stared at him.

"Jesus, John . . . These people . . . You know what they do to Germans?" Neumann shuffled up in the bed onto his elbows.

"They won't hurt you, Erhard."

"You don't know that."

"I'll tell them not to."

"You think that'll make a difference?"

"They'll do as I ask."

"These people, John . . ." Neumann tried again to make sense of it all. "You are just going to leave me here?"

Rossett stared at the damp concrete under his black leather shoes until he found a few words amid the grit and old straw.

"They took me to an execution."

"What? Who?"

"Dannecker. He told that big sergeant of his, Becker, to take me."

"And?"

Rossett shook his head as he continued. "It's . . . it's changed things for me. What happened today, it was like a slap in the face."

"They tried to kill you, but—"

"This isn't about me. It is about what is happening all over the country," Rossett interrupted. "It isn't just Dannecker, it's all of them. All those soldiers, all those officers, all the HDT. It's about them, and the things they are doing in the villages and towns all over Britain, all over Europe, to make this shit stick."

"I don't understand. What is—"

"I won't be part of it anymore."

"Part of what? John, please, you need to get me—"

"I'm not doing it anymore, any of it. I'm sorry."

"We aren't part of that, John, we're policemen."

"We are part of it."

"No, you're wrong." Neumann reached his free hand out and touched Rossett's arm. "You can't leave me here, we're partners." He looked around the cell. "Look at this place. Look at it. They'll kill me. These people are animals, John. You're my friend. Please. I'm begging you. You can't just go and leave me here."

"I have to change."

"You can't leave me here."

"They won't hurt you, Erhard. I'll kill them if they do. At the worst they'll probably use you in a prisoner swap down the line."

"No, no, John, you have to get me out now!"

Rossett went back to staring at his feet. "In the car, the other day, you sounded like a Nazi."

"I'm not a Nazi."

"You sounded like one when you said that your people just got rid of . . . rid of people like the girl." He looked at Neumann. "Do you remember?"

"I have children, John. At least think of them."

"Do you remember what you said?"

"Yes, but . . . that doesn't mean I agree with it. I was just saying what had happened back home. I'm not like that, John. You know me. How could I stop that stuff?"

"The only way to stop it is to stand up to it. That's the only way the madness ends."

"When you get me out of this, I promise, I will."

Rossett shook his head, then ran a weary hand down his face with a sigh.

"I'm just a dumb copper, Erhard. I just wanted to do my job and lock up bad people, but the war got in the way." He pushed himself up off the bed and walked toward the door.

"You can't leave me here, John."

Rossett hammered three times on the cold steel, paused, then turned back.

"That's just the problem . . . I can."

THE FIRE WAS roaring in the hearth. Someone had found two dusty armchairs and set them like bookends on either side of the fireplace.

Iris was in one of the chairs under an old army blanket, with her empty boots drying in front of the fire. Cavanagh nodded a silent greeting to Rossett and pointed to the other chair.

"Sit."

Rossett sat and stared at Iris. She looked exhausted, mouth hanging open, head tilted back. Her cheekbones were lit from below. They looked like knives, and her eyes were fluttering hollow sockets. She seemed to sense that he was looking at her and shifted an inch or two, blanket rising and falling as she found her dreams again.

"It takes it out of her." Cavanagh again. "She wasn't built for all of this."

"None of us are."

"Some are better at it than others." He passed Rossett a bowl of thick broth. "Eat."

"What is up with her?" Rossett asked after a minute or two.

"Cerebral palsy. She was born with it and she was supposed to die, but she didn't. Then they said she would never talk, and she did. Then they said she would never walk, and she did."

"She's a fighter."

"Every day of her life, she gets up and fights all over again."

"Does she have any family?"

"Just her dad, he ran this outfit, ex-army, a professional soldier, from the Great War through to 1936. He could have gone when the ships were leaving, but he stayed, and so did she."

"Her mother?"

"Died in childbirth." Cavanagh broke off so he could light a cigarette. "We're her family now."

He sounded a little shy, almost embarrassed, but Rossett saw that he meant it.

Rossett ate in silence until he finished the broth, then took a sip of cold tea from somebody else's mug.

"Iris said you should sleep, relax for a bit, you're safe here." Cavanagh was sitting at the table, staring into the fire. Rossett nodded and let the heat warm his face and hands. The fire seemed to breathe as the embers waxed and waned behind the flames.

Eventually, Cavanagh gave him a blanket and left Rossett to his thoughts. He sat straight, blanket on his legs, hands on the arms of the chair, staring at the fire as the fire watched him back.

He knew he was in shock.

He was used to it.

The empty thoughts, jumbling and tumbling, wondering why he was alive when so many others were dead. In the past, too long ago, he had first felt it while lying in a ditch in France. A bird, maybe an owl, had been calling in the trees. Rossett had listened to it, clinging to the sound, holding it as a sign that life went on, that mankind couldn't kill everything, and that he might survive and one day sit and listen to a bird singing and not be scared.

The fire popped. Rossett closed his eyes and saw the little boy at the Pier Head all over again. He drifted, thoughts, dreams, and nightmares. He didn't know where one ended and the others began.

They came to him, same as they always did as he was lost on the edge of sleep.

The Jews.

The ones who had looked to him for help. The ones who had held out a hand and not had it taken. People thought he was a hero; people thought he was a fighting machine, a big man, a killer.

He wasn't. He knew that. He knew how scared he was when he was left alone with the faces he had failed.

He thought about Neumann in the cell.

Another failure, or the start of getting it right?

"People need you." Iris snapped him back to life.

"What?"

"You are what Britain needs: y-you, Britain's hero." Her voice was sleepy, it sounded like she was calling to him across a dream, and Rossett wondered if he had fallen asleep and not realized it.

"I'm tired of fighting. Tired of having blood on my hands."

"Do something good. Join us. Be a hero again."

"I—" Rossett broke off, trying to decide if he should say what he had started to say. His mouth made the decision for him. "I shake sometimes. I don't know why, but my heart pounds and I start to shake. It's like I'm rattling apart from the inside out, and I don't know why. I hear voices, I see things . . . from my past. I see them like they are happening all over again in my head." Rossett lifted his hand from the arm of the chair, examined it in the shadows, then looked at Iris. "Does that sound like the hero you are looking for?"

"Are you complaining to me a-about shaking?"

"No." Rossett smiled and went back to staring at the fire. "What about Neumann and the others in the cells?"

Iris pulled the blanket tight around her.

"W-we're trying to be better than the Nazis."

"Neumann is a policeman."

The glow from the fire pooled in her eyes, danced, and then disappeared as she closed them again.

"He can g-go later, when this is over, you have my word. We don't want to harm the others, but we are f-fighting a war."

Rossett nodded and, satisfied, settled deeper into the chair. Eventually, after a minute or two, he spoke again.

"There was a little boy, a couple of years ago. He thought I was a hero."

"Your s-son?"

"No. A little boy I rescued from hell."

"So you are a hero." Iris turned to look at him. "You saved him from hell."

"I helped to create the hell he was in, and that's why I can never be a hero."

"Where is he?" She said it so quietly, Rossett could barely hear her over the crackle of the flames.

"He's with a woman who helped me. They are safe."

"You c-couldn't go with them?"

"I tried."

"And?"

"I failed. They got away, though, and that's all that matters."

"Did you l-love her?"

"I think so."

"Him?"

"Yes."

Iris nodded, then closed her eyes again.

"You'll see them one d-day, John." Her voice was distant as sleep carried her off.

"Maybe." Rossett let her go. "Maybe one day I will."

Silence again.

CHAPTER 14

MAY I GIVE you my condolences about the death of your father? It was terrible news, terrible indeed." Michael O'Kane lifted his arms to allow one of Iris's men to search him.

"Thank you, M-Michael."

"It was a real shame."

"We're in a dangerous business."

"Indeed we are." O'Kane dropped his arms, then nodded thanks to the other heavy who had been holding his coat and hat during the search. "Let me know if there is anything I can do for you down the line."

"I will."

O'Kane nodded, turned the hat in his hand, then looked around the living room of the tiny terraced house he was standing in. It was smart, but short of anything that could be called luxury. A four-lump coal fire was burning in the hearth, and a pot of tea and two cups sat steaming on the small table on the far side of the room.

The two heavies by the door were being so discreet, they almost matched the wallpaper. O'Kane had already forgotten about them until one leaned forward and gestured politely that he was free to move toward Iris. She was standing in the center of the room, her hands folded primly in front of her, one leg slightly tucked at an angle.

An awkward welcome committee.

O'Kane smiled again. "You're doing a fine job of leading the group in place of your father. He'd be very proud."

"Thank you."

"You've kept things moving along nicely. The people over the water will be impressed."

Iris smiled, then turned stiffly and pointed to the table.

"W-would you like to sit?"

"I would, thank you." O'Kane gestured that she should lead the way and watched as she wobbled across the room.

He joined her at the table and placed his hat on the floor when he saw that neither heavy was going to oblige by taking it from him.

"Should I be mother?" He reached for the pot.

Iris nodded.

O'Kane poured, held up a small milk jug, and when Iris nodded again, added a careful few drops for fear of overwhelming the weak tea.

"You English with your tea and your meetings. Don't you ever just drink a cup for pleasure?"

"It's called being c-civilized, Michael. I wouldn't expect you to understand."

"I'll take your word for it." O'Kane took a sip and daintily placed the cup back on its saucer. "It's good."

"L-liar. It's weak and the milk is powdered."

He smiled at her.

"It's terrible."

Iris smiled back, then wiped her hand in stuttering strokes to smooth the tablecloth. She paused, then looked up.

"Thank you for coming at such sh-short notice."

"I was hardly likely to stay away, was I?"

"No."

O'Kane took another sip of the tea.

"As you know, we're having trouble laying our hands on the gold."

"As you know, I have a ship waiting to sail with it."

"We are doing our b-best."

"Your best isn't good enough, I'm afraid." O'Kane put the cup down on the saucer. "I spoke to Dannecker this morning," he said quietly.

"Major Dannecker?"

"How many other Danneckers are there in Liverpool?"

Iris didn't answer, so O'Kane continued.

"Before he was shot, Hawthorn the consul had ensured that our ship wasn't going to be bothered while it was in port, and that the docks area where the gold was being stored was unpatrolled for a while. He did that by ensuring Dannecker was well paid."

"I know that."

"Hawthorn and your father thought they were being clever, but now that I think about it, I'm guessing keeping the area clear of Germans was what tipped the Bear off that something was going on."

"And that's how he found the gold and moved it."

"How he got it doesn't matter anymore. Fact is: he's got it, and we haven't. Now, cards on the table here." O'Kane rested his hands flat on the cloth, causing it to ruffle slightly between his fingers. "Dannecker doesn't have a clue where the gold is, and neither do you. So this leaves me in an awkward situation. My organization has invested a significant amount of time and money thus far. It isn't easy getting the sort of vessel we have acquired, and it is even harder making sure it is left alone while it waits. On top of that, I've got buyers waiting for the gold in America, plus we've bribed customs, police, senior naval officers, and politicians over there as well. So where does that leave us?"

Iris was silent.

"It leaves us in a race," he said. "That Dannecker, he's a smart fellow. Sure, he might like a drink and all, but he is a smart fellow all the same. He'll know that if he can find that gold before you lot . . . well, he'll know that I won't need you anymore." O'Kane pointed to the window. "It'll be him sitting in a first-class cabin on the same ship as the gold, crossing the Atlantic to New York with a much better drink than the stuff in your pot there." O'Kane paused, let the information sink in, and continued. "Now, even though we're talking business here, I'm not all that happy about making Nazis rich. I'll do it if I have to, but it is fair to say that I would rather not. Now, sitting here chatting as we are, I'd say you have one chance of staying part of this deal, and it is this: you've got to find the gold first. Now, Iris, don't take this the wrong way, but I don't see there being all that much chance of your raggle-taggle group finding it before two hundred SS soldiers, do you understand?"

"When does your ship sail?" Iris answered.

"I figure we've got a day, maybe two, before the German High Command in London send someone up here to see what the hell is going on. I don't want my ship here when that happens."

"W-when can it come back?"

O'Kane shrugged. "God knows. Organizing a thing like this is a mammoth operation. It has already cost us a fortune, but the hardest part of it is keeping it quiet. If the gold isn't on board when the ship sails, people involved in this matter will start to talk, and rumors don't take long to reach the wrong people. If the German High Command realize that there are a few tons of gold lying around, you can be pretty sure they are going to come looking. And they will be looking hard, and hard means people are going to die . . . lots of people."

Iris jerkily linked her fingers together on the tabletop and looked across to the heavies.

"G-go and get Detective Inspector Rossett."

One of the men left the room.

"Rossett?" O'Kane watched him go, then looked at Iris. "The policeman who came looking for the Bear?"

Iris nodded.

O'Kane lifted an eyebrow and leaned back, tapping his fingers on the edge of the table as he waited.

Not long after that, Rossett walked in.

The other heavy placed a hand on Rossett's chest and indicated that he wanted to search him.

"No," Rossett said quietly.

The heavy looked at Iris, then back at Rossett.

"Honestly . . . no." It seemed to rumble out of Rossett, and the heavy lowered his hand and took a step back.

Rossett crossed to the table and took the empty seat between Iris and O'Kane.

"We don't have a spare cup." O'Kane smiled. "But you can have some of mine if you don't mind sharing."

Rossett looked at Iris.

"Who is this?"

"Michael Mad Dog O'Kane," O'Kane said.

"H-he is helping us shift the gold."

"I'm not helping you shift it. I *am* shifting it." He looked at Rossett. "If they say that I'm helping, it implies that they could shift it on their own . . . and they can't."

"Do you have the gold?" Rossett asked O'Kane.

"Not yet I don't."

Rossett turned back to Iris.

"Does he know who I am?"

"I know who you are. I just don't know why you're here." O'Kane folded his arms.

"We n-need him." Iris moved her cup toward the center of the table.

"Why?"

"Because the Bear wants to kill me." Rossett looked at O'Kane.

"Which means he has to sh-show himself to do it."

"Which means we can catch him when he does." Rossett's turn to fold his arms.

O'Kane stared at them both while he considered this new information, then nodded. "Would you be able to catch him?"

"I'll catch him or kill him."

"If he's dead, how do we find the gold?"

"He has the location on him. I get him, you get your gold."

"Just like that?" O'Kane didn't sound convinced.

"You have a better idea?" Rossett tilted his head.

"Frankly, Mr. Rossett"—O'Kane looked at his watch—"I'm afraid I don't."

THERE WAS ANOTHER pot of tea on the table, this time surrounded by three cups and a small plate of pale cheese sandwiches.

Rossett had forced himself to eat. The bread was stale, the cheese was tasteless, and the tea was cold.

He'd had better afternoons.

O'Kane was smoking an American cigarette.

There was a clock on the mantelpiece ticking a restless rhythm. Every fifteen minutes the chime reminded them they were nearer to dying.

The fire had gone out. The room was colder than the tea, and the late afternoon was taking on the color of evening with the darkening of the street outside.

One of the heavies was snoring in an overstuffed armchair by the door, twitching occasionally with the odd smacking of lips.

O'Kane stubbed his cigarette in his ashtray, and then took out another in a long chain that was in danger of emptying the pack. He paused, looked at Rossett, and said the first words the room had heard for the last hour and a half.

"What are they like?"

"Who?"

"The Germans."

"In general?"

"To work for."

"Can I have a cigarette?"

O'Kane slid the packet toward him. "I thought you'd never ask."

"I thought you'd never offer."

O'Kane smiled. "You're a stubborn man, Inspector."

Rossett shook a smoke out and leaned forward for a light. "You have no idea, Mr. O'Kane."

The silver lighter flicked open and flared.

Rossett inhaled deeply on the cigarette, then leaned back. "They pay on time."

"Those Germans do everything on time." O'Kane lit his own cigarette and flicked the lighter closed. "But that wasn't what I was asking."

"What were you asking?"

"What I wanted to know is: Are they normal? Like me and you. Or are they all full of that heel-clicking and saluting shit?"

"Most of them, the ones I worked with, they've been pretty normal."

"I thought they would be. I've always thought it's the normal ones you have to watch. The madmen are easy to deal with, but the normal ones, the ones you can like, the ones you might want to go for a drink with, they are the ones to watch."

Rossett took another pull on the cigarette, thought for a moment, and then said, "One of them was my friend."

O'Kane looked surprised. "You don't strike me as a man who has many friends."

"I don't."

"So why would you become a friend with one of them?"

The heavy by the door farted, shifted, then settled again. They both looked at him, then Rossett continued.

"Beggars can't be choosers, I suppose."

"My mother used to say if you want to know someone, get to know their friends before you get to know them."

Rossett tapped the cigarette lightly on the edge of the saucer. "Your mother was right."

"So what about your German policeman? The one the resistance have over in their warehouse?"

"What about him?"

"These people are probably going to kill him."

Rossett ran his finger around the rim of his teacup as he gave it some thought. Finally he nodded.

"Maybe, maybe not."

"And you're just going to let them?"

Rossett didn't reply.

"You getting tired of rescuing Germans?"

"I'm getting tired of everything."

"Your problem is you haven't got a cause." O'Kane took a drag on his cigarette before continuing. "I think a man who fights for nothing runs out of energy the minute he realizes he hasn't got a cause. Whilst a man who is fighting for his life, his family, his country, or even his honor . . . well, that's a man who never stops, a man who never gets tired."

"Until he is dead."

"He might be dead, but he rests easier."

"What about you, Mr. O'Kane? What are you fighting for?"

"I'll tell you what, Inspector, when you get me the gold, I'll let you know. But until then, it's between me and my god." O'Kane pointed to the ceiling with his cigarette.

The door onto the street opened and let in a dash of cold rain that startled the sleeping heavy awake. Rossett and O'Kane looked up to see Iris and Cavanagh stumbling in.

"Well?" O'Kane beat Rossett to the question. "Did you hear anything?"

Iris shook off her coat and dropped it into the lap of the heavy.

"Nothing."

"So none of your people have heard anything about Bauer?" Rossett this time.

"N-not yet."

"Are your men looking for the gold?" O'Kane again.

"Everyone we have, men, w-women, and children. They are working their way through the docks, ch-checking warehouses, trucks, everything."

"If they get close to it and he knows, he'll kill them," said Rossett.

"These p-people are good; he'll not know what they are up to."

"He will, and he'll kill them." Rossett stubbed out the cigarette.

"Look on the bright side: if he does, then we'll know we're close." O'Kane picked up his hat from the floor.

"Our people know what they are d-doing," Iris chimed in.

"Like your father knew what he was doing? The Bear is capable of killing them from half a mile away. If they get anywhere near where he has the gold, he'll shoot them dead, get rid of the bodies, and we'll never know it even happened. Call them off. This man has killed enough innocent people as it is."

Iris looked at O'Kane, who shrugged his shoulders.

"So w-what should we do? We don't have a choice but to look." She looked back at Rossett.

"Don't go looking for him; make him come to us."

Iris made her way across the room and settled down in the chair to Rossett's right.

"I don't understand."

"Don't have people all over the city asking questions about him; have them all over the city talking about *us*."

"Disinformation?" O'Kane looked at Rossett.

"No. Why confuse matters? He wants a fight, and he isn't the kind of man who likes waiting. He knows the clock is ticking down, so he will make a move." Rossett looked at O'Kane.

"What kind of move?"

"We'll know when it happens, but at least we'll be outthinking him, not playing his game."

"And w-when it does happen, what do we do?" Iris again.

"I don't know what you are going to do." Rossett slid the cold teapot toward Cavanagh, then looked at Iris. "I'm going to go out and catch myself a bear."

CHAPTER 15

THE BEAR WAS as happy as he had ever been in his life.

There was a kid, maybe eight years old, right there, sitting in the rifle sight, center crosshairs.

Not a care in the world.

His aim drifted a fraction as the Bear breathed. His chest was barely moving, just enough to keep him alive. Just enough to make the rifle rise and fall like a horse quivering at the starting gate.

The kid had a small pile of stones. He was sorting them by size, biggest to smallest, left to right on the pavement at his feet. Every now and then he would finish, look up, look around, then mess them up and start over again.

The Bear smiled, then drifted the sight to the door behind the kid's head.

It looked solid, heavy, plated with steel, or maybe iron. Whatever it was, it wasn't going to open under the pressure of a bullet. He needed to get down there. He raised his head from the sight, stared at the scene, then lowered the rifle and placed it carefully on the half-empty sandbag he'd been using as a rest.

He looked at his wristwatch and got up on his feet. He stretched, his fingers reaching up to the dewdropped cobwebs hanging from the burnt ceiling joists above his head.

He held the stretch, saluting the morning sun that had finally elbowed its way through the clouds, then let his hands drop to his sides.

It was time.

———

THE KID WAS watching him out of the corner of his eye the moment he entered the street.

The Bear was walking quickly, but not too quickly. Hat pulled down, he moved like a man who knew where he was going and had been there a thousand times.

No drama.

That was always the best way. Look like you should be there, and most people will assume you should, and leave you alone.

Not this kid, though; he was too good for that.

He stood up, one hand in his pocket, the other hanging loose like he was playing Cowboys and Indians and was about to draw down on the stranger who'd just blown into town. The Bear smiled under his brim. The kid squinted, then looked at the pile of stones on the step. He picked up the biggest one and held it between his finger and thumb, like he was going to skim it into the sea.

The sea was a mile away, so instead, the kid hopped up to the iron door and used the stone to rap three times.

Rap!

Rap!

RAP!

The last one the loudest, each a second apart. The kid counted to three and then tapped again just once.

Rap.

A signal.

Watch out.

The kid dropped the stone, took another look at the Bear, and ran off in the other direction without looking back.

"Good boy," the Bear said under his breath.

The Bear didn't break step. He kept his arms swinging loose, his black raincoat wrapped tight, but not too tight, by the belt around his waist. His heels tip-tapped on the damp flagstones, right up until he stopped at the foot of the steps that led to the iron door.

He looked at the stones on the step.

Sixteen of them, like little upturned turtles in a line, all except the big one the kid had used as a knocker. It lay on the top step, all alone, waiting for someone to kick it down the road.

The Bear bent down and put the big stone at the end of the line. He restored order. It made him feel better, so he straightened his back and counted them again.

Sixteen.

He nodded.

He heard a window being opened above him.

"What do you want?"

The Bear stepped back and looked up at the man who was looking down.

"I've come for the German policeman." The Bear smiled and spoke in perfect English.

"Piss off."

The window rattled shut.

The Bear nodded, unfastened the belt on his coat, reached inside, and produced a potato masher grenade from the back of his trousers. He unscrewed the cap on the end of the handle, looked up at the window again, then walked a few paces toward the gutter at the edge of the curb.

He pulled the firing string on the grenade and tossed it at the window. He was already pressed up against the iron door when he heard the window smash.

He closed his eyes.

He felt the percussion of the explosion against his body as it thudded through the building. It felt gentler than it sounded, as if the building had skipped a heartbeat and put its hand upon his chest.

The glass scattered across the street behind him like silver snow.

He reached around under his coat again and this time produced the MP40 machine pistol that had been hanging by its strap against his back. Another rummage, and then his magician's hand produced a magazine, which in turn clacked into the gun.

The Bear stepped backward down the steps.

He checked that the stones were still lined up amid the debris that had been blown out of the window.

They were.

He smiled, worked the bolt on the MP40, spread his feet, stared at the door, and waited.

THE PHONE WAS dead.

Or at least Ken Houghton thought it was. He couldn't be certain because of the ringing in his ears from the hand grenade that had just blown him off his feet and down the flight of stairs. He rapped the edge of his hand against the telephone cradle, then listened again.

Definitely dead.

He dropped it onto the tabletop and wiped his eyes to get some of the dust out of them. He looked down at the hole in the left leg of his trousers where a piece of doorframe had ripped through and buried itself in his thigh. He should have pulled it out as soon as it had gone in and then wrapped it with a field dressing. He knew that now, now that it was too late to take the pain.

"Fuck."

He spat, gritty saliva that spotted the dusty floor.

"Fuck."

Once more for good luck.

He picked up his Thompson and limped across the room to check the front door. It was still locked. He wondered if the bloke who had thrown the hand grenade was still out there. Maybe there was more than one of them? He looked at the stairs he had just tumbled down and considered going up again to look, and then decided against it.

However many there were, they'd have to come through the door.

He looked over his shoulder to the staircase that led to the back of the building, and down to the cellar where the prisoners were being held. He could hear footsteps coming fast.

Ken wished he'd pulled out the wood splinter earlier.

———

THE BEAR LOOKED up into the sky and frowned.

He checked his watch, stared at the second hand, then shook his wrist and placed it to his ear.

A ratter-tatter tick-tock.

He looked up at the sky again. It was blue, much bluer than before. Finally it was going to be a nice day. He smiled, thought about throwing in another grenade, then stepped back from the door and down the steps onto the street again.

Eyes on the shattered window, then up to the sky, then finally, he saw the smoke from the fire he had set at the back of the warehouse twenty minutes earlier. He was going to flush them out, just like in the old days out east. Light the fire, fan the smoke, cover the exit, and kill some rats.

THERE WAS SMOKE. Neumann noticed it first.

It had started a minute or two after he'd heard the faint report of the explosion. It had been a wisp to start with. But now, thick black smoke that seemed to have mass was pushing its way under the door and into the cell. The young Brit on the bed closest to the door had produced a key from somewhere and had confirmed his cellmates' suspicions by unlocking his own cuff and climbing off his bed.

He'd been a plant, just like they knew he was. But now he was a plant who was panicking.

He had a key for the cuffs, but he didn't have one for the door.

He was banging on it with his fists and shouting for help.

Help wasn't coming.

"Use your blanket," said Neumann.

"What?" The banging stopped and the kid looked at him.

"Use your blanket to block the bottom of the door."

The Brit looked at the smoke snaking through, then grabbed his blanket and quickly got onto all fours and jammed it as tight as it would go against the narrow gap.

Neumann knew a blanket at the bottom was going to slow the smoke down, but it wasn't going to stop it.

"Take off our cuffs."

The Brit looked over.

"Fuck off."

"We'll die if you don't."

"I'll die if I do." The Brit nodded to the two German privates, who were sitting upright on their beds staring at him.

Neumann had to concede they didn't look happy, but tried again anyway.

"We might be able to break through the door with a bed frame as a ram."

"If there is a fire out there, someone will come and get us." The Brit went back to stuffing the blanket against the door.

"They'll be coming to get you."

"They'll get all of us." The Brit looked at Neumann. "I promise."

Neumann wasn't so certain.

"TRY THE PHONE again." Norman the jailer was pointing his shotgun up the stairs while Ken was covering the still-locked front door.

"I told you, they've cut the lines."

"We can't just sit 'ere waiting."

"The kid on lookout will have rung for backup."

"What if all the phones are off again?"

"Then he'll have run to get them, he knows the drill."

"They should never 'ave left just two of us in 'ere."

"Iris needed people on the streets. Stop worrying."

Norman looked over his shoulder toward Ken, who was sitting on a chair by the table, covering the iron door with his Thompson. "Stop worrying?" Norman's voice drifted up an octave. "The place is on fuckin' fire and we can't get out."

Ken was doing his best to close up the wound in his leg. Blood was pooling on the floor under the table.

"Go up, take a look if you can see anyone. It might just have been communists causing trouble."

"What if they're up there?" Norman didn't move.

"You said it yourself, the place is on fire. They're hardly likely to be playing hide-and-fucking-seek. Go and look if they are in the street. I'm bleeding bad here, go take a look."

Norman licked his lips. They tasted of burnt rubber from the smoke. He took another look at Ken, then set off slowly up the stairs, his shotgun leading the way.

It took him a full minute to reach the landing. He leaned against the wall, took a deep breath, and popped out his head into the short corridor.

Empty.

He leaned back against the wall, shotgun tight to his chest, barrel up high, cold metal against his right temple. He closed his eyes, took another breath, then moved fast toward the front room where the grenade had gone off five minutes earlier.

Empty.

He swooped the shotgun around once more for good luck.

Some of the floorboards were shredded from the grenade. He could see through to the empty room below, and as he crossed the floor he felt it give a little on its damaged joists.

He stopped short of the window and checked the doorway over his shoulder.

He could see the smoke in the hallway. Rubbery black, hanging by the gray ceiling and creeping across the room from the corridor. He felt the tickle of a cough and thought about young Porter downstairs in the cell with the Germans.

He should have released the kid before he had gone to investigate the sound of the grenade going off. Norman knew he didn't have much time, and judging by the blood on the floor downstairs, Ken didn't have much time either. But young Porter—the kid had less than the pair of them put together.

Norman moved toward the window.

He kept low, eyes on the buildings across the street. They stared back with boarded-up windows, same as they had done for the last few years. He knelt, shoulder level with the sill.

One ... two ... three!

He looked down into the street and then ducked back again. His breath was coming in short chunks. He didn't know if it was because of the smoke or his nerves, but he tried to steady it anyway. He shuffled forward a few inches to another position, paused. One ... two ... three!

Head up. This time a look left and right, then a bob, and then another check up and down the street.

Empty. He coughed. The smoke was getting worse by the second.

They needed to get out.

THE BEAR WAS pushed in so tight to the door, he felt like the knocker.

He could smell the smoke now as well as see it. The fire he had set at the back of the warehouse was doing well. The preparations he had made during the night had paid off. He'd collected wood and tires from the stockpiles he had hidden around the docks and then taken his time placing them carefully up against the boarded-up windows and cellar skylights.

The Bear knew people. He understood them better than they understood themselves. If you wanted to funnel people, you funneled fire: it worked every time.

All it took was a liter of petrol, and a degree of patience.

The Bear knew the front door was going to open.

And when it did, he knew he'd be ready.

"THERE'S NO FUCKER out there!" Norman was running down the stairs.

"You're sure?" Ken had rested the Thompson on the table.

"I'm telling you, the road is clear."

"What about opposite?" A slick of sweat sheened his face.

"Clear." Norman was looking down the corridor that led down to the cellar. It was blacker than ever. The smoke was so thick, it looked like the ceiling was a slow-moving thunder cloud. It was oil-slick black, searching for air, snaking past him and chasing up the staircase.

"Get the door." Ken's face looked gray.

"What about the kid in the cell?"

"I think I'm going to be sick."

Norman looked at Ken, considered his options, then went to get the kid from the cellar. Head low, shotgun in one hand, scarf pulled up to cover his mouth, he headed for the cells.

The smoke was bad, a thick, black, choking smog that stung his eyes and made them water. He tried to breathe in shallow gasps as he descended into the depths of the building, his eyes stung closed as he journeyed into hell.

KEN CURSED.

He left the Thompson as he lurched toward the door. His leg was slick with greasy blood. He tried to clamp a hand around the wound as he moved, but it slid like soap and made him cry out and drop to his good knee.

He took a look at the door: eight feet, two bolts, and one mortise. That was all it was, and then he'd be on the street and out of the smoke. He sucked it up, the pain, the smoke, the fear, and crawled to the door.

He was going to get out. He was going to be okay. He was going to go home and he was going to hold his wife and tell her she had been right. He was too old for this kind of shit.

He made it to the door and worked the bottom bolt.

IRON ON IRON.

What he had been waiting for.

The Bear leaned forward, risked a glance at the smoke-billowing window on the first floor, stepped down onto the curb, and checked the bolt on the MP40.

THE MORTISE TOOK the longest.

Ken didn't know how he had managed to get so much blood on his hands. The key had slid from his fingers twice before he had managed to insert and finally turn it. He was coughing now, coughing hard. He took a moment, lying at the foot of the door, sucking in the air that was leaking underneath, working up enough strength to get to his feet to pull that top bolt and then get outside.

He almost crawled up the metal, an inch at a time. The weight of his body leaning on the door made the bolt slide easily, with just one flick of his hand. He gripped the handle and pulled it open.

It seemed to take forever. He had to squirm out of the way as it pulled back on the old hinges he'd heard moan a hundred times before. The cold air of the street washed over him as he fell forward onto the top step, and he had to grab at the frame to stop himself from falling straight down onto the street.

He lifted his head.

The Bear.

Standing at the bottom of the steps, holding an MP40.

Ken knew who it was. Iris had talked about the German. She had warned him to be careful, and yet here he was, and Ken was about to die.

The Bear smiled.

"You're bleeding."

"Fuck you."

"How many others are inside?"

Ken wanted to say fuck you again, but his teeth were clenched too tightly together.

He was scared, not as brave as he thought he would be, and a little disappointed in himself.

He didn't want to die.

"How many?" the Bear asked again.

The best Ken could do was shake his head.

The Bear nodded, like he understood, and then shot Ken Houghton dead to put him out of his misery.

———

THE BEAR TOSSED another grenade past Ken into the building, just in case there was anyone hiding in the room behind the door.

The door slammed into Ken's legs and then hammered back open as the air rushed back into the room. The Bear hopped over the Englishman and dropped to one knee at the threshold.

He stared into the room. It looked empty because of the smoke, but that didn't mean it was. The Bear entered quickly and stepped to one side before dropping to his knee again, eyes on the stairs through the smoke. He took one hand off the magazine of the MP40 and pulled the damp silk scarf he had worn especially over his mouth and nose.

Hand back on the magazine, he waited.

NORMAN HAD NEARLY not made it to the cell.

He was dizzy, disorientated, and almost on his belly as he edged across the flagstone floor. He'd spent months in the cellar. He knew it like the back of his hand, but as the smoke pushed down, he realized he was struggling to find his way.

He'd long since lost the shotgun, but long since stopped caring. What good was a gun when you were dead?

He was now certain he was going to die, but it was too far to go back now, so he carried on.

Maybe the kid could make it out? He could hear them banging on the door. Properly banging. Terrified banging. The sort of banging that sounded like drowning.

He found the keys by memory. On the chain, fastened to the same loop, kept in the same pocket; comforting to know he could remember that, despite everything. He knelt in front of the door, eyes closed, feeling for the lock, inserting the key. The door opened and he fell into the cell.

The air was clearer. He could feel hands pulling him inside as the door slammed shut behind him. Someone threw water over his face and he revived a little. It was the policeman, the one they had brought in the night before. Porter must have released the others.

The kid must be crazy.

The copper slapped him, so Norman lifted his hand to stop him doing it again.

"It's all right . . . I'm all right." Norman was coughing hard, and his eyes were stinging. He squeezed them tight, and then used his hand to wipe some of the splashed water into them.

"We need to get out."

Norman looked around and saw the kid, Porter, standing next to the door, a ripped-up sheet wrapped around his face.

"Can you stand?" The German copper was calm.

Norman nodded, so they helped him up off the floor. Someone tied a scrap of sheet around his mouth, and the copper gave him a shake.

"Can you show us the quickest way out?"

Norman nodded as another coughing fit took hold.

"We all have to hold on to each other, but move quick, yes?" The copper was shouting at the others while helping Norman to stand up.

Everyone nodded.

"Are you ready?" The copper took a handful of the back of Norman's jacket.

"Yeah."

"Okay, let's go."

THE BEAR WATCHED them walk past him as if he weren't even there. He'd been listening to the coughing for six seconds before he'd made them out through the fumes. They'd been hunched, hands holding on to each other like a chain of elephants as they shuffled past, then down the steps and out into the street.

They collapsed in a heap of huffing and puffing.

He gave them a few seconds to get their breath, then followed them out.

He shot Norman first. The jailer was still lying on the ground where he had fallen down the steps. The remaining men stared back at him, rags still over their faces, sucking in and out with each shock-snatched breath.

The Bear pulled down his scarf. "Neumann?" he asked in German as the MP40 came back up to his shoulder.

Nobody moved an inch.

The Bear gestured to Norman on the ground, then back at the group in front of him.

"Tell me, or one of you will join him."

Neumann lifted one hand. "Me."

"Your mask." The Bear indicated with the muzzle of the MP40, wafting it up and down as he brought it to bear on Neumann. "Remove it."

Neumann did as he was told. The Bear nodded, then opened fire on the others with three short bursts. He emptied the magazine, dropped it, flicked the tail of his coat, inserted a fresh clip, and worked the bolt in less than three seconds.

The sights settled back on Neumann, who started scuttling backward away from him in shock.

"Stop."

Neumann lifted one hand to stop the bullets he thought were about to come. He looked at the men on the ground around him and then back at the Bear.

"They were German!"

"I'm not going to kill you."

"They were the same as you."

The Bear lowered the MP40. He'd seen this confusion before on the battlefield. He turned slightly at the waist so that the gun was pointing up the street.

"They weren't the same as me."

"They were German. They were SS." Neumann started to cough.

"Trust me, they weren't the same as me." The Bear smiled, then held out a hand to help Neumann up. "Come with me."

"They . . . they were German." Neumann pointed at the corpses bleeding out on the wet cobbles.

"We don't have much time for what I need to do, and they would have slowed us down."

"You're a murderer."

"Get up or die."

Two cars came around the corner at the far end of the street. They were traveling fast, and one of them fishtailed slightly on the wet road as its engine raced.

They watched the cars approaching, until the Bear lifted the MP40 again and opened fire.

He was good.

Short bursts, controlled, leaning into the recoil, feet planted, breathing steady, eye on the driver of the car on the right.

The windscreen shattered and dropped into the car. The Bear watched as the driver's head rocked and dipped and the car lurched. The front-seat passenger was leaning across, firing a pistol wild with his left hand while trying to grab the steering wheel with his right.

The Bear looked down at where Neumann had been two seconds earlier.

He was gone.

CHAPTER 16

NEUMANN WAS RUNNING.

Clattering, scattering, stumbling steps along back alleys and across wide warehouse streets.

He could just about hear the sound of shooting over the thunder of his feet, the blood in his ears, and the gasp of his smoke-soaked breath. He knew he didn't have far left in his legs. He was slower than he used to be. His lungs had taken a beating, and the chair in his office was just a little too comfy.

His throat burned cold with the morning air. He kept going, not looking back, lost in enemy territory and running out of steam. He ran flat out for what felt like an hour, but in truth was less than a minute and a half.

He tried not to think about the pain in his chest. He kept looking for the end of another alleyway, another bent lamppost. Something to reach, something to aim for, something to get him farther away.

He finally ground to a halt with his hands on his knees, at the corner of another empty street. He swallowed down some vomit and felt like he was breathing through a straw. He stood up straight, looked around, then bent double again and tried to slow down his gasping.

He failed.

He straightened up again, hands on the back of his hips now, arching his back and looking up into the blue sky as he started to walk. Slowly for the first few steps, then he lowered his head and started to move as fast as he could again.

He tilted his head and listened for the sound of gunfire over his wheezing. He heard nothing but the sound of his footsteps bouncing off the buildings around him. He tried every dark door that he passed. Checking over his shoulder and then eventually starting a slow jog, using the shallow slope of the street to keep him moving.

He needed a phone or a car. He took another turn, left this time, a wide back alley that ran behind some more warehouses.

This alleyway was worse than the others. Thick, dirty wet, scruffy brambles clung to the cracks in the cobbles like alley cats looking for a fight. They grabbed at the bottom of his trousers as he passed, thorns like claws, itching and scratching and tearing his skin.

He tested a few gates to the backyards on either side of the alley. Some of them opened, but none of them offered any hope of genuine refuge.

He stopped walking and tilted his head, turning in a slow circle as he listened.

He could hear a car somewhere.

Neumann ran. His lungs alive again, heading for the sound of the engine, his breath blowing white and cold toward the blue sky. Fifty yards later he skidded to a halt at the end of the alley where it met the street.

There was a van coming toward him, slow, creeping along, like it was looking for something, maybe fifty yards away. He peeked around the corner with one eye only, pressing his body to the wall as tight as he could.

He checked over his shoulder and saw there was a gate open, maybe twenty feet behind him. He would watch the van approach, and if he couldn't decide whether it was safe, he'd hide in the yard until it passed. Not much of a plan, but it was all he had to hold on to.

He looked out one more time.

The van had stopped.

Neumann placed his hands flat on the wall. It was cold. Some grit fell through his fingers and then down his right sleeve. He dangled his arm to shake it free, checked over his shoulder again, then looked back at the van. The driver was out, pulling at some empty packing cases stacked against a wall.

Neumann watched as the driver was joined by the passenger. They lifted one of the cases to look behind them, and then the driver leaned out of sight for a second. The men were carrying something that looked like scrap metal back to the van.

They weren't looking for him. He was safe.

He broke cover and shouted to them.

"Hey!"

They looked at him, then the passenger let go of his end of the load so it fell to the ground. Neumann lifted his hands.

"Hey!"

They were fifty feet away. He saw them look at each other, then the driver also let go of the metal. It landed with a whump that Neumann heard clearly.

"We found it." The driver pointed at what Neumann could now see was a pile of folded lead sheet. "We didn't rob it."

"I need your help." Neumann stopped just short of them with his hands held out, calming the men. "I need to get into the city center."

The men looked at each other, then back at Neumann.

"You foreign?" the passenger asked.

"Dutch," Neumann lied.

"What you doing around 'ere?"

"I'm lost."

"What happened to your face?"

Neumann didn't understand what the passenger meant, so he reached up and touched a finger to his cheek and then inspected it. The soot from the fire stared back at him.

Neumann gave it a moment, then tried an explanation.

"There was an accident."

It was a bad explanation. The driver put his hands on his hips.

"We saw the smoke. Did you light the fire?"

"I was trapped but I escaped."

"Why didn't you wait for the fire brigade then?"

Neumann opened his mouth and then closed it without speaking.

The driver squinted.

"You scamming the insurance? Burn the place down and then claim for it?"

Neumann shook his head.

"We won't tell anyone, mate, we know the score," the passenger chipped in.

"I can pay you."

"How much?" The driver.

"Whatever you want, just get me back to the city."

The driver nodded to the lead on the ground.

"Give us a hand with this first."

THERE WERE RAILS on either side of the van where Neumann guessed there had once been sliding doors. The doors were long gone, so he wondered if they were under the pile of scrap in the back where the lead had been thrown. The driver had tried to make Neumann climb onto the old metal for the journey, but he had refused, and instead was squeezed onto a narrow bench seat with the passenger.

Both men stank.

Not just with the smell of a hard worker, either. There was a mix of sweat, rotten food, rotten teeth, and foul tobacco hanging over them as a reminder of how grim their lives were.

The van wouldn't start.

It whined and whined like someone was cutting wood slowly under the hood. The driver cursed as he stabbed at the accelerator so hard, Neumann worried that his foot was going to push through the rusty floor under it.

"Bleedin' thing!" The driver punched the steering wheel, then looked at Neumann and the passenger. "You'll have to get out and push the fucker."

The passenger was out before the sentence was finished. Neumann wondered if that was why they had lost the doors, for convenience at getaways. He got out and saw that the passenger was already at the back of the van, two hands high, head down low, getting ready. Neumann braced his shoulder against the doorframe and the windscreen.

"Push!" the driver shouted, and the van started to roll.

The incline helped; the van picked up speed quickly until it bucked, jolted, and then fired up. Thick black fumes belched from the back as the engine revved, stuttered, and then revved again.

Neumann looked back and saw that the passenger hadn't been pushing.

He was laughing, walking along with his hands in his pockets, enjoying the joke he had just played on him.

There was a squeak of brakes as the van stopped and waited for them to catch up. Neumann walked quickly, almost a jog, until he reached the van, looked in at the driver, and then past him through the open doorway.

The Bear.

Emerging from the alleyway Neumann had come from two minutes earlier.

The MP40 was gone, in its place what looked like a Browning automatic pistol down low at his side. He was walking fast, a quick look left and right, and then the pistol came up and fired one shot.

The driver bucked.

Neumann flinched as a fine spray wet his face. The van started to roll as the dead driver pitched forward, his lifeless foot sliding off the brake and onto the accelerator next to it.

The engine roared.

Neumann stepped back as he heard another shot.

He looked right and saw the passenger crumpling straight down into the road. His head hit hard with a hollow crack. He turned onto his side and tried to get back up to his feet like a fallen drunk.

The Bear fired again.

Dead.

The van was still rolling down the street. The steering wheel was turned slightly to the left, so it was drifting slowly to the curb. Neumann watched it, then looked at the Bear.

He was pointing the Browning at him. The pistol flicked toward the van, which had just bumped up onto the curb and rolled to a stop against the front wall of an empty warehouse.

The Bear shouted over the sound of the racing engine.

"Get in the van or die right here, right now. Your choice."

They stared at each other as Neumann clenched and unclenched his fists. Seconds passed, and then Neumann deflated and started walking toward the van. He looked through the passenger door at the dead driver, who had half slipped off his seat onto the floor.

The Bear appeared, grabbed the driver's shoulder, and dragged him out.

"In." The pistol flicked again, so Neumann did as he was told and climbed into the van.

The Bear produced about eighteen inches of looped string. "Hands." He held up the string. "Put them through the big loop. Do it now."

Neumann did as he was told. He flinched as the Bear yanked on the loose end of string. The loop tightened around his wrists and locked them together.

"Put your hands on the windscreen."

Neumann had to sit on the edge of the seat and lean forward to do it.

"This is hurting my back." Neumann tried to bargain a better position for himself.

"It won't be for long." The Bear climbed into the van, crunched a gear, and got the van rolling again.

"I'm no threat to you."

"I know," the Bear replied without looking at him.

"Please, if I could—"

"Be quiet, or I'll kill you."

The glass was cold against Neumann's palms as he considered his options, and then he lowered his head as the van bounced off the curb and accelerated away down the road.

THE BEAR DROVE well. The van moved quickly and smoothly along the main road toward the city center from the docks. The closer they got to the city, the heavier the flow of traffic, until finally the Bear was having to flick the steering wheel left and right as he searched out fleeting gaps between the cars all around them.

Not once did they stop at a set of traffic lights, and not once did their speed drop below twenty miles an hour. Neumann stared past his hands out of the windscreen, desperately searching for a safe place to bail out of the van, but the Bear gave him no time to find one.

Occasionally Neumann glanced down at the pistol, which was now jammed between the Bear's legs, as he used both hands for driving. The fourth time he did it the Bear looked at him and shook his head.

"I'll kill you if you go for it, so don't."

"Where are you taking me?"

The Bear dropped another gear, then dived into a too-small space between two cars that blared their horns. He switched back up a gear and smiled at Neumann.

"I need you to help me."

"I'm not going to help you."

"Oh, don't worry, you don't have to do much. You just need to sit and wait."

"I don't understand."

The Bear glanced across. "You know how they catch birds by putting seed under a basket and then pulling away the stick?"

Neumann shook his head. "No."

"It's simple. They leave a trail of seed, and the dumb chicken follows it until it is under the basket. And then they pull away the stick and trap the chicken. I want you to be the seed under the basket."

"Why?" The van rocked and Neumann's head rolled a little.

"So the chicken can come and peck you up." The Bear dropped another gear as they approached an intersection.

"What the hell are you talking about?"

The Bear floored the accelerator. The van bucked, belched some black smoke, and blasted through the intersection. Neumann dipped his head as a car skidded to their right and missed the van by less than a few feet.

The Bear looked across at Neumann as they picked up speed.

"It isn't difficult. You are bait to catch Rossett with."

"Bait for Rossett?" Neumann chuckled despite himself. "He already had his chance to rescue me and he didn't bother."

The Bear looked across at Neumann.

"What?"

"He came to the cell last night. We spoke, but he refused to help me. As far as I can guess, he's with the resistance, but either way, he seemed happy to leave me there."

The van dipped and swerved again. The Bear glanced a few times from the windscreen to Neumann and back again before he spoke.

"Rossett was happy for them to kill you?"

"He told me they wouldn't hurt me, that he wouldn't let them. But he was happy for me to stay there, like some sort of hostage or something."

"So he won't try to rescue you from me?"

"I think it is more that you just rescued me from him."

The van slowed a little. Neumann glanced across at the Bear, then went back to searching for a likely escape point in the distance.

"But he would have been angry if they had hurt you?"

"He said they wouldn't hurt me. He said he would kill them if they did."

With no warning at all, the van braked suddenly and slewed into the car park of what looked like a low office block. Neumann looked out the windscreen at the building in front of them.

Big white letters on the brownstone walls spelled out the company name: CHESTNUT SUPPLY

Through the windows he could see people working, some on telephones, another typing, another drinking tea from a mug.

Neumann looked at the Bear.

"What are we—?"

"Come." The Bear grabbed Neumann's jacket collar and jerked him over the seat and out the driver's door.

Neumann fell onto the ground, stood, and scrambled, still with his hands tied, across the asphalt as the Bear dragged him around the front of the van by his jacket collar. He could feel the heat of the engine behind him as the Bear forced him down onto his knees facing the building.

Neumann looked up at the offices. A fat man was standing at a first-floor window looking out. He was lowering a mug from his lips slowly as he watched Neumann and the Bear below.

The Bear lifted the pistol and fired one shot into the air. It cracked and echoed, and drew the attention of anyone in the office block who was near a window.

Neumann counted maybe eleven faces, then looked at the Bear again.

"What are you doing?"

The Bear ignored him.

"This is Generalmajor Erhard Neumann of the German police!" he shouted like some sort of town crier as he pointed at Neumann. He paused, and then shouted again. "Erhard Neumann, did you hear that?"

Two or three people in the building nodded, despite the confused look on their faces.

"I am Captain Karl Bauer of the Waffen SS. They call me the Bear!" He raised the pistol and fired another shot into the sky. "Remember this, tell everyone what happened, word for word, or I will come back and kill you all."

A few people backed away from their windows, and Neumann saw one woman talking frantically into a telephone.

Neumann looked up at the Bear.

"Are you ready?" the Bear asked quietly.

"For what?" Neumann asked back.

The Bear placed the pistol against the right side of Neumann's head and shot him dead.

CHAPTER 17

MICHAEL O'KANE HAD been given very specific instructions before he left for Liverpool:

"Bring back the gold, or don't come back yourself."

Many people would have been put off by the direct threat, but not Michael O'Kane.

He liked simplicity; it left little room for confusion.

This was why they had chosen him. He was good at what he did. He worked for them, and he would die for them, but most of all, they chose him because he never failed.

He needed the gold, he didn't have the gold, so he would get the gold. Simplicity.

He sipped his tea and gently placed the cup back on the saucer.

Who had the gold? The Bear. He needed the Bear.

Maybe the Bear wasn't as crazy as these people were making out? Maybe he could talk some sense into him?

If he couldn't, it would have to be torture and then murder. Now, while that was a solution, it was a messy one, and messy was seldom simple.

O'Kane lifted a finger to attract the waitress's attention.

It didn't him take long to get it; he was the only customer in the hotel dining room taking afternoon tea.

"Could you get me a telephone, please?"

"Of course, sir."

O'Kane picked up something that looked like cake off the tea trolley she had left next to his table. He sniffed it, tapped it twice on the side of his plate, and put it down when it sounded like it was going to break the china.

At least the tea was warm.

He took another sip and looked around the room. It reminded him of the liner upon which he had crossed the Atlantic. It was all high mirrored ceilings, gilded chandeliers, and wood paneling so polished it made the mirrors jealous.

They were trying, he had to give them that. The problem was that their efforts looked like makeup on a corpse. It worked from a distance, but if you got up close, you could see the cracks in the skin and the details being lost to decay.

There was a three-inch hole in the carpet by the door. In the corner, high up on the wall, a stain of damp was spreading like a frown. The chandelier had more bulbs missing than were there, and the string quartet in the corner was now down to three, because the cello player was taking a nap in his chair.

O'Kane watched them warming up for their second set of the lunchtime concert. The viola player had one loose string snapped and hanging from the instrument's head. It wafted as he tuned up, like a horse's tail swatting flies away from its ass.

There were no flies here, even though the band were shit.

"Hey, boys," O'Kane called across to them. "Why don't you take the afternoon off? There's only me here."

"If we don't play, we don't get paid." The lead violinist shrugged like he meant it.

The sound of voices caused the cello player to wake up and look around confused. He seemed surprised to be there, and then a little disappointed that he was.

O'Kane knew how he felt.

"How about I pay you not to play?"

"Are we that bad?"

"Let's just say I like my peace and quiet."

"It'll cost you a tenner."

O'Kane took out his wallet.

"I'll give you twenty."

The quartet looked at each other and then nearly fell over themselves to get to the table first.

"Thanks." The lead violinist took the four five-pound notes.

"It'll be my pleasure." O'Kane waved them away and watched as they packed up their instruments and left the dining room quickly, just in case he changed his mind.

The phone trolley squeaked across the empty hardwood floor as the waitress pushed it slowly toward him. He waited as she uncoiled its cable and plugged it into a socket by the wall.

"Anything else, sir?"

"Just some privacy."

"You'll get it here, sir. It's about all we've got left."

"What about more tea?"

"That's the other thing we have."

"Well, I'll take some of that as well then."

She almost curtsied, then primly left the dining room on a pair of legs so good he made a mental note to leave her a decent tip.

He waited till the gilded doors swung shut behind her, then dialed Dannecker's direct number. It rang once before the admin corporal picked it up.

"Major Dannecker's office."

"O'Kane here, put me through to the major."

"I'm afraid he isn't here, sir."

"Where is he?"

"He said if you called I was to tell you to wait for him to contact you, and to see if you required men for protection purposes."

"I don't need protection. Where is he?"

"With Captain Bauer being on the loose, he thought that—"

"Where is Dannecker?"

"I'm not at liberty to say, sir."

"Tell me."

"I'm only instructed to provide you with protection."

"Is it the Bear?"

There was a pause.

"You met me yesterday?"

"I did, sir."

"Do I look like the kind of man you want to withhold information from?"

"Sir, this is very difficult for me."

"Son, your boss is so scared of me he can't sleep at night, so imagine what I would do to you."

Another pause, then the corporal broke.

"The major has received a tip-off as to Captain Bauer's location, sir."

"Tell me where he is, and tell me quick."

SCOTLAND ROAD WAS the main road to the north out of the city center. It was no grand boulevard in the European tradition, though. It was a jam-packed tide of humanity squeezed so tight it seemed to squeak every time somebody took a breath.

O'Kane wondered why so many people seemed to be loitering on the street, until he took a look at the housing.

Dirty brown buildings with tiny windows and ramshackle walls that looked in danger of collapse overlooked oil-slicked cobbles the color of eel skin. In the center of the road empty tram lines stretched off into infinity, while down the sides ran row after row of tall tenements, shops, and pubs, all full of dust and despair.

Kids darted through legs, bone-bag urchins scratching a life in the grime. Black-swaddled women wandered with empty string shopping bags, and men stood on street corners, glassy eyed, hands deep in pockets, fags in slack mouths, wrinkles full of shadows and shame at their worthlessness.

O'Kane watched the world pass outside the taxi window.

"You sure you got the right address, mate?" the taxi driver called over his shoulder.

"Just go there."

"It's rough round 'ere, y'know. Do you want me to wait?"

"No."

"You might want me to look after yer coat and that. Good stuff stands out a mile here, and there's plenty who'll want it."

"How much farther?"

"These aren't bad people, but they've got nothin'."

O'Kane leaned forward to shut the flap between him and the driver, but stopped when he saw a line of SS troops blocking the road maybe one hundred yards ahead.

"Stop here."

"'Ere?"

"Here."

"But we're—"

"Here."

The cab pulled to the curb. O'Kane paid, climbed out, slammed the door, and looked around.

He'd been dropped outside what passed for a fruit and veg shop. A small glass sign was in the window: TOMMY YOUR GROCER.

Tommy the grocer was leaning against a wooden rack that in better times might have contained brightly colored fruit, but today contained three cabbages and two trays of soft green potatoes.

He looked at O'Kane, then took his cigarette out of his mouth.

"Cabbage?"

"Back entrance?"

Tommy looked at the troops up the road, then back at O'Kane.

"It might be locked."

"How much to open it?"

"Ten bob?"

"Go find the key."

THE ALLEY WAS medieval in its stench.

Down the center of the smooth flagstones was a stagnant brown river of filth, lying like foul gloss paint in the gully.

O'Kane picked his way through the rubbish until he was well clear of the backyard from which he had emerged. He looked up at the tenements that crowded him and layered him in shadow.

O'Kane took out his Browning and worked the slide. He was in bandit country, and he could feel it.

He walked slowly, working parallel to Scotland Road, using the alley to keep off the streets until he could outflank the roadblock.

He wanted to find a spot where he could observe the operation to find the Bear and not be part of it.

He wasn't a rusher. Rushing got you killed, just the same as trusting got you killed.

O'Kane wanted to watch from the sidelines. He knew that if Dannecker had found something, he had found it, and there was nothing O'Kane could do about it.

But he also knew that if Dannecker was following a lead—or, even worse, a hunch—O'Kane would be able to learn more from the people who lived in the area if he wasn't seen hanging around with Germans.

He stepped over a puddle and then was blown backward into it as a building sixty feet in front of him exploded.

ROSSETT COULD WRITE a book on patience. He was a man who knew all about biding his time, and he knew his time had come the second the message arrived in Iris's living room.

Neumann was dead.

He'd been executed in public with a single shot to the head in a wet car park. Left lying facedown, bleeding out till he was cold on the concrete. Just like one of the rabid dogs that sometimes turned up on the streets and had to be dealt with and then thrown away.

Death and Rossett.

Like an old unhappily married couple, tied together and hating each other every time they walked into the same room.

Death and Rossett.

Same old same old.

"The Bear killed seven of our men at the warehouse, plus the two German prisoners, two civilians nearby, and then, finally, Neumann, a few miles away." Cavanagh said it quietly, as if he couldn't believe it was true.

"Why take N-Neumann so far from the warehouse just to kill him? Why not kill him with the others?" Iris looked at Rossett.

Rossett took a moment to steady his breathing before he replied.

"He changed his mind."

"Who did?" Cavanagh this time.

"The Bear. He took Neumann as a prisoner, then changed his mind and killed him."

"How do you know?"

"Neumann must have told him that I wouldn't be interested in rescuing him. The Bear realized that Neumann was no good to him alive, so he wants to see if he is good to him dead."

"How can he be?"

"The Bear wants me angry. He wants me to hunt him."

"It's just killing for k-killing's sake." Iris had sat down in the armchair and rested her chin in her hand. "It makes no sense."

"He's pushing me, squeezing the pressure on and making it personal." Rossett was sitting at the table next to a half-full ashtray.

"Those men were my friends. It is personal," Cavanagh said quietly.

"Make it personal and you make mistakes."

"You don't care that he killed Neumann?"

Rossett slid the ashtray away from him, then looked at Cavanagh. "I care. I feel responsible for Neumann's death and I want justice, but I'll not play the Bear's game. He shot Neumann to make me come after him. He wants me angry with him. He wants to draw me out into a careless fight."

"But you're not going to fight him?"

"I'm going to catch him."

"So you're not angry with him?"

"I'm angry with him, but not for killing Neumann. That death is on me."

"Why?"

"I should have made you release him. I should have stood up for him, but I didn't."

"And now he is dead."

"And it is my fault."

The clock ticked on the mantelpiece for a few moments, and then the bomb, a quarter mile away on Scotland Road, went off and shook the room. Everyone looked toward the window—everyone except Rossett, who was heading for the door.

THE EXPLOSION KNOCKED Dannecker off his feet behind his staff car. He lay there, staring at the sky for a moment, before finally managing to push himself up onto an elbow. He looked around for Becker as dust and debris slowly fell to earth all around him. He saw his men and the nearby civilians either running for cover or lying in the road.

He was confused, struggling to process what had just happened.

He lay down again. He realized his ears were ringing. He wiped a hand across his nose and looked at his fingers.

There was blood.

He pushed himself back up to his elbows.

It was a bomb.

Some of the men around him were also getting to their feet. He could see one soldier emerging from the front of the blown-up property minus an arm. He looked even more confused than Dannecker and was covered in red dust. A thick, matte daub of blood was running down the soldier's face and onto his uniform.

He fell.

Dannecker wanted to help the kid. He tried to get up. First onto all fours and then, staggering, to his feet. He rested his hand against the roof of the car and felt grit dusting the paintwork.

He looked at his hand and saw it was gray, then noticed his uniform was the same color, coated in dirt thrown by the blast.

He swiped at it to clean it and looked at his car. The windscreen was smashed through, and several lumps of rubble were on the front seats and hood. He wiped his face. The explosion had nearly got him; he'd been lucky.

This time.

He remembered the boy with one arm, who hadn't been as lucky, and walked toward him.

Dannecker's ears were whistling. He dug a finger into his left ear and waggled it. It didn't work. He was still deaf by the time he reached the soldier on the ground.

The soldier had gone into shock. His teeth were clamped, his eyes shut tighter still, and he was shaking. Dannecker tried to remember the kid's name as he squatted, patted him lightly on the shoulder, and shouted that everything would be okay.

He looked around the scene as the kid grabbed his tunic tightly.

"Medic!" Dannecker didn't know how loud he was shouting, so he tried again. "Medic!"

There was no medic, there was only chaos.

Civilians, soldiers, men, women, and children lying all around. Dannecker felt like he was waking from a dream, only to find himself in a nightmare as his senses slowly cleared.

There were a few tending to the dead and dying, but not many. The wounded soldier shook him, and Dannecker looked down.

He was mouthing something, but Dannecker was still deaf. He tried to pull free, couldn't, so used his free hand to unpeel the kid's fingers from his uniform.

Dannecker stood, looked around again, and realized he had fucked up badly.

He had rushed when he should have taken his time. The tip had come from someone he had considered reputable. Well, as reputable as an English informant could be, and the wording had been clear and concise.

"The Bear is holed up on the top floor of the derelict Parrot Pub, and he is there right this minute."

Dannecker had moved fast because the operation had seemed simple enough.

The pub had long been closed for business. The informant had told him the rear was boarded up, and that there was only one way in.

Through the front door.

Dannecker had known that the Bear posed a risk, so he had brought fifty men with him and they had hit hard and fast.

He looked around him.

He reckoned twenty of his men were dead all around.

Shit.

He looked down.

The soldier had stopped moving.

Twenty-one.

Dannecker started walking toward the pub. He stumbled on some debris, then leaned in through what was left of the doorway. Smoke and rubble, but no fire, thank God. His ears were whistling now, and he could hear shouting, muffled, far away, as he rubbed his right ear and tried to clear it.

He looked up at what was left of the front of the building, decided it wasn't going to fall down on him, and entered the pub. Half of the floor was pretty much totally gone, along with most of the ceiling above. Some of the front wall and all the windows had blown out onto the street, and here and there loose bricks hung at angles like ribs sticking out from a carcass.

It had been a trap laid for an idiot. The Bear had lured him, and Dannecker had come running like a fool and tripped the wire that had blown it all to hell. He guessed the Bear had wanted him in the building when the bomb went off. Maybe to get him out of the way. Maybe to prove he was a superior soldier, a better man, and not the fool he thought Dannecker had taken him for. Or maybe, and this was the option that worried Dannecker the most, the Bear wanted the gold for himself, and he knew the only two people who could stop the ship from sailing with it on board were Dannecker and Becker.

There was an arm in the corner of the pub. Lying there without a body, bent at the elbow like it was hitching a lift. Dannecker looked back at the kid in the street and decided to leave it where it was.

It wasn't like the kid was going to need it.

The dust and smoke were clearing a little on the breeze, but Dannecker still had to cover his mouth with his hand as he moved through the debris. He saw movement on the far side of the bar, over by where the back wall was. He skirted the hole in the floor, and as he drew closer, watched as a blinking gray ghost came staggering out of the gloom.

Corporal Lange, wide eyed, covered head to foot in dirt and dust, except for the whites of his eyes and what looked like yellow teeth. He was confused and had one hand out in front of him like an Egyptian mummy from the movies. He was being followed by a few more men who had somehow survived the blast, and at the rear of the line was Becker.

He looked a mess.

His uniform was torn and his weapon was gone. There was a gash on his face and another on his neck. Dannecker could see blood running down onto his uniform and staining it black.

Becker staggered and grabbed at the splintered bar. Dannecker went to him, hooked his arm around his waist, and helped him out into the road. Once they were outside Becker paused, gathered himself, then took his weight off his boss and stood up under his own steam.

Dannecker waited to see if Becker was going to fall over. When he saw that he wasn't, he looked around and took stock.

There were more civilians around now, picking through the detritus as the few fit Germans tended to their colleagues with dressings and canteens of water. An Englishman was collecting some of the weapons that were strewn around.

Dannecker pulled his pistol, having to shake it free from its holster with a hand that felt like it could barely hold on to it.

He worked the slide, but Becker reached across and pushed it away. "Don't."

Dannecker realized he could hear what his staff sergeant was saying. "What?"

"Don't. They'll turn on us."

Dannecker looked around and realized how outnumbered his troops were. He lowered the gun. "We can't just let them—" He looked around at the crowds again and wiped his hand across his mouth. "How did you survive?"

"We were on our way up to the first floor. I was at the front. Then the place exploded." Becker wiped his face clear of a fresh trickle of blood and clamped his hand to the wound on his throat. "The bend on the staircase, it took the force out of the explosion. We were trapped by part of the fallen ceiling until we could shift it." Becker looked at the palm of his hand and then pressed it to his neck again. "Did anyone else make it out?"

"No." Dannecker didn't see the point in mentioning the one-armed corpse lying five feet away.

"We need to get moving, sir." A corporal, one of those who had been manning the roadblock, appeared next to them.

"How many injured?"

"Fourteen walking, plus two serious. I've not been in the pub, but—"

"You don't need to go in the pub. There is nobody alive in there," Becker said quietly.

The corporal glanced at the pub and awaited his orders.

"Get the trucks." Dannecker scanned the buildings on the far side of Scotland Road. Most of the windows had been blown out by the blast. The holes would make perfect sniping platforms for the resistance, or the Bear, or whoever else came along to claim his soul. He turned back to the corporal. "Get everyone on board, including the dead, as quick as you can. We're moving out."

The corporal saluted and spun to start gathering men as Dannecker turned back to Becker.

"He nearly got us."

"It may have been resistance."

"It was Bauer. He wants us dead. He wants the gold for himself, so he needs us out of the way if he is going to get it out of the city."

"So what do we do?"

"We find him, we find the gold, we kill him, then we get the gold. Simple as that."

———

O'KANE LIFTED HIS head, then rolled out of the puddle and onto his side. Debris was still falling around him, fluttering to earth like leaves in autumn, most of it landing silently in the backyards of the tenements to either side of him.

He stood up, then pulled at his wet trousers as he tried to release their grip on his legs. He looked all around him in a slow circle and started to walk cautiously toward the back of what was left of the pub.

The high wall that had bordered its yard was no longer high. In truth, it was pretty much no longer there. The force of the blast had thrown most of it into the alleyway.

Through the dust, and the gap, O'Kane could see into the interior of the building. The first and second floors were exposed to the outside, and the whole pub looked close to collapse.

The torso of a young SS private was lying near a drain in the backyard. A short ribbon of backbone was hanging out like a tongue lapping at the pool of blood that dripped down into the sewer.

The soldier stared at O'Kane with dead eyes. His mouth was open a fraction, and perfect white teeth half showed through the gap.

O'Kane looked past the boy. He could see people moving around inside. It looked like they were making ready to clear the scene.

He looked back at the boy and felt slight panic that they would miss him and that he would be left to rot in a bombed-out backyard in Liverpool.

He shook his head.

What did it matter?

The boy was dead.

He turned away. It was time to go. The only thing he had learned from the journey was that Dannecker was a man on the ropes and prone to making mistakes.

O'Kane started to jog back to where he had come from.

The Bear was winning. O'Kane needed to do something about it, and do it quick.

Tommy the grocer had locked his back gate, so O'Kane had to walk another block before he came across a way to get back out onto Scotland Road. The route he found was a narrow alley, less than two feet wide, barely a slit, threaded between two tall buildings. A blinkered strip of the street lay ahead of him. He could see people walking to and fro, appearing and disappearing behind the walls like frames in a movie.

Ten feet from the end of the alleyway, O'Kane stopped, pulled at his wet trouser leg again, and dusted himself off. He looked up. A kid was watching him, standing silhouetted at the end of the alley. Barely an urchin, with a flat cap pulled down low over hollow cheeks and black eyes. O'Kane stared at him, wondering if he had seen the pistol he was still holding, now tucked behind his leg.

The kid had his hands in the pockets of his short pants, and after a second or two he lifted his chin in greeting.

O'Kane nodded back.

The kid walked away.

O'Kane breathed, engaged the safety on the Browning, and slipped it into the waistband at the back of his trousers. He walked to the end of the alley, checked the street, and then stood on tiptoe so that he could look over the heads of the people on the pavement, back toward the pub.

He could see the canvas backs of two of the SS trucks. Either they had been abandoned or they were still being loaded. He thought about asking for a lift, then decided it would be best if Dannecker didn't know he was there.

Assuming Dannecker was still alive.

O'Kane knew how quickly those who weren't directly affected by a bomb could get back to their lives again. People were all the same, and Scotland Road was proving that already. It was almost as if the explosion had never happened. The world had got over the shock and was already going back to normal.

All except the kid in the yard who had been cut in half.

He wasn't going back to normal.

He wasn't going anywhere.

O'Kane glanced back toward the pub and started walking in the other direction back to town. It was time to figure out what he should do next. Things were moving too quickly; the situation was burning through his hands like he was sliding down a rope fast.

He needed to put the brake on, and put it on fast.

It was four minutes before he realized he was being followed.

He hadn't seen anyone directly, but he knew it all the same.

O'Kane had been around long enough to know every trick in the book when it came to spotting a tail. Looking in shop windows, stopping to light a cigarette and turning your head against the wind, crossing the road, crossing back again, speeding up, slowing down.

He knew them all.

He just didn't see the point in them.

He just reached up under the back of his coat, grabbed the butt of the Browning, stopped walking, and turned around.

The Bear.

Even though O'Kane had never met him, he knew who it was the second their eyes met. With fifteen feet between them, the Bear had his hands in his overcoat pockets, feet planted.

Ready.

They were frozen in a river of time that flowed around them. Vehicles drove past, people crossed their lines of sight, car horns sounded, crates crashed, shop bells rang, and newspaper vendors called.

But Bauer and O'Kane stood still and stared.

"Who are you?" the Bear called to him across the gap.

"Michael O'Kane."

"What do you want?"

"I want to make you rich."

"I have more money than you could ever count."

"You don't have money, Captain Bauer, you have gold."

"Gold is worth money."

"Gold is worth nothing if you can't spend it."

"And you can help me with that."

"I can help you with a lot of things."

The Bear smiled. "And what do you want?"

"I want the gold, and in return I will give you your money and your safety."

The Bear nodded. "Always the gold."

"Always the gold." O'Kane shrugged.

"Where are you from?"

"What does it matter?"

"I killed an American a few days ago. Was he your friend?"

"I don't have any friends."

"We have something in common then."

"Maybe we could be friends?" O'Kane tightened his grip on the Browning behind his back.

An old lady stopped in between them for a moment as she thumbed through some small change in her hand. Neither of them seemed to see her, but they both stood waiting for her to move. It took ten seconds for her to realize she was interrupting their conversation. She looked first at Bauer, then at O'Kane. Then she scurried away as if shocked by the electricity that was passing between them.

The Bear smiled.

"You aren't going to give me money for that gold, Mr. O'Kane. We both know it. The minute the last crate is taken off the lorry, you will try to kill me."

"Captain Bauer, I can assure you, I am a man of my word. If I wasn't, I wouldn't be able to operate in the manner that I do. If I say I will do something for you, I will do it, so the offer I gave to the resistance stands for you. That gold buys a passage out and a tenth of its value in U.S. dollars. You will be a very rich man if you accept."

"And in America? What would they say to a man like me stepping off a ship in New York?"

"They'd say, 'Can I carry your bag, sir?'" O'Kane smiled. "Money in America has a habit of making people look the other way. You'll find that over there, rich people don't break the law, they buy it. If you give me the chance, I'll prove it to you."

———

DANNECKER WAS RIDING in the front of the truck next to the still-disheveled Becker. The cab stunk of diesel and exhaust fumes, mixed with the grit everyone inside it was covered with. Every now and then Becker nudged Dannecker when he lowered the field dressing he was holding to his throat and checked it for fresh blood.

The driver crunched a gear and the truck lurched. Becker caught Dannecker on the shoulder again with his elbow.

"Stop playing with it." Dannecker was staring out the window, but turned to nod his head toward the dressing. "Leave it on."

"I want to see if it is still bleeding."

"It won't stop if you keep moving it."

"It hurts."

"Don't be such a—" Dannecker broke off. He leaned forward, squinted, then pointed out through the windscreen. "There."

"Sir?" The driver looked across.

"Stop the truck." Dannecker reached across Becker and grabbed the driver's arm. "Stop now!"

The driver stamped the brakes and Dannecker and Becker slammed into the windscreen.

Becker landed half on top of his boss, and it took him a moment to pull himself off. As soon as he moved, Dannecker grabbed the door handle and jumped out of the cab.

He dropped down onto the tram line, checked nothing was coming, and called up to Becker.

"Get the men."

"Sir?"

"Over there! It's Bauer and O'Kane!"

Dannecker pointed across the street again and started running. He pulled out his Mauser, then realized there was no point. He couldn't shoot either of them. Just the same as he couldn't let one of them kill the other.

He could see from their stances that they were seconds away from drawing on each other. He shouted again and fired a shot in the air. "No!"

It was his shot that did it.

The soldiers piling out of the back of the wagon heard it and started shooting. The shop window next to O'Kane and the Bear exploded as people darted for cover from the rapid rat-a-tat and splintering timber, glass, and brickwork.

O'KANE DIDN'T KNOW where it was coming from at first. His reflexes threw him to the ground, gun in hand.

He sprawled, Browning out in front, face flat on the concrete as rounds skittered and danced around him. He saw a few civilians drop, some hit, some hiding, as he looked around for a target to shoot at.

And then he saw them. The SS, blasting away like amateurs.

Fucking Germans.

DANNECKER SPUN TO see who was shooting.

He saw Becker and started screaming. "What are you doing?" He stumbled as his feet failed to keep up with his sudden change of direction. "Don't shoot at them, you idiot!"

Becker lowered his weapon a few inches and waved for the troops at the back of the wagon to cease fire.

He looked back at Dannecker and shrugged.

Dannecker turned, dropped to one knee, and raised his pistol.

The Bear was gone.

O'Kane was lying in the gutter, his head down, covered by one ineffectual hand as his pistol remained outstretched, pointing at nobody in particular.

A few of the troops from the back of the second wagon opened up at the shop with their assault rifles when they saw O'Kane and his pistol. The heavy fire sent shards flying as they unloaded wildly, their nerves shredded after the explosion.

Dannecker started to wave his hands and scream at them.

"Stop fucking shooting! Hold your fire! Hold your fire!"

The firing stopped, and an awkward, angular silence settled on the street.

Dannecker started running.

IT HAD TAKEN less than six minutes to get to within walking distance of the pub after the explosion. As soon as they had got near, Rossett had dismissed the driver and jogged the rest of the way on foot, doing his best to blend in with the crowd that was gathering around him.

They had been still clearing up. Through the drifting smoke he had seen Dannecker and Becker rallying their men in the confusion. Rossett had watched them for a moment, and then he had started to search for the Bear.

He knew the Bear would want to watch the explosion.

Whether it was for the enjoyment of death or a cold calculation of the forces left standing against him, Rossett knew the Bear was near.

He also knew that the Bear was good. He was a man who left little to chance. He was a man who planned and prepared, as any good soldier should.

Rossett just had to figure out the details.

He got as close as he could and saw that pretty much every window for fifty yards in either direction was blown through. The blast had been channeled by the tall, tightly packed buildings, and the shock wave had had nowhere to go.

The Bear would have known that the windows would blow in, so he wouldn't have been in front of the blast for fear of getting cut by flying glass.

He would either be behind it or to the side.

Rossett crossed the road and looked at the shops on the same side as the bomb site. More glass was smashed, and curtains fluttered through broken windows like flirtatious eyelashes.

Even though they were closer to the blast than those opposite, the buildings had taken less of its force. They were a better option, but Rossett doubted they provided a good enough view of the aftermath.

The field of vision was too narrow, unless you risked standing right at what was left of a window. That would make you a potential target, and potential targets would have stood out a mile to the men who were covering the rescue operation with their StG 44s.

Rossett had spun on the spot. The Bear wasn't in front, to the side, or behind the blast. Rossett was confused. The Bear had to be there, somewhere. Faces swam, voices drowned out thought. Rossett had focused on the windows and doorways, the turned backs, the hands over mouths. He saw them all, but he didn't see the Bear.

And then he'd heard an engine firing up, off to his right.

An old Bedford box van belched some smoke and pulled away. It had been parked about fifty yards up the road, just far enough to blend in with the crowd that was gathering to watch the fallout after the bomb.

The Bear.

Rossett cursed himself for sending the driver back to the safe house. The van was moving away, slowly, almost too slowly. If he'd been able to run, Rossett reckoned he would have been able to catch it. But he couldn't run, not with so many German guns around.

He started to walk, skirting the back of the crowd, watching the van, and wondering why it was going so slowly until it stopped. Rossett kept walking, hand on his Webley in his pocket, his pulse and his feet quickening as he drew nearer.

Thirty yards.

The Bear got out, checked the street, then jogged across it through the thin line of traffic that was building up due to the blockage up ahead.

Rossett followed the Bear across the road at a safe distance.

The engine of the van was still running and the door was still open. Rossett was aware that the Bear might be heading back to it at any moment and prepared himself for the confrontation.

The Bear was walking slowly, taking his time, one hand in his pocket. Stalking.

The Bear stopped, and the man in front of him turned.

O'Kane.

Rossett stepped into the lee of the buildings to get out of a potential line of fire.

He waited, keeping the Webley in his pocket and leaning in close to a doorway, watching from a position of safety. If the Bear lived and made for the van, Rossett would take him as he crossed the road.

Rossett checked the people around him. Nobody seemed to notice the almost silent confrontation taking place in front of them. Life went on as usual, and it struck Rossett that maybe the suddenness of unexpected death was a blessing.

He finally slipped the Webley out of his pocket and tucked it behind his leg as two SS trucks skidded to a halt across the road. He glanced back to the Bear and O'Kane, who hadn't noticed. He looked back toward the trucks and saw Dannecker running toward his side of the road. The troops in the back of the wagons were jumping down, and he watched as Becker pointed toward the Bear and O'Kane.

Rossett knew what was coming next.

He ducked.

The SS started firing.

The scene in front of him broke down into chaos. The soldiers were opening up at anything and everything. The people crouching around Rossett started to push past to get to the safety of the shop behind him. He lost sight of the shooting and had to straighten a little, making room to be able to see what was going on.

O'Kane was in the gutter, and the Bear was gone.

There was only one place for him to have disappeared so quickly. Through the shop and out the back. Rossett took the same route through the shop where he was sheltering.

The chase was on again.

O'KANE GINGERLY SHOOK off the debris that had landed on him. He lifted his head, saw Dannecker running toward him, and instinctively leveled the Browning.

"No!" Dannecker skidded to a stop fifty feet away and threw up his hands. "Don't shoot! It was a mistake!"

Dannecker was shouting across the distance between them. O'Kane stared down the sight for a second or two, then lowered the pistol and looked around.

At least four dead, several more injured, and a shop front blown apart by rounds of automatic fire.

That was one hell of a mistake.

He pushed himself up onto one elbow and shook his head to shake off a few pieces of broken glass that had landed in his hair. He stopped, looked back at the shop, and realized the Bear was gone.

Shit.

O'Kane was up and running into the shop in a flash. Once inside, it took his eyes a moment to adjust to the gloom. There were bullet holes all over the back wall and the counter in front of it. Children's treats and broken glass jars littered the shelves and floor.

Down to O'Kane's right, crouching below the frame of the window, three women stared up at him. O'Kane pointed to the back of the shop, where he could see an open door, and held a finger to his lips.

One of the women nodded and pointed at the door herself.

He heard Dannecker shouting orders at his men outside, and O'Kane frowned at the thought of having twenty nervous machine guns behind him.

He moved through the shop slowly, over the broken glass. His feet crunched as if he were on a woodland walk, and he grimaced with every step. His head was twitching left and right as he tried to see into the room beyond the doorway.

As he drew level with the shop counter, he saw the shopkeeper slumped behind it. His dead eyes stared up at what was left of his life's work. O'Kane stepped to the left of the doorway, then took a look over his shoulder to see who had followed him into the shop.

Three SS privates who had the look of fodder on their faces.

O'Kane signaled them to stop moving and to be quiet.

He crouched, then bobbed his head around the door to take a look into the other room. It was almost pitch black. He thought about asking the shopkeeper if there was a light, then remembered the man had just started decomposing behind him.

He looked at the private closest to him and pointed to the back room.

You go first.

The private shook his head.

You go fucking first.

This time O'Kane jabbed a finger.

The private looked at his colleagues behind him, swallowed, and did as he was told.

PRIVATE GUNTHER WALTZ was seventeen years old, a long way from home, and very, very scared.

He'd been conscripted, the same as every other sixteen-year-old, the moment that he had left school and informed the local government that he wasn't intending to go to university.

That was why he was shitting himself in the back of a shop in Liverpool.

He swallowed. It was dark, and no matter how hard he tried to open his eyes wider, he couldn't grab enough light to see into the gloom. O'Kane, who was right behind him with one hand on his shoulder, was wearing such strong cologne, it seemed to crowd Gunther's senses and hush them up.

O'Kane gave him a gentle shove and let go of his shoulder.

It was the kind of shove that said "Get moving."

So Gunther got moving.

The place was full of shadows, shadows that messed with his depth perception and made him feel like he was falling off a cliff.

The light switch Gunther found when he had passed through the second door just clicked with no result. A few seconds later he heard the crunch of the lightbulb under his boot as he crossed the floor toward where he hoped a back wall was.

He wanted to look over his shoulder to see if anyone was behind him, but fear had made his neck stiff and his head dip, so he just kept moving forward.

Just keep going, it'll be okay, just keep going.

His hands gripping and then flexing, then gripping and flexing again. The cold steel of the StG made them ache with the effort, but he kept doing it until finally he turned a corner and saw a sliver of light.

A door.

Ajar, maybe two centimeters. Whoever they were chasing had fled the building. Gunther breathed out, relaxed his hands on his rifle, swallowed, and called out to his colleagues back in the shop, almost twenty yards behind him.

"It's okay, there is a door, he's gone out the back!"

He heard them coming, moving through the shop a lot quicker than he had done. He took off his helmet, wiped his forehead with his sleeve, then put the helmet back on his head.

He'd made it through one more minute in a war zone.

He pushed open the door and heard a click.

He looked down, and saw the potato masher grenade booby trap, which was about to explode.

Gunther realized he wasn't going to make it through the next minute.

O'KANE HEARD THE explosion but didn't feel the blast as the two soldiers in front of him blocked the wave.

He guessed it was a hand grenade, probably a potato masher tied to the door handle. Just another booby trap catching someone who took his mind off what he was supposed to be doing.

Didn't they teach these kids anything?

He moved past the men on the ground without looking at them.

He was on point again.

ROSSETT WAS IN the alleyway, straining his ears and eyes, trying to catch sight or sound of the Bear. It took a few seconds, and then he heard the back door to a yard being dragged open somewhere up ahead.

The Bear was coming.

Rossett crouched down behind some metal rubbish bins against the moss-covered wall and thumbed the hammer on the Webley.

He waited, pistol ready, letting the Bear come out of whichever backyard he was hiding in.

Rossett had a plan. It wasn't much of one, but it was the kind he liked the best. Simple.

He would make it quick, a straight choice.

Be arrested or die.

The gold didn't matter to Rossett. What mattered was doing his job. The right thing, the simple thing. He wasn't going to give in to anger, he wasn't going to give in to revenge, he wasn't going to give in to violence.

Not this time.

He just wanted to do his job.

Rossett would sooner snap on the handcuffs than pull a trigger, but he was certain he could do either with a clear conscience, for the first time in a long time.

The Bear came out the backyard up the alleyway at a full-on sprint.

Rossett caught sight of him and ducked down unseen. He couldn't see the Bear, but he could hear him. Splashing through puddles, getting closer, closer to justice with every step.

There was a whump of an explosion.

Rossett ducked, then recognized the percussion as a grenade, probably left as a booby trap. He knew German potato mashers came with a string in the handle that made setting a trap a ten-second job.

He'd done it himself in another life.

It was a sound he'd heard so many times, he could imagine the scene of the explosion without having to close his eyes.

The Bear had killed someone else.

Rossett stood up and pointed the Webley down the alley at where the Bear should have been.

There was no one there.

He crouched back down behind the bins, cursed, then lifted his head again.

The alley was still empty, but Rossett guessed it was going to be filling up shortly with German soldiers. He had to get moving.

He started to make his way in the same direction he figured the Bear had headed. He stopped when he heard the sound of falling rubble and scrambling boots up ahead, maybe forty feet past where the booby trap had been. It sounded like it was coming from the bombed-out houses that backed onto the alleyway.

The Bear climbing for cover, or maybe heading up to a sniping platform?

Rossett dodged flat against the left-hand wall. It was seven feet high, on the same side as the scrabbling. Seconds passed. Silence. Rossett slowly moved forward. He reached a yard gate, half propped up by a rotten frame and rusted hinges.

The gate had scraped an arc of grit against the flagstones when it had last been opened.

The shifted dirt looked fresh, so fresh it must have been moved in the last minute or so.

The Bear.

Rossett stared at the gate but didn't touch it. The sound of the recent explosion was still ringing in his ears, making him cautious. He checked for signs of a trap and listened for sounds of movement in the backyard beyond it.

Sudden scrambling again. Feet on rubble. Someone was climbing up to the first floor of the bombed-out tenement behind the gate.

Rossett gripped the Webley a little harder and considered shoving the gate open and shooting at the Bear as he climbed. He rocked on his toes, the cold wall flat against his back, then gone, flat against his back, then gone.

Wait.

He stopped rocking. The Bear had a reputation for being the best. If Rossett was going to catch him, he'd have to be better. Blasting into the yard would probably get him killed, and Rossett was better than that.

This was chess, not bowling.

Rossett looked around. Each of the tenements had identical yards and adjoining back walls. He counted off two backyards down the alley, then moved silently toward it.

He gripped the top of the wall, climbed, then rolled over the top. He was in the yard two buildings to the right of where the Bear had gone.

He pulled the Webley, scanned the yard and then what was left of the building it backed onto. The house was almost as badly damaged as all the others.

It was as though someone had ripped the guts out of the buildings and dragged them out into the backyards. A few outhouses remained standing, but pretty much everything else was buried under the bricks that had been blasted out of the back walls.

Rossett moved slowly across them. He kept close to the building line, eyes looking up into the carcass of the houses as he passed. It took him a minute of creeping before he made it to the house next door to where he believed the Bear had gone.

The whole of the back of the tenement was missing. Plaster hung from splintered slats, and dark smears of soot alluded to the fire that had gutted the place after the bomb blast. Rossett climbed the rubble to the first floor as quietly as he could. Once there he found remnants of a rug still lying on the floorboards. He stepped onto it off the rubble. The floor moved under his fcct as he crossed to the front of the property. The boards on the windows were thin, and in places too small to cover the gaps. Rossett gripped the bottom of one and eased it back a few inches.

He looked out onto the street. It was deserted, blitzed until nearly all of the buildings looked like rotten teeth in a skull. Behind him he could now hear German voices in the alleyway. They were looking for the Bear, which meant they might discover Rossett by accident. He tried a door and found a narrow stairwell that looked fairly undamaged.

He climbed the stairs, pistol out in front, ducking as he passed holes blasted in the wall that ran between the two houses. He paused at a rear window on the third floor and looked through the shattered glass down into the alley. There were squads of SS moving along it in both directions.

Rossett caught sight of O'Kane.

He was working with the Germans.

You learn something every day.

No time to think about that now. Concentrate on the Bear. He was the one that mattered. He was the one who had to pay for what he had done.

Rossett started moving again, silent, slow, each step a whisper of menace into an unhearing ear.

He came to a gap in the wall that separated the two houses. Four bricks, a diamond-shaped hole through to the other side, a space just big enough to stick his head through. He didn't have to; he could smell the Bear on the other side.

A faint whiff of cordite and body odor. Rossett listened. He could hear the other man breathing.

They were inches apart.

Rossett didn't move. He waited.

Patience was a virtue.

CHAPTER 18

THE BEAR HAD heard the grenade booby trap going off, but he'd taken no satisfaction from it.

He'd made a mistake.

He'd allowed himself to be drawn out.

He'd confronted O'Kane on the street instead of following him back home, and that had nearly cost him his life. He'd behaved like an amateur, a fool, and he was angry. He'd nearly missed out on the duel with the Lion because he'd allowed himself to be distracted by the gold.

He was supposed to be better than that.

Rossett was the only thing that mattered. He was the test, the worthy opponent, the one who would finally prove that the Bear had nobody left to beat in Great Britain.

When Rossett was dead, then he could think about the future, about the gold, about America.

But only after Rossett was dead.

Only after he knew he was the best.

He wouldn't make another mistake. The prize was almost in his hands; he wouldn't drop it now.

He'd recced and established the safe house that morning, before he had primed the bomb in the pub. It was eighty yards and an eleven-second sprint from where he had almost been pinned down outside the shop. In case of emergency he'd scouted four routes to, and six routes from it. He knew that some people might think it was too close to where he had been shot at, but the Bear liked close. Close meant that he would have less time to wait for them to pass by when they started the search.

At the safe house he had a change of clothes, a store of ammunition, and, in the event of the worst-case scenario, food and water to last a couple of days. Staying alive was all about patience and preparation, and the Bear had a gift for both. He'd picked the place carefully. It was an old tenement, the center of which had taken a few artillery strikes during the fall of the city. The roof was mostly gone, the back wall was three-quarters missing, and the back rooms that remained were exposed to the elements.

From the alleyway, if you were to take time to look up, the whole place looked like a tumbledown doll's house with the walls removed. Tattered pale-blue-striped wallpaper wafted in the breeze, while odds and ends of furniture had slid down slanted floors and hung off the edge as if they were too scared to jump down to the rubble below.

It didn't look like it would shelter a rat, let alone a Bear.

He had stashed his stores on the fourth floor, after he had found that the stairwell was mostly clear at the front of the house. Only the two ground floors had been boarded up at the front, which meant that if he climbed up to the top, he had an option to escape with a rope from a front window. In a real emergency, say an assault from the back and the front at the same time, he could reach the roof and run almost the full length of the road. He'd be a full four stories above anyone searching for him, and he could drop through one of the many skylights to safety below.

Preparation would keep him alive, just as it always did.

After the booby trap had gone off he had ducked into the backyard of the tenement and, once on the other side, skidded to a stop, spun, then lifted the wooden back gate into the hole in the wall.

The grenade had made them cautious. He'd slowed them down, but he hadn't set another trap. The alley had several exits; he wanted them to think he had gone out of one of them, moving fast without stopping.

He'd wanted them to chase his ghost.

The night before he'd marked out a route to the first floor and practiced it a few times. Today, he'd paused halfway, listened, then finished making his way into the safety of the ruin. Once inside he'd ducked through a smashed doorway and on through the first room, with its delicately balanced floor and furniture. There was enough light from the back of the house to move along the narrow corridor, and then to the front of the building with its boarded-up windows.

At the foot of the stairs he'd stopped, checked the fine trip wire he had set carefully the day before, and then finally, when certain all was well, headed up.

He climbed to the top of the stairs, crouched, then craned his neck over another pile of fallen bricks. From his vantage point, his head low behind the cover, he could just see into the backyard and the alley beyond.

Soldiers, moving slowly, looking over walls and testing gates. He edged forward so he could see farther along the alleyway.

O'Kane, directing the soldiers with gestures and silent points of his hand.

The Bear had considered O'Kane and his offer about the gold.

Who was he? He wasn't a Liverpool policeman. The Bear knew every police detective in the city by sight, and he'd never seen O'Kane before.

He wasn't resistance. He was working with the SS.

The Bear tried to place O'Kane's accent. American? Canadian? Irish maybe? Hard to tell, all of them and yet none of them. A little like the Bear's own English.

Whoever O'Kane was, he was dangerous, but the question was: Could he be trusted?

If the Bear wanted out of the city after he had bested Rossett, it seemed like O'Kane was the one ticket on sale.

He just had to be careful he didn't get shortchanged.

The Bear found a spot, cleared his mind, and calmed the waters.

He thought about his childhood, the same memory he always used when he had to wait and think at times like this.

He heard his mother singing in the kitchen. He was in the back room of their little house in Essen. He could feel the room, every detail.

He was sitting on the floor; he could hear her and smell the strudel she was baking. Her voice was so clear and so crisp. She was through the doorway, just out of sight, except for her shadow on the floor, put there by the sunshine through the window in the kitchen.

The song drifted back to him like a warm breeze that made him lift his chin a little and smile.

"Das Bucklige Männlein."

The Hunchbacked Little Man.

The words were ugly, but her voice . . . oh, her voice . . . it was beautiful. He wanted to tell her that she sounded like an angel, but he couldn't go to her because he was so small, stuck there on the floor.

> *I want to go into my little garden,*
> *I want to water my flowers,*
> *There's a hunchbacked little man there,*
> *About to start to sneeze.*

The years slipped away. The Bear didn't move an inch. He listened to the soldiers in the alleyway, the crunch of the boots, the hush of their voices, the same as he listened to his mother in memory.

> *I want to go to my little cellar,*
> *I want to draw my little wine from the keg,*
> *A hunchbacked little man stands there,*
> *He's already snatched a jug from me.*

She was beautiful, smiling as she sang, the sun lighting her blond hair, like golden wisps of angel's thread.

> *I want to go into my little bedroom,*
> *I want to make my bed,*
> *A hunchbacked little man stands there*
> *And starts to laugh.*

He could hear the soldiers below him grumbling. They were tired, scared, on a wild-goose chase after searching for almost two hours now.

"We've got casualties in the truck, we should be looking after them . . ."

He heard the back gate being shoved by a reluctant shoulder and standing firm.

They were moving down the alley again.

He smiled as he listened.

And then they were gone.

Dear little child, please
Pray for the hunchbacked little man . . .

The song ended.

HOURS PASSED, AND like the soldiers the afternoon was long gone.

The smile faded, just like it always did as he came back to life.

He remembered her body in the bathtub.

He didn't want to remember.

He didn't want to find her dead.

But he had.

The blood in the water.

He blinked and saw her hair, splayed out around her head, like she was falling away from him off a cliff. She stared up, lips apart, as she lay beneath the surface.

Pray for the hunchbacked little man . . .

He wished he had gone to the doorway to watch her sing in the kitchen instead of listening to her voice. He wished she had taken him with her.

That way he wouldn't hate her.

He wouldn't hate her for leaving him to the men in the children's home. The men with their rough hands, stubbly chins, and snorting midnight drunken breath that blew against the back of his neck and sounded like a bull bearing down on him.

He hated her more than he hated them.

And he hated them a lot.

The Bear lifted his head. He'd been there almost three hours, according to his watch. He took a look into the backyard and the alleyway. Empty. Slightly softer, slightly longer shadows as the sun set behind the houses.

There was a cat, oblivious, sitting on the wall, watching a bird on a rooftop. It looked bored and hungry, but not disturbed by searching Germans.

The Bear watched it closely.

He'd learned long ago that a watched animal could tell you a lot more than your own senses could. Their senses were sharper, they smelled people hiding, they heard the beat of a human heart and saw the twitch of a human hair, long before he could.

The cat yawned.

They'd gone.

He was safe.

He slipped his pistol into his pocket and slowly got to his feet, then stretched out his stiff limbs.

There was plenty of cover from where half of the roof had fallen in to make what amounted to a lean-to. The Bear had stashed his provisions there, including an MP40 in case of emergency.

He was cold, but it was still too light to start up a fire. He was hungry, but instead of eating, he decided to prepare some wood while there was still enough light to do so.

The fallen roof provided a few boards, but kindling was scarce, so he checked that the coast was clear and then stepped out of his shelter to rip some of the tattered wallpaper from the floor below.

He saw the fist coming, hard and fast. He felt like a rabbit in the headlamps.

John Henry Rossett punched him in the face.

It was a good punch. A Rossett punch. Straight, economical, and whip-crack fast. Most men would have been out like a light. Most men would have woken up five minutes later and wondered what truck had run them over.

The Bear wasn't most men.

He managed to dip his chin two inches. That was all it took. Rossett's right fist connected with his forehead instead of his nose. The Bear staggered back; forehead or not, the punch was hard enough to give his brain a shake and dull his senses.

His instincts were still good, though. They snapped up his hands and lifted his elbows. He dipped his head under their cover. Rossett stepped in, following the Bear as he went backward. The Bear blinked off the shock of the first punch and felt a left fist thud into the back of his right hand and pin it against his head.

Another good punch. A brain-numbing punch, but still not enough to put him down. He feinted another step back, then stepped forward.

He met Rossett halfway through throwing another right.

This time the Bear was close enough to duck under it and into Rossett's chest. The hands that had been held high protecting his head now became levers to slam into Rossett and rock him backward to open a gap between the Lion and the Bear.

The fight was on.

ROSSETT WOULD HAVE bet a hundred pounds on the Bear going down after that first punch. His hand was stinging from slamming it into the German's forehead, and he had a nagging feeling that he might just have broken a bone or two.

It didn't stop him throwing the left, though. The one that normally finished the job.

The Bear fended it off with a high elbow and forearm. They took out most of the power of the punch and left it landing limply against the hand protecting his head.

Rossett was surprised. The Bear protected himself like a boxer. He knew that winning a fight wasn't all about the punches you threw; it was about how you dealt with the punches you drew.

And he was dealing with them well.

Rossett stepped in, drawing back his right. He'd find out if it was broken the second it landed on the Bear, but either way, Rossett knew it should be the punch to end the fight.

The Bear stepped inside the punch almost the second it was thrown. It flashed past his left ear and left Rossett's torso exposed in its wake.

The Bear slammed Rossett's chest with the flats of both hands and drove him back eighteen inches. The Bear threw a good right, and Rossett hooked it away. The Bear threw a sharp left; Rossett took it on the shoulder and rolled with it a few inches.

The Bear stepped in, hooked the left again, and caught Rossett with a good kidney punch.

Rossett started to regret not just shooting the Bear when he had the chance.

THE BEAR DUG his knuckles hard into Rossett's back, grabbed at the Englishman's raincoat, and tried to pull him upright so that he could land a head butt.

It was his first mistake of the fight.

He had to step across Rossett. He was in too close. He realized it the second he felt Rossett wrap his arm around his then use his momentum against him. The Bear hit the wall face-first.

He felt the already weakened plaster crack under his cheek. His right arm was locked up and behind him by Rossett.

He couldn't shake it free. He felt Rossett pulling on his shoulder, trying to lift him a few inches off the wall. He guessed he was going to be slammed again.

He wasn't.

It was a trick designed to get him to bring his leg forward to brace himself.

It worked.

Rossett kicked down on the outside of his knee. It buckled, and screamed with pain the second it gave way. The Bear dropped into the rubble. Rossett slammed his face back into the wall and then pulled him back. The Bear looked up.

Rossett knocked him out.

THE BEAR BLINKED.

The world spun, disappeared, then spun again as he squinted up at the muzzle of a Webley revolver. He closed his eyes, squeezed them so tight it ratcheted up the dull ache in his head a notch, and opened them again.

Rossett stared back at him from behind the Webley.

"Oh," the Bear said quietly, because it was all he could think to say.

"You're under arrest."

"Arrest?"

"Arrest." Rossett dropped the cuffs onto his chest.

The Bear sighed and closed his eyes again for a moment. Eventually he swallowed, licked his tongue around his dry lips, and looked back up at Rossett.

"Where were you?"

"Other side of the wall next door."

"How did you know I was here?"

"I saw you talking in the street, before the shooting started."

"In the street?"

"In the street. Put the cuffs on."

"If I don't?"

"I'll shoot you in the right elbow."

The Bear considered that option, then slipped the cuffs on and held them up for Rossett to inspect. They passed muster, so the Bear dropped his hands back onto his chest.

"I killed your partner."

"I know."

"I shot him like a dog."

"I know."

"He whimpered like a dog."

"I don't care."

"Just because these cuffs are on doesn't mean you've won. There is a long way to go yet."

Rossett lowered the Webley a few inches. "Get up."

"You aren't going to make me pay for what I've done?"

"Not the way you think, no."

"Why?"

"Because I am better than you."

The Bear sighed. "I think you broke my nose."

"Good. Now get up."

The Bear got up to his feet unsteadily, tested his nose again, and looked at Rossett.

"They won't stop; they want that gold more than anything else on earth."

"Then they will have to go through me to get it."

"They'll walk right through you and out the other side without stopping. They will want the address of the gold, and there is nothing you can do about it. I promise you that."

"Like you promised you'd written it down and put it in your pocket?" Rossett took hold of the Bear's arm and pushed him ahead as they made their way out of the building.

The Bear looked back at him over his shoulder. "You searched me?"

"You lied."

The Bear laughed. "Were you disappointed, Lion? Were you going to kill me if you found it?"

"I don't want your gold, Bauer."

"You looked, though."

"I just wanted to see if you were telling the truth."

"Yeah, Lion." The Bear stumbled forward a few paces, then cast a glance over his shoulder as Rossett shoved him again. "You keep telling yourself that."

CHAPTER 19

'M A POLICE officer and I need your car."

The driver stared up at Rossett through the half-open window of the tiny Standard Eight motorcar, then craned his neck a little to look at the Bear.

"I'm a port agent and I need the car more than you, so piss off." The driver wasn't too keen on walking home.

Rossett pulled out the Webley and shoved it through the window.

"This needs it too, so you are outvoted."

The port agent stared at the Webley and then opened the door. Rossett gripped his collar and half dragged him out of his seat into the road. The agent stumbled, righted himself, looked at the Bear, who gave him a shrug, then back at Rossett.

"I need that car."

It was the Bear's turn to be grabbed by the collar and dragged around. He was compliant, especially because now his hands were handcuffed behind him and his options for resistance were pretty much zero.

Rossett opened the front passenger door of the car, shoved the Bear in, and slammed the door behind him. The port agent lifted his hands and tried again.

"If I lose that car, I'll lose my job!"

"You'll find it at the central police station."

Rossett got in the driver's seat. He crunched a gear and pulled away with a small wheel spin on the wet cobbles, but squealed to a halt after a few seconds.

Rossett leaned out the window and called back to the port agent.

"Do you know where the central police station is?"

"Of course I do!"

The driver's door flew open and Rossett got out, then reached in and manhandled the Bear into the backseat with the Webley as encouragement. He gestured that the port agent should get back in the driver's seat, then walked around the car and got in the other side.

Rossett looked over his shoulder at the Bear.

"One move, one twitch, one thing I don't like, and I will put a round in you. Understand?"

"Perfectly."

"Don't doubt me."

"I wouldn't dream of it."

Rossett looked at the port agent, who was looking in through the driver's door.

"What's your name?"

"Brian."

"Well, Brian, if you drive us to the central police station you'll be free to go with my thanks."

"I'd rather just go without you shooting me."

"So would I."

Brian considered his options, then climbed in. He looked over his shoulder at the Bear, who smiled at him and said, "He's actually quite nice when you get to know him."

IT HAD STARTED to rain again. Not heavily, just enough to speckle the streets and mist the edges of the windscreen as they headed across town.

Nobody spoke.

Rossett was watching the Bear. Who, in turn, was simply staring out the side window at the passing streets. They had driven for almost ten minutes, hardly stopping at traffic lights or slowing for corners as Rossett encouraged speed with gentle waves of the hand whenever they looked to be in danger of reducing speed.

Brian finally spoke.

"I drive home this way six days a week."

"Just drive."

Brian glanced over his left shoulder at the Bear, and then at Rossett, before looking back out the windscreen.

"I think we're being followed."

Rossett looked out through the back window. There was a car, maybe a hundred yards back, with its headlamps on, the only other moving vehicle on the street.

The Bear spoke softly. "It seems that even if you don't care about the gold . . . someone else does."

Rossett did his best to ignore him and turned to Brian.

"Take the next right-hand turn as quick as you can. When you're clear of the intersection, stand on the brakes. I want you to stop, but keep the engine running."

"Did he say gold?"

"Just turn the down the next street."

Brian did as he was told as soon as they reached the next right-hand turn. For a moment Rossett thought they were going to skid, but Brian was a better driver than he looked. He countered the slide with a flick of the steering wheel, and then, once they had rounded the corner, stamped on the brakes and brought the car to a halt.

"Lights."

Brian turned them off as Rossett stepped out the already-open passenger door and pointed the Webley over the car roof toward the corner.

He waited.

A moment, then another, then the car that had been behind them drove past the intersection at about thirty miles an hour and speeded on out of sight.

Rossett lifted the Webley, released the hammer with his thumb, and blew out his cheeks. He glanced around at the side street they were in, checked the Bear through the back window, then placed his Webley on the roof of the car and started to pat himself down for a cigarette.

He didn't have one.

He picked up the Webley and got back into the car.

"Turn around and head for the police station."

"We going to be driving around all night like this?"

"Don't make me shoot you, Brian."

Brian shook his head, jabbed at the clutch, and finally found first gear.

They'd moved less than twenty feet when two cars came around the corner in procession and fanned out to block the road.

Brian stamped on the foot brake.

"Oh dear," the Bear said quietly.

ROSSETT KNEW IT was pointless pointing the pistol at them, but he did it anyway. Behind the headlamps he could count eight men, and he guessed there were eight guns as well.

He could feel the cold from the car roof leaching through the thin material of his coat as he rested his arms on it, the Webley outstretched in front of him in a double-handed grip.

Iris came out of the lights. He recognized the walk long before he heard her voice calling to him from the silhouette.

"John?"

"Yes."

"Y-you have the Bear?"

"Yes."

"But you aren't g-giving him to us?"

"No."

"You're s-stealing the gold?"

"No."

After a moment Iris called out again.

"You're protecting h-him?"

Rossett saw the tilt of her head silhouetted by the headlamps as she waited for his answer.

"I'm arresting him."

Iris looked over her shoulder at the guns behind her, then back at Rossett.

"You're not d-doing a very good job."

"He's wearing handcuffs."

"Not for long."

"We'll see." Rossett shifted the Webley slightly.

"He killed your partner."

"He didn't do anything you weren't going to do eventually."

"That's not t-true."

"You kept him alive long enough to get me over to your side."

"The r-right side."

Rossett spread his feet a few inches wider, settling into his shooting stance.

"You know, Iris, if there's one thing I've learned over the last couple of years it is that there isn't really such a thing as a good side and a bad side. There's just people fighting for the edge of the same coin from opposite sides."

"You th-think we're as bad as the Nazis?"

"No, but being less bad than something doesn't mean you are better than it."

"So you carry on working for them?"

"I carry on being a policeman."

"Just like that?"

Rossett took a breath, held it, thought for a moment, and then called back to her.

"There's a police warrant card in my pocket, Iris. To some people it is just a bit of card. I'll be honest: for a while, that's all it was to me, but . . ." Rossett wiped his forehead on his upper arm and felt the sting of the cut there as it scraped against his coat. He paused again, watching her through the sights of the Webley for a moment before he spoke again. "I realized that I made an oath to uphold the law. I keep telling

people that's all I want to do, but I then keep forgetting to do it. The
Bear, Bauer, he's a murderer. Consul Hawthorn, Neumann, your people,
and the countless others he's put to death—he has to face justice for that,
and I have to play by the rules, even if nobody else does. I'm going to put
him in a cell, I'm going to do my job, and I am going to start worrying
about the people I swore to protect. Maybe then I can start sleeping at
night."

Iris took a tiny step to the side as her left leg twitched. She rested her
right hand on her hip and looked over her shoulder at her men. A second
passed, then she turned back to Rossett and took a few paces forward.
She finally stopped when she was less than four feet from Brian's door.
He leaned out the open window a few inches and whispered to her.

"This is nothing to do with me, love, I was just drivin' home. He's a
nutter; reckons he is a copper but he hasn't shown me a badge or nothing. Can I get out? I love Churchill, can I go? God save King George and
all that."

She didn't reply. Instead, she stared at the Bear in the backseat for a
moment, then at Rossett.

"I could just t-take him."

"I'll shoot him, or your men will shoot him, but either way you don't
get the gold."

"John, w-we don't have much time."

"Let the Germans have the gold." Rossett said it quietly.

"What?"

"How long do you think Dannecker can keep a lid on this for? I
figure you've got maybe a day before reinforcements start to head up
from London, or even closer. When the new men arrive and find out
what's been going on, Dannecker will be in a cell before nightfall. He'll
tell them about the gold and they will rip this city apart to find it."

"We can kill D-Dannecker, and his bosses will never know the gold
existed. That'll buy us time to find it and arrange another ship."

"Kill him and there'll be a crackdown so heavy, the people of Liverpool will be lucky if they make it out the other side. The Germans will
land hard, Iris, harder than you can imagine. I've seen what they can do."

"We need that gold to keep on fighting."

"Sometimes you need to stop fighting. Sometimes you need to think about the people you are fighting for and whether you are doing more harm than good."

"I'm fighting for their freedom."

"They aren't free when they're dead, Iris. They are just dead. You don't want the crackdown, it'll destroy this place, kill hundreds, maybe thousands of people. The only way around it is to lose the gold and make Dannecker look corrupt, and I think that is a price worth paying."

"You're helping them win the war."

"They already won the war, you just haven't realized it yet."

"You don't kn-know how wrong you are, John." Iris looked at the Bear again. She chewed her lip, then ran a fluttering hand through her cropped hair. "O'Kane will come after you."

"I have to try to save the people of this city."

She looked at the Bear again. The men behind her were like greyhounds in the traps, straining to let fly.

"I can just t-take him."

"Then you'll make me kill him. And you'll kill the city you love."

Iris stared at Rossett, then turned to her men and lifted a featherlight hand.

"Let them pass."

CHAPTER 20

'M NOT SUPPOSED to let people in at night." The police constable on the other side of the glass didn't look entirely happy with the conversation he was having with Rossett.

"Open the door, son, before I kick it in and then kick you in."

"I've been given strict orders."

Rossett stepped back from the door of the central police station, lowered his warrant card, and raised the Webley. He jerked the Bear around so that he was close to the glass panel and kicked the back of his leg gently to force him down onto his knees.

The bobby watched the Bear sink to the floor.

Rossett placed the Webley against the back of the Bear's skull.

"Open the door."

"I'm not allowed to. I—"

"Open the fucking door."

"I'd appreciate it," the Bear added for good measure.

The bobby took a step back.

Rossett thumbed the hammer on the Webley.

The bobby held up his hands.

"All right! Okay!"

It was only when the door was finally opened that Rossett lifted the pistol up off the back of the Bear's head.

"Thank you," he said quietly as he dragged the Bear back up to his feet and propelled him in through the door.

———

THE POLICE STATION was mostly in darkness. Rossett and the Bear had waited at the back of the enquiry office as the bobby relocked the door, then followed him down to the cells in the basement.

"I shouldn't be doing this. We have procedures for prisoners, records, paperwork. I shouldn't be just flinging someone in a cell without doing things properly." The bobby pulled open a cell door and stepped back.

Rossett pushed the Bear through the doorway and shoved him face-first up against the nearest wall. He took out a handcuff key, slipped it into the lock, and paused.

"I can leave these on all night just as easily as I can take them off, do you understand?"

"Yes," the Bear just about managed to answer.

"One move, one twitch, they stay on."

"Okay."

Rossett turned the key, released one cuff, and stepped back toward the door.

The Bear leaned back off the wall and then turned around. He finished uncuffing himself, and then held them up for Rossett to take back. "They'll know you've brought me here."

"Who will?" The bobby looked at Rossett.

"Dannecker probably already knows." The Bear looked at the bobby. "I'll wager he's already on his way."

"Who is?" The bobby started to feed his key chain through his fingers.

"You're going to have one hundred guns trying to get to me."

"How many?"

"Throw the cuffs and key over here." Rossett took a step out of the cell.

"You should have run for the hills, Lion, while you could."

"The cuffs."

The Bear tossed them to Rossett, who let them land on the floor, then kicked them away from the door.

"Shut the door." Rossett lowered the Webley and the bobby did as he was told.

"Too late now, Lion," the Bear called through the crack in the door as it started to swing shut. "They are coming."

The cell door slammed.

"Who is that?" The bobby leaned back against the door.

"Death," said Rossett as he walked away.

THE LINE WAS dead.

Rossett had guessed it would be, but he still felt a sting of disappointment. He put the phone down, placed the Webley on the desk next to it, and looked at the young bobby and the old police sergeant standing next to him.

"What's your name?"

"Jimmy Warner," the sergeant replied.

"How long have the phones been down, Jimmy?"

"Two hours or so."

"Has it happened before?"

"It's always happening, sir. We don't know if it is the resistance or just that we don't have anyone maintaining the system anymore."

"Is there a call box around here?"

"Yes, but it's knackered as well. When they go down, they go down far and wide."

Rossett clicked on the green-shaded lamp next to his pistol and sank down onto the leather chair behind the desk. He ran his hand down his face, then pulled open a few of the drawers in a vain search for the policeman's friend.

Scotch.

He came up empty and looked back at Jimmy.

"My name is Detective Inspector John Rossett. I'm from the Metropolitan Police."

"I know."

"How?"

"You came to speak to my prisoner, sir, Captain Bauer."

"You arrested Bauer?"

"Yes, sir."

"That was good work."

"Thank you." Jimmy was holding the police station keys, running the long chain they were attached to like worry beads through his fingers, then twisting it around his hand before repeating the process in the other direction. "People are trying to kill you, sir."

"You know about that?" Rossett looked up from a fresh search for some Scotch.

"We hear everything, all the rumors."

"But you don't act on them?"

Jimmy shook his head. "It's difficult to know who to trust, sir."

"You can trust me, Sergeant. Downstairs is the man who killed my partner, and he is under arrest."

"Your partner was a German."

"He was a policeman, same as you and me. The Germans and the resistance want me the same way, and chances are they are coming here."

Jimmy didn't reply.

"I'm just trying to do my job," Rossett said quietly.

"I know, sir; I'm just not used to people trying to act like police officers anymore. That's all."

Rossett smiled and closed the drawers in the desk. "Do you have a radio here, Jimmy?"

"We have a set for getting in touch with the patrol cars."

"What's the range?"

"I don't know, maybe fifteen miles?" The key chain started to worry its way through his fingers again.

"How many cars do you have out tonight?"

"Just the one, it's all we've got."

"You've only got one patrol car?"

"We've only got one patrol car that's working."

"How many on board?"

"Two."

"How many in the station?"

"Two, including me." Jimmy looked at the young bobby. "And him."

Rossett rubbed his eyes hard with his index finger and thumb. He sat, pressing his eyes shut, taking a moment to ease the dry sting from the fatigue he was drenched in.

Eventually he lifted his head and blinked a few times to clear his vision.

"Is there a way I can relay a message to somewhere? Via the radio room to the car, and then via the car to an outside force? Maybe Manchester?"

"Maybe, but Manchester isn't any better than Liverpool. The North is falling apart, sir. To be honest, Manchester is in worse shape than we are. At least we have a decent-sized garrison of SS here to protect the docks and the railways. Manchester is pretty much abandoned now that the industry and most of the young lads have gone to the Continent."

"Call the car back into the station. I'm going to need it."

"If you're thinking of making a run for it, sir, I'd suggest you go careful. The lads have been reporting roadblocks springing up on the routes out of the city center."

Rossett started to rub his eyes again, then dipped his head into the palm of his hand.

"Call the car in," he said without looking up.

"Yes, sir."

Jimmy and the bobby made for the door, but Jimmy stopped and turned.

"Sir?"

"What?" Rossett looked up.

"We might not have much of a police force here, but I still remember what it is to be a decent copper."

Rossett looked up. "I'll remember that."

Jimmy nodded his head to the far corner of the office.

"The Scotch is in the bottom drawer of the filing cabinet, sir. You look like you could do with one."

CHAPTER 21

HELLO?" DANNECKER DIDN'T bother lifting his forehead out of his hand as he spoke into the telephone.

"Hello, sir. This is Leutnant Brecht from Liverpool Aerodrome Luftwaffe Station."

"What do you want?"

"This is rather delicate, sir."

"What is?"

"We've received a message from London, sir."

"And?" Dannecker picked up an enamel mug of cold coffee.

"They were trying to contact you, so they asked me to check everything was all right."

"We're having some problems with the long-distance lines, that's all."

"They mentioned that they'd been trying to get you on the wireless as well."

"Like I said, we've been having problems with communication. We're down to field telephones at the moment, as you can see."

"Yes, sir. Of course, sir. I understand. I told them that, but . . . well, since they called—"

"What?" Dannecker put the mug down, and a little coffee made a break for it and splashed onto his desk.

"They've had a report of an explosion."

"Like I said, everything is okay here. There's nothing out of the ordinary." Dannecker wiped up the spill with his thumb.

"It's just that . . ."

"What?" Dannecker wiped his thumb on his leg.

"This is embarrassing, sir."

"Speak."

"Well, one of my men, a solid chap, he's engaged to the sister-in-law of one of your Home Defense Troops. He said this girl was injured in an explosion yesterday, quite badly apparently. It took a while for her family to get in touch to let him know. Apparently some of them don't approve of the relationship. You'd think they'd be grateful for it; with her German connections she was able to get treatment at the Royal Hospital. Her family didn't complain about that—"

"Leutnant, just fucking tell me what you called to tell me."

"I'm sorry, sir. My man spoke to her family, and they told him there were lots of German soldiers killed and injured in the explosion."

"There was no explosion."

"He said—" Brecht cleared his throat again. "There were at least eighteen bodies, sir, maybe more."

"Nonsense."

"He's seen them, sir."

Dannecker lifted his head and looked across the table to where Becker was slumped in the chair opposite him. The staff sergeant's face still had traces of the dust and dirt cragged in the wrinkles around his eyes. A thick black smudge of blood peeked out from his hairline and dodged down his right temple an inch. Just above his collar, a pure-white dressing seemed to light his corner of the room and it looked out of place, a little sign of weakness.

Becker seemed to read his boss's mind. He reached up and dabbed at the dressing with a dirty fingertip.

Dannecker leaned back in his chair and looked at the ceiling. He'd forgotten that the garrison didn't have a morgue, or for that matter, much of a medical facility at all. The injured would have been transferred to the Royal Hospital along with the dead.

"Like I said,"—Dannecker continued staring at the ceiling—"it is business as usual here. Your man must be mistaken. There's nothing to worry about."

"He's very experienced, sir. He came straight back here and told me himself."

"Well, I'm telling you, it never happened."

"I had to inform London about the casualties."

"What?" Dannecker closed his eyes.

"I had to, sir, and they've given me instructions."

"About what?"

"Well, sir, in view of the problems you've been having with Major Bauer, and your not notifying London of the casualties . . . London have told me that if you are uncooperative, or if I have any doubts about your command, I'm to relieve you of it."

"Relieve me of my command?"

"Yes, sir."

"Are you mad? Every city in Britain is falling apart outside of London." Dannecker picked up the coffee mug, remembered what it was filled with, put it down again, and shoved it away. "You tell those bastards everything is in order, and to leave me to get on with my job."

"This is embarrassing for me, sir, and you are making it very difficult—"

"Brecht, I swear to God." Dannecker leaned forward in his chair and dropped his voice to a growl. "If you don't get to the point I am going to come over there and kick seven shades of shit out of you."

Brecht gave a little cough.

"Major, in view of your attitude in this matter, and in accordance with the direct orders of General Gilsa, the military governor of Northern Sector, I am ordering you to stand down and confine yourself to your quarters until such time as I arrive at the garrison and place you under formal arrest."

"What?"

Brecht coughed again, then came back on the line sounding a little more confident.

"I'm placing you under arrest, as per General Gilsa's orders."

"Are you fucking mad?"

"I've had my orders."

"I'm a Waffen SS major, you little shit."

"My orders come from—"

"Leutnant, I dare you . . . honestly . . . I fucking dare you to come into my city and try and arrest me."

"As I said, sir, I've had my orders."

Dannecker slammed the phone onto the cradle and ended the call.

He looked at Becker. "We've got a few hours and then it's all over."

"It?"

"Everything. The gold, our careers . . . our lives. Everything . . . all over."

Becker had known Dannecker long enough to know when to stay quiet and when to speak.

They sat for two full minutes before Dannecker spoke again.

"Did we set up the roadblocks?"

"Yes, sir."

"Everywhere?"

"We've got every route out of the city covered with HDT, and I've assigned two squads to the docks to look for the gold."

"How many are still here in the garrison?"

"I've held back thirty men for security."

"Thirty?"

"It's all we've got."

"How many men did we lose today?"

"Twenty-two dead, twenty-eight injured, and of those twenty-eight, seventeen hospitalized long term."

"Jesus." Dannecker buried his face in his hands, then looked up. "If that ship sails without the gold or us on board, all this is going to come tumbling down, and you and I are dead men." Dannecker took out his pistol and ejected the magazine. "How many do you reckon are in the airfield defense field division?"

Becker shrugged. "A hundred, maybe? Plus, the same in HDT."

"What's their quality?"

"Not good. Young conscripts mostly. The rest is made up of technicians who haven't fired a rifle since training. Although our men aren't much better, sir; we're down to the bottom of the barrel."

"Brecht wants to arrest me." Dannecker pulled open a desk drawer and placed two fresh magazines of ammunition on the tabletop.

Becker didn't reply.

"He says London told him we've lost the city. He says we're out of control."

"I'm not sure it would be wise to ask our men to fight the Luftwaffe, sir."

"We need that gold, old friend." Dannecker picked up a magazine and slammed it home. "And we need it quick."

CHAPTER 22

H E'S WHERE?" O'KANE was halfway through packing his small suitcase and was holding a crumpled shirt as he stared at Iris, who was on the other side of the hotel room by the door.

"The c-central police station. He's arrested the Bear."

"What?"

Iris gulped like a fish out of water, took a moment to compose herself, and then spoke again. "He's a policeman. He wants to do it right."

"I thought he was on our side now?"

"He said he d-doesn't want the Germans to destroy the city."

"They already have." O'Kane threw the shirt into the case.

"He's worried the Germans will blame us for the bomb yesterday. He thinks that by producing the Bear, he can save lives." Iris took a few paces toward a chair by the window and leaned against it for support.

"Has he forgotten about the gold?" O'Kane turned to face her.

Iris took another breath, went to speak, hesitated, and started again. "I suppose he doesn't care about it."

O'Kane looked at the ceiling.

"God save us from the people who lose sight of what's important in life. Iris, we need that gold, girl, or it'll be us worrying about saving our own lives."

"Maybe R-Rossett has a p-point." Iris squeezed her fist as her stammer almost overtook her. She took a moment, then tried again. "A bomb as large as the one yesterday will cause a hell of a crackdown. That, plus

Neumann's death . . . w-we could be talking hundreds killed, maybe m-more."

O'Kane walked around the room a little. He rolled his broad shoulders as he moved, trying to ease the tension that had been knotting them for hours. From over by the door Cavanagh made eye contact with Iris and nodded reassurance.

Finally O'Kane closed on Iris. He stopped just short, took a breath, and then spoke quietly to her.

"Listen to me, Iris. The Nazis are killing people left, right, and center as it is. We need to think long term."

"I'm not sure there's e-enough money and guns that'll let me do that."

"It's short-term pain for long-term gain. People have gone to a hell of a lot of trouble to organize this operation, and the window is slamming shut even as we speak. How long do you think I can hold a U.S. Navy ship in port here?"

"I don't know."

"Not fucking long, that's how long." The pressure was starting to show again as O'Kane's voice grew louder.

"Maybe w-we're beaten?"

O'Kane pointed at her.

"You want to give up? Is that it? You want to fucking run away?"

Cavanagh slipped his hand into his coat pocket. O'Kane saw the move and his finger swept the room until it was aimed at Cavanagh's chest.

"You take your hand right out of that pocket, boy, and you take it out right now."

Cavanagh looked at Iris. She nodded, and Cavanagh did as he was told.

O'Kane turned back to Iris. "If you want to stop, if you want to give up and walk away with your little tiptoe limp and your stuttering talk, you do it. Go on." O'Kane pointed at the door. "But if you give up now I can promise you one thing, and one thing only: the day will come soon when it's you who is thrown into the back of one of them trains, because these Nazis will soon get sick of looking at you, and people like you, wobbling around the place and making it look untidy."

"Hey." Cavanagh took a step forward.

"If you want to protect her, son, you tell her to keep fighting, because that's the only way she'll stay alive." He looked at Iris. "If people die tomorrow in Liverpool, or if they die in a week's time, they die. Simple as that. It doesn't matter. This is a long game, and that gold is paying for the extra time. You accept it and you listen to me when I tell you: we can't let Rossett get away because we need Bauer, so get fucking organized and get ready."

"You want me to assault the p-police station?"

"I want you to be on standby if they try to move the Bear."

"Ambush?"

"Maybe, but I'll need you to be close whatever happens, so where's good?"

"L-Lime Street station."

"A station will be too busy."

"It's b-bombed out. They never rebuilt it because it was a passenger station."

"Is it close?"

"Very."

"And you can get in there?"

"There are tunnels," said Cavanagh. "They lead off to all parts of the city. We use them a lot."

"Go wait there for my orders."

Iris looked at the floor for so long O'Kane thought she was going to defy him. Eventually she looked up at him, and spoke without her stammer.

"Just because I'm taking your orders now, it doesn't mean you are running this operation."

"No, girl. If you want your money, and your war, I'm running it, and you had better get used to the idea. Now fuck off, and leave me a car downstairs with a driver."

———

O'KANE GAVE IT two minutes after they'd gone before he picked up the telephone and rang downstairs to the lobby.

"Operator?"

"Yes, sir?"

"I need you to connect me to the duty officer at the SS garrison."

"I'm afraid the lines are down, sir."

O'Kane looked up at the ceiling and clenched a fist to his forehead. The operator spoke again and broke his agony.

"I can get one of the porters to take a message for you."

"How long will that take?"

"Five minutes, sir. Would that be all right?"

"That, my dear, would be grand."

CHAPTER 23

HOW MANY GUNS do you have in this place?"

"You can just fuck right off." One of the three coppers standing on the other side of the desk from Rossett couldn't contain himself. "If you think I'm going to take on the SS, you can piss off. I've got a family to think of."

Rossett stared at the three of them blankly.

"Sir." The copper at the end of the line looked at his partner and then tried to inject some reason into the situation. "We're not paid enough to get into a shooting match with trained soldiers. We wouldn't last two minutes."

"I can order you."

"You can't order us to commit suicide, sir."

"You are police officers. You have a duty. You took an oath."

"I took an oath to King George, but that didn't matter when they asked me to take one for King Edward a few years later, did it?" The first copper pulled at his tunic collar and looked at his mates for backup.

It came.

"I've a family, sir. I'll not fight, either," said the middle one.

Rossett turned his head to the window, stared out for a moment, and then looked back at Jimmy the sergeant, who was standing to his left.

"What time does the morning shift come on?"

"Seven."

"How many?"

"Five, plus a sergeant and inspector, assuming they don't get turned around by the roadblocks. I'll tell you this, though: if they do make it here, they will be even less keen than this lot."

"What about the chief superintendent I spoke to a few days ago?"

Jimmy pulled at his right ear.

"He comes and goes."

"More go than come," the middle bobby chimed in, then regretted it when Rossett and Jimmy looked at him.

Rossett checked his Rolex.

3:30 A.M.

Three hours at least until the skies began to lighten, and three hours was a long time to wait.

He looked at Jimmy.

"How long are the phones normally out?"

"Nobody will look at them overnight, it's too dangerous. If they come on at all, it'll be lunchtime at the earliest."

"Did you reach anyone on the wireless?"

"No."

Rossett sighed.

"You're sure there is no way through the roadblocks?" He looked at the thin blue line in front of him.

The bobbies looked at each other, and then the middle one replied.

"They were everywhere, SS and HDT covering every road out as far as we could tell. They even stopped us, then turned us back when we tried to pass through."

"Trains?"

"There are checkpoints at Central, Exchange, and Edge Hill stations, and they don't run at night anyway."

"Trains out of Liverpool are nearly all cargo. Most of them don't stop till they reach the docks, and it is the same when they leave," the youngest copper added.

"So what you're telling me is one of the biggest cities in England is totally cut off?" Rossett addressed the question to all of them.

All of them nodded back.

"Fuck me," Rossett said under his breath, then rubbed his forehead with the heel of his hand.

The three bobbies and their sergeant took the opportunity to exchange glances. Finally, the middle bobby cleared his throat loud enough for Rossett to look up.

"You could just let him go, sir."

"What?"

"The Bear, sir. Captain Bauer. You could just let him go."

"What's your name?" Rossett said quietly.

"Barnes, sir."

"How many kids have you got, Barnes?"

"Three, sir. Two girls and a lad."

"Do you want to be able to look them in the eye next time you see them?"

"Sir, with respect, if we try to hold off the SS, I'll not be looking anyone in the eye ever again."

Rossett stared across the table.

"If I let Bauer go, Major Dannecker is going to cover up what he has been doing here."

The oldest bobby looked at Jimmy and then back at Rossett.

"So?"

"If he does that, the first thing he will do is cover up that Bauer has been killing Germans, planting bombs, and causing mayhem for the last few days. Dannecker will kill Bauer, then blame the British for the damage his men have taken. As a result of that, the High Command will exact retribution on those they perceive to have caused the trouble."

"The people of Liverpool," Jimmy said quietly.

"The people of Liverpool," Rossett repeated. "The Germans will come down hard, and we all know how hard that can be." Rossett looked at the medal ribbons on Jimmy's tunic, then at the bobbies opposite him. "You joined this job to protect people, to uphold the law and do the right thing. Well, now is the time to do it."

The bobbies exchanged glances, and then the youngest one spoke. "I joined this job to pay my rent, mate."

"Get out." Rossett said it so softly, the three bobbies weren't sure they had heard him correctly.

"Sir?" The oldest one leaned forward an inch or two, just to check.

"Get out." Rossett flicked his head toward the door for good measure. "Just go. If you want to go home, go."

There was a moment, just a fraction of a second, when Rossett wondered if they might surprise him.

They didn't.

The shuffle of boots on boards signaled that the three bobbies were taking the opportunity Rossett had presented to them. The oldest one held the door open for his two colleagues. Once they had passed through, he paused and looked back at Rossett.

"The job's not worth it, sir."

"What?" Rossett lifted his head.

"The job, sir, it's not worth it. You should go home to your family, sir."

"I haven't got a family."

"Well then, go home to your cat or something, because you can't win this fight. Not even the British Lion can win this fight."

Rossett moved a pencil that was lying on the desk a couple of inches to the left, stared at it a moment, and then looked up at the bobby.

"Sometimes it isn't about winning. Sometimes it's about just having the guts to fight."

"FOUR LEE-ENFIELD .303 rifles with one hundred rounds of ammunition in five round stripper clips. Six Enfield .38 revolvers and . . ." Jimmy lifted the two boxes of pistol ammunition from the back of the station gun safe. "One hundred rounds of ammunition." He turned and looked at Rossett. "Plus whatever you have on you."

"Webley and twelve rounds."

"Not much to stop the German army with."

Rossett reached into the cabinet and pulled out one of the .303's ammunition clips. He turned it in his hands and tried to remember how many times he had shoved one into the breech magazine of a .303 while under fire.

"It looks clumsy, but they work well." Jimmy was watching Rossett.

"I know," Rossett replied as he slipped the clip into his jacket pocket and took out one of the rifles. He worked the bolt, checked the breech, and tried twice to close it before, at the third go, the bolt clicked home. Rossett replaced the rifle and took out another. This time the bolt was even more reluctant to operate. "When was the last time someone cleaned these things?"

Jimmy took out a third rifle and took his turn at working one of the rusty bolts.

"Nobody uses them because nobody wants to be seen out with a long weapon. Even in uniform, there's a chance a nervous Jerry will mistake you for resistance. We use the pistols; they should be in better condition."

"I've got a pistol." Rossett took out the fourth rifle.

"I haven't." Jimmy put down his rifle on the counter next to the safe, then took out a revolver and cracked it open.

Rossett stopped testing the Lee-Enfield and looked up.

"You're staying?"

Jimmy shook open the box of .38 revolver ammo on the counter and started to load the pistol. "I'm not off duty until seven." He didn't look up.

Rossett drove home the bolt on the .303, flicked it open, and drove it home again. He pointed the gun toward the far corner of the room.

The Lee-Enfield clicked as he pulled the trigger on the empty chamber.

He looked at Jimmy.

"At least one works."

"Yeah, but watch out for the rust. It's been a while."

ROSSETT AND JIMMY were standing at the open door of the cell. The Bear was lying on top of a straw mattress up on one elbow, staring at them.

Rossett stared back at the Bear, but carried on speaking to Jimmy. "This man will kill you as soon as look at you. You cannot relax for one minute."

Jimmy didn't reply. He stared at the Bear for a moment, placed his rifle on the floor outside the cell, and handed Rossett his pistol.

"I've been dealing with prisoners for the last twenty-five years."

"This one is different."

"We'll see." Jimmy threw a pair of handcuffs into the cell. "Hey, Adolf, put them on."

The handcuffs hit the Bear on the chest and bounced onto the floor. He looked at the cuffs, Jimmy, and then Rossett.

"Why have you brought your father down here?"

"I'm warning you." Jimmy pointed at the Bear, then at the cuffs. "Put them on, or else I'll kick you up the arse so hard, you'll have to take your hat off to have a shite."

The Bear smiled, sat up on the bunk, and then picked up the cuffs.

He looked at Rossett. "I like him." He snapped on the cuffs and held them out for Jimmy to inspect.

Jimmy entered the cell and approached the Bear slowly. He reached out with his left hand to check that the cuffs were tight enough to prevent them being slipped over the Bear's hands. As he drew close, the Bear jerked forward a couple of inches in an attempt to scare him.

It didn't scare him.

Jimmy swiped hard and fast with a short leather cosh that had been concealed in his right hand. It connected with the Bear's temple and spun him down onto the mattress face-first.

Jimmy stepped back and waited a few seconds for the Bear to look up. He blinked, reached up to his temple and dabbed a finger at the quarter-inch cut above his eye, then looked at the blood on it.

"That was my head, not my arse."

Jimmy slipped the cosh back into his pocket and gestured that the Bear should hold out his hands again.

"I'm sorry." Jimmy ratcheted the cuffs tighter by a few notches, then took a step back. "I couldn't tell the difference."

ROSSETT STOOD IN the enquiry office and looked out through the glass in the door.

The street looked empty.

There were still the odd piles of rubbish waiting in vain for a refuse collection, and the few streetlamps that were working lit the cobbles silver-star white. Away at the edges of the street, where the soft light blurred, shadows skulked away in the corners and cracks, hinting at danger.

In one of the office buildings on the other side of the street, whoever had been last to leave had left a desk lamp burning away and holding the night at bay until morning.

"Well?" Jimmy asked from over by the counter.

Rossett didn't answer. Instead, he shifted position to the other side of the door and checked the other end of the street.

It was just as dead.

"This is the best car you've got?" Rossett finally said.

"It's the only car we've got." Jimmy got to the point quickly.

"Is it fueled up?"

"It'll have a couple of gallons in it."

Rossett looked at the keys in his hand, then out through the glass at the old Ford Model C sitting outside. It had more scars than he did, and it looked about as capable of moving quickly on a cold morning.

"They'll have roadblocks, Lion," the Bear chimed in. "Running is a mistake. That window closed hours ago."

"Sitting still is a bigger one." Rossett noticed a stray dog dragging at some of the rubbish up the street. It scratched at some old sacking, gave a wag of the tail, then stopped and sniffed the air.

Rossett turned to Jimmy.

"When I go outside, bring him to the door so I can see you both through the glass. Once the car is started, come out. Put him in the passenger front seat, and you sit behind. Okay?"

"Yes."

Rossett looked at the Bear.

"I want to take you in alive. Do you understand that?"

"Yes."

"Just because I want that doesn't mean it's going to happen. If I have to, I will shoot you. Do you understand?"

"Obviously."

Rossett nodded, grabbed hold of the door handle, then turned back around as the Bear called to him.

"Lion?"

"What?"

"You don't really think you will be able to do this, do you?"

"You'd be surprised at what I can do." Rossett picked up his rifle and opened the door.

"If I know Dannecker, you won't even make it to that car," the Bear said.

Rossett paused, looked out into the street, and then flicked his fingers toward Jimmy.

"Bring him over."

Jimmy did as he was told.

Rossett took hold of the Bear's arm and pulled him around so that he became a human shield.

"How about we see if he lets *you* make it to the car instead?"

EVEN THOUGH ROSSETT had been standing next to the half-open door, the shock of the cold morning air still made him shiver. They moved as one, a tightly packed bunch of three heading for the Ford, which was parked twenty feet away across the pavement.

Out of the corner of his eye Rossett saw the stray dog watching them from up the street, and then he saw the first of the open windows.

Three floors up, a hundred yards away, right above the dog, and open just enough for a sniper to shoot through. The building had been out of his sightline when he had been in the station.

He'd made a mistake.

The second he saw the window he knew it.

He was already pulling the Bear and Jimmy back toward the police station as the first round hit the near side of the Ford. Their tight group split a little as the second, then the third, then the fourth shot slammed into the old metal or onto the cobbles.

By the time the sixth, seventh, and eighth rounds had hit, Rossett, the Bear, and Jimmy were falling through the front door of the police station and sprawling onto the office floor.

Rossett kicked the door shut with his heel, then rolled onto his stomach and looked for the Bear. He was lying underneath Jimmy, who was shoving his revolver hard into the back of his neck.

They all lay on the floor for a few seconds listening to the shooting outside. Eventually, it stopped. They waited in silence until the Bear finally broke it.

"That went well."

IT TOOK DANNECKER two or three attempts to get his men to stop shooting. The air in the office stank of cordite, and the sudden silence seemed as deafening as the gunfire that had gone before it.

He lifted his field glasses to check the car and pavement in front of the police station.

The Ford was peppered with silver flecks and looked like it had a flat tire. Dannecker scanned the stretch of road between the car and the station. He squinted but didn't think he could see blood on the pavement. He breathed out, then lowered the glasses and shouted over his shoulder.

"Where's the field telephone?"

He hadn't wanted to start shooting. Dannecker didn't want a dead Bear.

His original plan had been to make contact with Rossett and try to reason with him. If that failed, like he guessed it was going to, he was going to send Becker and a squad into the rear of the police station while he and his team assaulted the front.

That was the plan, and he knew it was a bad one, but it was all he had been able to come up with as the clock ticked down and the pressure squeezed tighter.

He was just going to shout for the phone again when a private ran up the stairs and held out the receiver to him.

"They're ready to go, sir."

Dannecker took the phone and ducked his head a little as he looked out through the window toward the police station again. He checked his watch, then spoke into the field telephone.

"Becker?"

"Sir?"

"I'm going to try to talk some sense into them. If it fails, I want you to storm that place as fast as you can."

"Yes, sir."

"Do not kill Bauer, do you understand?"

"Yes, sir."

"If he dies—"

"I understand, sir."

Dannecker passed the phone back to the private and turned back to the window.

A few seconds later, on the street directly below him, he saw a three-man squad moving toward the police station under the cover of a white flag. One of them was laying out wire while the second was carrying a field telephone.

Dannecker checked his watch. It seemed to be speeding up, just like his heart rate.

"BACK ENTRANCES AND windows?" Rossett was looking out the front door as everyone caught their breath.

"The cells have their own entrance, but there's no way through unless they have a tank." Jimmy had taken up station with the Bear by the desk again. "There's the fire exit for the main building, and then one door to the backyard. I told the lads to check everywhere was secure before they left."

Rossett stared at the car. It was going nowhere. Underneath, a slick of oil was staining the street, running past the flat tire, and pooling in the gutter.

He strained to look up at the building where the snipers had been sited. He couldn't see the open windows from where he was, but he could tell that they would give a field of fire right down to the intersection at the other end of the road. There was little or no cover if Rossett were stupid enough to try to make a break for it.

He moved back, then knelt down on one knee next to Jimmy and the Bear.

"Where did you get those medals?" Rossett nodded his head toward Jimmy's chest.

"The Great War. The Somme, and then Cambrai."

"Regiment?"

"The Kings."

"I was in the Guards, joined up in '39."

"I know. I read about you."

"I'm sorry for dragging you into this."

"My job dragged me into it, not you."

Rossett nodded, glanced back at the door, and then looked at Jimmy again.

"They want him alive." Rossett pointed at the Bear. "So I don't think they will come in heavy to get him. We just need to wait this out until the phones come back on and I can call London."

"And if they don't come back on?"

"Dannecker can't keep the entire city in lockdown. He's got a ship to catch, and if he misses it, it won't take long for people to realize something is wrong. When that happens, they'll start to investigate."

"Dannecker won't sit and wait." The Bear was sitting with his back to the counter and his eyes closed. "When the pressure is on, he only has one way of dealing with it."

"Which is?" Jimmy looked at the Bear.

"Violently." The Bear shrugged.

"I thought it might be." Jimmy turned back to Rossett. "Well?"

"We just need time," Rossett said. "They won't try to come in until they've used up all the other options. We just need to keep them talking."

"What ship?" Jimmy asked.

"There is a ship that sails in the morning. Dannecker needs to be on it."

"If he's on it, won't the Nazis just radio the ship and turn it around?"

"Not this ship. Even if they know he is on it, it's American navy. The Germans won't want to go near it for fear of causing an incident. If Dannecker gets on it, Dannecker won't be getting off until he is across the Atlantic."

"And if he doesn't?"

"This whole thing will come tumbling down around him, and we will have saved a lot of lives."

"You think?" The Bear opened his eyes.

"When I tell the authorities about the gold, Dannecker, and what you've done, the people you have killed and why you have killed them . . ."

The Bear looked at Rossett.

"You know, I honestly thought that you were going to be a challenge. I thought you'd be a threat to me, and yet . . ." The Bear paused, looking for the words as he stared at the exit onto the street. "And yet . . . you're just so fucking stupid it hurts my brain."

Jimmy looked at Rossett, then back at the Bear as he continued.

"They made you out to be some sort of super warrior, all the stories about you fighting us, and then fighting the resistance for us. And yet when I finally have to face you, you're just a dumb grunt of a man."

Rossett stared at him a moment, then returned to his position by the door.

"We need to barricade this entrance."

The Bear carried on speaking as if Rossett hadn't spoken.

"You're brave, I'll give you that, but bravery doesn't make you clever." The Bear looked at Jimmy. "I normally find that those who show extreme bravery on the battlefield are either brain dead or just plain dead."

The Bear turned back to Rossett.

"If Dannecker isn't on the boat, he isn't simply going to go home and wait to be arrested. He is going to make sure you and I—and, sadly for this old man, him—are all dead so that we can't talk."

"So what would you do?" Finally Rossett looked around at the Bear.

"I'd speak to him on a field telephone. Like the one his men are leaving on the bottom step right behind you."

Rossett spun and pointed his Webley at the three Germans outside. The one with the white flag waved it furiously as they backed away. Rossett lifted his pistol an inch or two and watched them go.

Rossett glanced up toward the sniping windows, then gestured that Jimmy should move the Bear to behind the counter. Jimmy did as he was told, grabbing the Bear by the collar and dragging him before he could struggle to his feet. The Bear slid on the polished wooden floor, banging his head on the counter door as he was shoved through it.

Rossett waited.

Outside on the steps, the field telephone started to ring.

Rossett opened the door.

The ringing of the phone grew louder. It was on the third step, just close enough to reach for, but far enough away for a good sniper to put a hole in his head if he was careless.

Rossett took a deep breath and grabbed it.

He was back inside before it had time to ring again.

"Hello?"

"Rossett?"

"Who else would it be?"

"This is Dannecker."

"I know."

"Is everyone all right in there?"

"What do you want?"

"You know what I want."

"You can't have him."

Dannecker paused, and Rossett glanced over to the counter to check on Jimmy. He was standing up, slightly bent at the waist, watching him back.

Dannecker crackled back on the line.

"We need to try to resolve this situation, John. It isn't doing either of us any favors."

"Don't call me John."

"I need Captain Bauer, and if you—"

"Dannecker. You're not getting your gold, and you aren't getting on that ship, either. It's over for you. Enjoy your last night of freedom."

"I have enough men here to take him from you."

"You have no idea, do you?"

"What?" Dannecker sounded unsure.

"I'm a force of nature." Rossett turned away from the door and stalked around the enquiry office as he growled. "You aren't coming for me. I'm coming for you. I'm going to end you. I'm going to get justice for all the people you've killed, all the lives you've ruined, all the crimes you've committed."

"You don't—"

"I'm coming for the children and the men and women of this city."

"Inspector."

"Know this, Major: I'm coming for you and I am going to make you pay."

Rossett opened the door and tossed the telephone out into the street. He turned, picked up his .303 and the canvas ammo shoulder bag, and looked over it at the Bear.

"You want to fight me?"

"Yes."

"Okay, I promise you'll get your chance, but only if you do as I say right now. Yes?"

"It depends on what you say."

"Run."

The Bear considered the offer, looked at Jimmy, and nodded.

THEY CROUCHED JUST inside the doorway, Rossett and Jimmy, with the handcuffed Bear between them.

"The office opposite."

"Which one?"

"That one." Rossett pointed at the building directly across the road.

"It used to be an insurance company. They've long gone, though. You sometimes see a caretaker coming and going, but other than that, the place is empty." Jimmy shifted a few inches to allow the Bear a view of the place they were talking about.

"We're going through that door."

"It'll be locked."

"It'll be open by the time you get there. Just run, don't stop. If one of you goes down, keep running. I'll be behind you, and I'll get the door open and the other person up before you get there."

"And then?" The Bear stared across the street.

"We go right through the building fast, until we make it out the other side."

"What's on the other side?" The Bear again.

"Us, in about one minute." Rossett shuffled back half a pace, then got up to his feet. He looked at his watch and then at Jimmy. "You ready?"

Jimmy adjusted the ammo bag on his shoulder, checked the Bear's handcuffs, and picked up his .303.

"Yes."

"You?"

The Bear shrugged. "As I'll ever be."

"Okay . . . run!" Rossett kicked open the front door.

The Bear and Jimmy were gone almost before Rossett had finished saying it. Both of them darted down the steps and ran for their lives. They didn't stop, they did as they were told. Running hard, the Bear in the lead, hands handcuffed in front of him. Jimmy five feet behind, holding the .303 across his chest.

Rossett gave them a start.

Then shot at the plate glass door across the street. His rifle was down by his hip, his right hand a blur as it fired, flicking the bolt, firing again, flicking the bolt.

Three rounds. The plate glass door shuddered, then shattered in a million shards that dropped straight down like diamond snow.

The Bear and Jimmy were through.

DANNECKER WAS ON the field phone to Becker.

"Smash windows, set fires, and we'll drive them out the fro—"

The sound of shooting made him drop the phone, then stand up so he could see into the room where he'd set the snipers.

Rounds were flying and empty cases were pooling as his men let loose with their StG 44s out the windows.

"Cease firing!" Dannecker ran to the nearest window, dropped to one knee, and looked out. "What was it?" He had to shout over the voices of the men at the windows calling to their colleagues to cease firing.

The fire-team corporal pushed back his helmet and pointed to the window.

"They ran sir, two and then one, straight out the police station and across the road."

"Where?"

"Into the other building, all three of them."

Dannecker was already running for the door.

THE BEAR VAULTED the dusty reception desk, slid across its wide surface, then dropped to the other side in one fluid movement. He kept on running, heading toward the huge green-and-gold-painted swing doors at the back of the reception area.

He hit them hard.

They were locked.

He bounced off, stumbled backward, and looked around for Jimmy and Rossett. Jimmy was lifting the flap on the counter, but Rossett followed the Bear's lead and skidded over the counter surface holding the .303 high.

Rossett landed and worked the bolt as he ran.

The Bear stepped to the side a half second before Rossett fired a shot into the lock. The big .303 round punched the lock barrel straight through the thick wooden doors and six feet into the next room. Rossett kicked the doors open on the run. What remained of the lock splintered, and he was through and still running before the doors had fully swung open.

They were now through to a darkened atrium, which was lit by dim emergency lighting and nothing else. Concentric circles of dusty desks spun out around a raised central dais, and as Rossett and the Bear ran past them, leaves of paper whipped and whirled in their wake. At the far wall they stopped at another two doors, exactly the same as the set they had passed through on entering the room.

This time they waited for Jimmy to catch up.

The Bear gave Rossett a broad smile. "This is living, Lion, finally. This is what people like us are bred for."

Rossett had to stop himself from smiling back.

This *was* living.

The fire in his belly was lit again. His heart was pounding, and his veins crackled with adrenaline.

The fast flick of the rifle bolt had been a muscle memory, but the kick of the rifle in his hands as he'd fired was more than that.

It was a part of him.

He hated himself for it, but he felt alive.

Jimmy wheezed to a halt next to them. He adjusted the bag on his shoulder and shifted the weight of his rifle as he leaned forward and snatched short breaths.

"You okay?" Rossett tried to not sound as concerned as he was.

"Yeah."

"He's not okay," said the Bear. "He's old and out of shape. We should leave him."

"Fuck." Jimmy took a breath. "Off." The old policeman straightened a little and adjusted his tunic. "I'm all right," he told Rossett. "I can keep up."

"Stand back from the door." Rossett fired a round through the lock.

This time it took a couple of shoves to get the doors to open as the lock struggled to hold on. Rossett gestured that Jimmy should lead the way, then looked at the Bear.

"He won't make it." The German nodded his head toward Jimmy as he moved into the building.

"Just keep moving."

"Okay, but don't say I didn't warn you." The Bear headed off.

Rossett checked over his shoulder, then followed them.

JIMMY HAD HIS lighter out.

There was no emergency lighting. They were walking down what looked like a service corridor, and the contrast with the dark wood and high ceiling of the atrium was stark. Utilitarian floor tiles and matte cream walls crowded them in with the flicker of the lighter's flame.

They dropped down a short flight of stairs, took a right, then a left, and emerged at a metal shuttered door chained and locked. Rossett stepped to the side of the shutters and smashed the padlock off the chain.

Jimmy pulled on the chain and noisily lifted the shutter a few feet off the ground.

Rossett pushed the Bear through the gap, then ducked under himself. Jimmy followed, still holding the end of the chain, then released it so that the shutter fell to the ground with a crash.

They were outside. A soft drizzle of rain had started to fall. Rossett felt a breeze brush his cheek, and it made him look into the air and then around.

An empty yard, brick walled, maybe twenty feet long by sixty feet wide. At the center of the far wall was a set of padlocked iron gates. The three of them jogged toward the gates, and Rossett used another round to pop off the padlock.

"Do you just use that to open doors?" The Bear watched as Rossett loaded another stripper clip into the magazine.

Rossett drove home the bolt, then looked back at him.

"Keep asking questions and you'll find out."

IRIS SIPPED COLD tea and looked up at where the glass roof of Lime Street station had once been. One of the million pigeons that flittered and fluttered in the darkness softly cooed to her from seventy feet above as rain fell silently and dusted her face.

The station felt like dinosaur bones in a desert. A relic, left lying there to serve as a reminder of the majesty that had gone before.

Iris looked toward the old ticket office. A sign, held up by one remaining chain, swung loose like a hanged man. It twisted in the breeze, edges burned by the blasts that had half destroyed the station and reduced it to its current state of dereliction.

"Did you know this was once the biggest train station in the world?"

Iris looked at Cavanagh.

"W-what?"

"This." He pointed up into the darkness and drew his hand in a wide arc above his head. "This was the biggest iron and glass roof in the world."

The oil lamp at his feet popped, then flickered in the silence between them.

"I just thought it was interesting, that's all." Cavanagh shrugged, then looked off down the platform toward the tunnels that had once taken trains away from the station and off across the British Empire.

Iris didn't reply, but she did follow his gaze toward the three tunnels. In the mouth of the center tunnel was a group of eighteen men and women. They were standing around a small campfire made on the tracks. The darkness of the tunnel rose above them like a serpent's mouth waiting to swallow them up. They looked tiny, easy prey to the blackness as their shadows danced on the walls.

She watched them awhile. A silhouette passed in front of the fire and blocked it from her view. She heard a laugh, then a shush, and then someone threw on some more wood. The fire belched and sparked, then lit the area like a flare before it faded back to a glow again.

"I'll go tell them to keep it down." Cavanagh made to stand.

"They're okay. Nobody is h-hunting us tonight."

Cavanagh slumped back onto the seat.

"Do you want a blanket?"

"No."

"Let me know if you do."

Silence.

They stared straight ahead like strangers waiting for a train that was never going to come. Above them, another pigeon took to the air, giving itself a round of applause as it flew across the glass roof and up into the night sky.

"My f-father used to bring me here."

"What?" Cavanagh looked at Iris.

"I used to like the trains. He u-used to buy a platform ticket, then take me out of my chair and make me walk to see the engines at the far end of the trains."

More sparks belched from the campfire as something popped in its depths, and Iris imagined she saw the soot, steam, and sparks of a straining phantom steam train.

"It was the only way he c-could get me to walk and talk." Iris smiled at Cavanagh, all lopsided beautiful shadows.

"You were a train spotter?"

She laughed. "I was a cripple."

Cavanagh smiled, then brushed a hand over the Thompson in his lap to wipe off the spots of drizzle.

Iris was enjoying the rain. She gave a thin smile as she lifted her chin to the night.

"I don't have l-long left."

"What?"

"They w-will come for people like me soon."

"We can hide you."

"I'm not a mouse. I'll not hide."

"I won't let them take you."

"You can't stop an army."

"You could leave," Cavanagh said quietly. "Go to America with the gold."

She lifted her chin again and stared up to the roof, where the pigeons were cooing.

"I know," she said quietly.

———

THE MESSAGE WAS brought to them by a young girl wearing a torn raincoat tied with string. She had skidded the last few feet on the dust and fallen glass from the roof, then stamped her feet to attention and hooked one thumb into the string that was holding her coat closed.

"There's Jerries shooting up Hope Street police station."

"Which ones?" Cavanagh waved his hand to the resistance down by the tunnel entrance and beckoned them closer.

"Dannecker's lot." The girl had been running, and her breath hadn't yet caught up with her. "There were three fellas who they were shootin' at. They legged it, though."

"Who ran?"

"An old copper, and two blokes in suits. One of the blokes in a suit was wearin' cuffs." The girl held up her hands and mimed handcuffs. "And the other one looked like that hard copper from London."

"R-Rossett?" Iris leaned forward a little.

"Yeah."

"Which way did they run?" Cavanagh glanced at the fire again.

"To the building across the road."

"And then?"

"Out the back. Then up to Crown Street."

"You're sure?"

"I ran behind where the Jerries were." The girl snatched another breath. "And then along the alley. I heard a shot, and then another one. I reckon it was the gate at the back. All the places are locked round there."

"Did you see what the Germans did?"

"No."

"They'll chase them." Cavanagh looked at Iris.

"W-which way, though?"

The kid answered the question. "If we get chased round there by the coppers, we leg it toward the old coal yard."

"Crown Street Goods Yard?"

The kid nodded.

Iris nodded.

Cavanagh stood up and shouted to the group making their way toward them up the platform.

"Crown Street, go!"

They stopped, spun, and ran past the open fire and off down the tunnel.

The one that led to Crown Street.

CHAPTER 24

FLANKED BY TALL Georgian townhouses, Rossett, the Bear, and Jimmy ran along tramlines set into the cobbles. All the streetlamps were out, and not one light shone in the windows of the four- and five-story buildings on either side of them.

Jimmy missed a step and stumbled onto the cobbles. His .303 rattled ahead of him and the spare clips spewed out of his canvas bag and onto the cobbles. Rossett stopped, grabbed the Bear's arm, and dragged him back to Jimmy, who was still on the floor.

"Bullets," Rossett said to the Bear, who in turn crouched and started collecting the clips and placing them in the bag.

Jimmy rolled onto his back. "I'm knackered." He was gasping for air.

Rossett looked at where they had come from, then over his shoulder at where they were going.

"We should leave him." The Bear placed the last of the rounds into the satchel, then placed it around his own neck.

Rossett picked up Jimmy's .303.

"How far is the goods yard?"

"Quarter of a mile?" Jimmy pointed down the street. "Maybe less?"

"Get up." Rossett slung the rifle over his shoulder.

"Honestly, I'm finished." Jimmy remained on his back, oblivious to the water on the ground that was soaking through his police tunic.

Rossett leaned down and dragged him up.

"We have to keep moving."

"I can hide." Jimmy pointed to the house closest to him, then dropped both hands to his knees as he started to cough.

Rossett started to pull him down the street. "If Dannecker decides to start searching houses, do you want the family who sheltered you killed?"

Jimmy stumbled, then straightened a little as he snatched another breath. He took a few more steps, pushed away Rossett's hand, and broke into a jog so slow that it was almost a walk.

ROSSETT HEARD THE engines coming from a few streets away.

Trucks. Probably the ones that had held the men from the Pier Head shooting the day before, getting closer, engines racing, coming fast.

"How much farther to the yard?" he shouted to Jimmy, who had now dropped back a little again.

"Around the corner, one minute."

Rossett could hear the trucks clearly now; they sounded no more than one street away. He slowed, grabbed Jimmy's sleeve, then started dragging him along as fast as he could.

They turned the final corner and saw a dirty painted sign: CROWN STREET GOODS YARD.

Rossett pulled Jimmy's arm in the other direction to stop him from running across the wide, empty street toward the gate. The old sergeant's momentum spun him around.

"What?"

"Wait," Rossett whispered as he noticed the Bear was already crouching in the shadows to his right.

"What for?"

"I don't know, which is why we wait."

One spotlight shone over a pair of rusted wrought-iron gates, which would have been wide enough for three trucks to pass through had they been open. But they were chained and blocked from behind by what looked like twisted iron tank traps dumped behind them.

To the right of the gates, just inside the wall, was a watchman's hut, with its windows smashed and door missing.

"What do they use this place for?" Rossett whispered.

"Cargo from the port on its way in and out of the south docks passes through here, but it doesn't stop anymore," Jimmy said. "They used to store coal here, but because there's no surplus and everything goes straight for export, it's pretty much unused."

"Isn't it guarded?"

"Not really." Jimmy was wheezing, his buzz-saw breath coming in snatches. "The resistance leaves it alone because whenever they used to sabotage it, the Germans came down heavy on the locals. The locals got sick of it and withdrew support for the resistance and—"

"So it's empty?" Rossett cut Jimmy off.

"Probably." Jimmy coughed. "And if not, it'll only be a watchman, and I'll know him if it is. There's a hole in the wall, just around the corner, where the kids get in when they're looking for bits of coal that have fell off the trains as they pass through. We can get in through that."

THEY WERE HALFWAY across the street when the Opel Blitz turned the corner, seventy yards away on their right-hand side. At first Rossett could only see the headlamps cutting through the drizzle, but after a moment he saw the first of the soldiers fanned out behind the slow-moving truck.

Rossett figured they would make it into the yard unseen.

Rossett figured wrong.

Voices shouted. The truck engine roared, but Rossett didn't shoot. He dropped his head and raced for the cover of the yard wall. He got there before Jimmy and the Bear, dropped to one knee, then fired a covering shot toward the truck's windscreen.

Barely a second later he fired another round at the same spot.

The headlamps bobbed as the driver jabbed the brake and stopped the truck.

As the Bear and Jimmy made their way around the corner of the yard, Rossett tried to see past the headlamps through the sights of the rifle. He drifted to the left searching for a target, keeping his aim low in case the men had made a dive for the ground.

Nothing.

He scanned back, this time a little quicker. The driver's door of the cab was open. They were either trying to get him out because he was injured, or trying to force him to stay in because he wasn't. Either way, Rossett could see pairs of legs poking out from under it.

He shot at the door, then saw someone drop. The Lee-Enfield's heavy round had punched through the thin steel and then through the man standing behind it.

He heard more shouting, then fired two rounds into the engine of the truck.

That was enough to keep them low and get them guessing. Rossett rose and followed the line of the wall until he came to a gap in the concrete, the result of a bomb blast.

It was fifteen feet wide and had been covered with a chain-link fence. At first the wire looked intact all the way across. Rossett felt a mild panic in the pit of his stomach as he pulled and pushed against the wire looking for the hole that Jimmy and the Bear had used to get in.

He stepped back, studying the fence as the sound of shouting around the corner got louder. At the far end, finally, close to the ground, he saw in the shadows that the wire was folded back, and held up by a short piece of timber. Rossett dropped to his stomach to squeeze through the space and felt the wire catch on the strap of the canvas ammo bag. He twisted and pulled at the bag to free it from behind him and then froze.

A scuffle of feet in the darkness, ahead of him in the yard.

Jimmy and the Bear.

Rossett yanked at the bag and dragged himself forward, pushing the .303 out from under him as he went.

He was through.

The spotlight over by the gates barely cast enough light to see fifteen feet in front of him. He looked left and right, then crouched down to see straight ahead. Outside, the Germans were shouting on the other side of the wall.

They wouldn't be long.

The scuffle again, somewhere ahead.

Rossett moved slowly, keeping low, eyes wide to capture as much light as possible. The yard was a maze of shadows and shapes. Rossett could make out the odd pile of bricks and rubble. Over on the far side, a line of bombed-out, half-demolished offices and warehouses loomed out of the night. Here and there on track sidings sat empty train cars, including the occasional burned-out passenger coach.

At the end of the yard, farthest from the road, Rossett had seen a line of train tunnel entrances, set into what looked like a bluff limestone cliff face.

There was a strong smell of coal, and even the puddles on the ground sounded dirty when Rossett stepped in them.

The German voices were getting closer.

He didn't have much time.

The dull knife edge of panic he'd felt at the fence started to sharpen itself in his chest as he moved at a crouch. His pace increased as he flicked his head left and right.

Jimmy.

There on the ground. Spread eagle, staring up at the rain that was washing the blood off his face.

Rossett knelt next to him, looked around, and moved off again.

There was no point checking the pulse of a dead man.

THAT OLD COPPER had been tougher than he looked.

He'd not gone down until the third strike from the brick the Bear had picked up as they crawled through the fence. The copper had still been trying to defend himself after the sixth time it hit him.

Impressive stuff.

The seventh had finally knocked him out, but the ninth was the one that killed him.

He was a tough old, dead old, memorable old, bastard.

The Bear had to give him that.

No time for congratulations, though. Not with Rossett breathing down his neck.

This was what the Bear had been waiting for. This was the moment he had been dreaming of since he had seen Rossett walking through the doorway of his cell.

The Bear finally had a worthy opponent.

He lay under one of the old abandoned train cars struggling to get the key he had taken from Jimmy into the handcuff lock. The Bear had it in his mouth and was holding the cuffs up to it. He cursed as the key dropped onto his chest for the third time, picked it up again, and then froze.

Footsteps.

To his left. Careful, slow, searching steps.

Rossett?

The Bear gripped the key between his teeth again, then took hold of the revolver he had taken from Jimmy. The hammer was already back and raring to go as he rolled silently onto his left side. He looked toward the footsteps.

It was painfully dark.

There was nothing now, just silence.

The Bear moved so that he could see out from under the other side of the train car. One of the stones between the crossties made a noise as he rolled. He froze. Waited. Listened. And then slowly, ever so slowly, completed the maneuver to look out toward the gates.

The floodlight was still burning bright about fifty yards away. The Bear scanned the open spaces, then the shadows. The sound of the voices on the other side of the wall was louder now. The Germans were nearly inside.

He needed to get moving.

He rolled back, took a slow breath through his nose, and calmed himself.

This was what he wanted.

All his life, every step, every moment, every decision large or small, they all led to this.

He breathed, focused, adjusted the key with his tongue against his teeth, and tried once again with the cuffs. This time he forgot about Rossett, about the Germans outside, about the games, the challenges, the fights, and the blood that had been pounding in his ears since he had beaten Jimmy to death.

He closed his eyes.

He just thought about the key and the lock.

Cuffs pulled as far apart as he could get them. Searching for the key-hole with the tip of the key. Slowly slipping it in, twisting it, then holding it tight with his teeth and tongue.

Slow.

Slow.

The key turned. The Bear breathed. Ten seconds later the cuffs were on the ground and he was out from under the train and running.

ROSSETT HEARD THE Bear go.

He spun and dropped to one knee, Webley out in front of him, .303 on the ground at his feet. The drizzle was turning to rain, and it tasted of coal dust. He slowly traced the bead of the Webley's sight through the shadows and sparkling rain.

Nothing.

To his right, through a gap between freight cars, he could see one of the Germans peering through the iron gates, dodging back, then peeking in again.

It wouldn't be long until they entered.

He needed to get moving.

He needed to find the Bear.

CORPORAL WILLY KOHL was an eleven-year veteran, and he had a theory that the soldiers who got the medals were often the soldiers who got shot.

Willy didn't want any medals, and Willy didn't want to get shot.

That night, when Becker had been dispatching squads to go out and search for Rossett and Captain Bauer, Willy had taken his men in the direction he thought was least likely to lead them into trouble.

His men hadn't complained. They wanted to go home just as much as he did, so they had followed him without question.

The problem was, it had been the wrong direction.

His driver was lying next to his truck leaking blood onto the street. The truck was also leaking, and neither of them was going to be moving anyplace soon.

Both shot by whichever bastard had been heading into the goods yard Willy had been stupid enough to stumble upon.

He and his men had sprawled on the ground as the first of the shots had come in, and by the time the second one had hit home, most of them were hiding behind the truck wishing they were on the boat home.

It had taken Willy nearly two minutes to get himself moving again, and if you added the minute it had taken him to encourage his men out of hiding, a lot of time had passed.

Enough time for whoever had shot at them to get clear of the scene. Enough time to make it safe to search the area.

Willy dodged his head around the gatepost and peered into the yard.

The darkness beyond the solitary floodlight gave him no clues as to what to do next. He leaned back and looked at his men, who were pressed tight against the wall behind him. Eight of them, armed to the chattering teeth, and not one of them over the age of twenty-three.

He looked through the gates again, then gestured with a flick of the hand that the man nearest to him should come closer.

"Corp?" The kid was trying to sound like he wasn't scared, and failing badly. His helmet looked like a soup pan balanced on his head, and he had to keep pushing it back to keep it above his eyes.

"Did Becker say how long he would be?" Willy nodded his head to the radio operator crouching behind them.

"Ten minutes."

Willy looked back into the yard, then at the chain on the gate. He had to go in. If Becker turned up and they were still hiding outside the yard, he'd skin him alive.

"We are going in," Willy said to the private, who nodded unconvincingly. "Blow the lock."

Even in the shadows Willy saw the kid swallow.

There was a pause before the kid eased past him, pushed back his helmet again, and then approached the lock at a crouch. Willy gestured that the rest of the squad should move back. He watched as the private unscrewed the caps on a couple of grenades and carefully hooked them into the chain holding the gates shut.

The kid looked at Willy and nodded. Then he pulled the string and ran like hell.

IRIS AND THE resistance froze in the mouth of the tunnel when they heard the grenades go off.

They'd been steadily climbing the half mile of track that ran from Lime Street station through the Crown Street tunnel to the goods yard.

Everyone looked at Iris. She was holding out a wobbling hand.

Wait.

Whoever had chiseled the tunnel out of the limestone ridge had dug out square refuges for people to use in case they were trapped with a train coming at them. The trains had long gone, but the refuges were deep enough to provide cover for the resistance. They fanned out silently to both sides of the entrance to the tunnel, just far enough back to be in the shadows, just far enough forward to give them a field of fire into the yard.

Iris remained near the entrance, close to the wall, her black coat blending with the soot she had smeared on her cheeks.

She felt Cavanagh lean in close.

"We should fall back to the station." He was so close to her she felt his lips brush her ear.

"Wait."

"The Germans might already be here."

"I know."

Cavanagh looked past her into the yard, and then leaned in close again.

"This isn't a good position to defend. We'll be exposed if we have to fall back. This tunnel is too straight, we'll have no cover."

Whispering didn't come easy to Iris. She breathed in through her nose, composed exactly what she had to say, and rested her hand on his shoulder to pull him close.

"S-sometimes the result is worth the risk." She took another breath. "If the Bear is here, we aren't leaving without him."

Cavanagh nodded. The order was given, so he would do as he was told and stay at her side.

Iris turned back to the yard. The rain was getting heavier. It was slanting past the mouth of the tunnel, and a few drops brushed her cheeks. She thought about taking a step farther back into the shelter.

She didn't.

She could just see the top of the gates over the piles of rubble. They flexed occasionally, twitching like fish on a riverbank. Whoever was out there was climbing through the hole made by the grenades.

She counted the twitches of the gate.

Fewer than fifteen men, a small force, definitely German, definitely coming into the yard.

She looked at her people behind and to the side of her.

They were well armed and well trained.

They could take them, but in doing so they might lose the Bear.

And some things couldn't afford to be lost.

ROSSETT HIT THE deck when he heard the grenades go off. He lay still for as long as it took the sound of the explosion to echo back off the buildings to his right, then rolled across the wet ground and under one of the abandoned train cars to his left.

He had left the .303 behind. As good as the old rifle was, it was useless for creeping around in the dark with. He needed something he could bring to bear quickly and silently.

His Webley was back in his hand.

Close-up killing might be on the menu.

The hole in the fence was sixty yards away to his rear. Around him was the litter of train cars, rubble piles, and shell craters. Ahead of him three tunnels, and to his right a derelict three-story office block and outbuildings.

Rossett had lost count of the possible escape routes, which meant there was a good chance the Bear was already half a mile away. He rested his chin on his forearm.

Should he run?

The Germans outside would have radioed for backup, and Dannecker would be coming with more troops to shut down the site. The net was closing, and if Rossett didn't want to be in it, he should get moving.

He wondered if the Bear was out there, thinking the same thing.

The rain was getting heavier. It was hissing, patting, and puttering just beyond the shelter of the freight car he was under.

He thought about Jimmy, lying in the dirt, staring up into the rain, not feeling it landing on his face and rolling down his cheeks. He thought about Neumann, kneeling, the ache of cold concrete through his trousers, grit digging into his knees as the muzzle dug into his head.

Rossett felt tired.

He was tired.

He could quit if he wanted to.

He could drop the hammer on the Webley and then drop the pistol itself.

He could run, lie low, see it out until Dannecker was either called to account for what he'd done or got away with the gold and headed into the sunset.

It wouldn't be long, just a week, maybe less?

The rest would do him good.

Rossett shifted and rubbed his forehead on his sleeve, then looked up and out from under the train.

He thought about the little girl outside the hotel. He thought about the people being lined up in front of the guns down by the river, the people of Liverpool. He thought about the Bear laughing at him.

He thought about himself.

He wasn't going to quit.

He never quit.

THE BEAR HAD seen the office building at the far side of the yard the moment he'd crawled under the fence. It was brooding, looming out of the shadows like a three-story-high tombstone.

The back and front of it had been pockmarked by shrapnel strikes during the bombing of the city. The soot on the brickwork hadn't just been left by passing trains, either; somewhere along the line, a fire had partially gutted what was left after the bombs had stopped falling.

Three stories. Soot crusted, bombed out, burned out, and perfect for sniping from.

Old habits die hard.

It looked like it had once been offices for the railyard staff. The ground floor looked like it had been some sort of large enquiry office. Dotted around, charred cubicles sat empty, while over on the far side, a wide flight of stairs led up to the first floor and beyond.

The Bear headed for the stairs.

He moved like a panther. The distant spotlight shone through the gaps where the windows had once been, making his raincoat look like a swelling sea with a surface coat of oil.

He stopped at the foot of the stairs, listened, and slowly started up them. At the top, he turned left, then crossed the landing to the first office he guessed looked out onto the yard.

It did.

The office was square, with four desks spaced around the floor, each of them facing toward the center of the room. The Bear picked up a chair and carried it with one hand across to one of the desks farthest from the window.

He put the chair on the desk, slipped the pistol he had taken from Jimmy into his pocket, and then unslung the .303.

A brass cartridge shone in the half-light, then slid home ahead of the bolt.

He lifted the rear sight, adjusted it a fraction, and took up position next to the desk before resting the rifle on the back of a chair.

"When you are being chased . . ." the Bear said in a whisper.

He adjusted his position.

". . . it is generally because the thing that is chasing you . . ."

He rolled his neck and then planted the stock into his shoulder.

". . . isn't scared of you."

He looked down the sights of the .303 and adjusted them once more with his thumb and forefinger.

"The trick of not being caught . . ."

He leaned in closer to the rifle and spread his feet a little.

". . . is to make the person chasing you . . ."

He started to slowly pan the rifle a few inches to the left, then to the right, searching out a target through the window across the room.

". . . shit scared of you."

He pulled the trigger.

Two soldiers, crouching by a wall.

He shot the one farthest from him, worked the bolt, and shot the second one, all in less than three seconds.

He smiled, then drove another round home.

The sound of the second soldier screaming carried across the night. The Bear panned toward the gate by the floodlight and searched for another target.

They were lying low.

He shifted again, breathing through his nose, able to hear the water falling through the holes in the roof now that the second soldier had stopped screaming. He thought about shooting out the spotlight, but decided it would do him more harm than good.

He wanted to kill one more person.

He wanted them too scared to move; he wanted them too scared to breathe.

He waited.

Saw the medic.

Then shot him.

The Bear was heading out of the room before the medic hit the ground. He took the stairs three at a time, slinging the .303 over his shoulder and pulling the revolver as he went. He didn't worry about noise as he ran through the foyer of the building, heading for the yard and the tunnels he knew so well.

He ducked out through the door without looking toward the gates, running at a half crouch to the corner of the building. He turned, dipped, then straightened as the rain lashed his face.

He broke into a sprint, and then the world turned upside down.

Rossett hit him hard from the side.

A solid rugby tackle that blasted the breath out of his lungs and hung both men in the air for a second before they plowed into the ground in a heap.

The butt of the .303 slammed into the Bear's ribs.

He swiped with the revolver and managed to catch a stinging strike against Rossett's left temple as he came around and on top of him. They rolled, again, and the Bear felt Rossett's knuckles dig into his throat, as the Englishman grasped the collar of his shirt.

The Bear lifted his elbow, then whipped it down to break Rossett's grip.

For an instant, he thought he had the upper hand, but Rossett used their momentum to roll them through another 180 degrees, so that he was on top again.

Rossett punched the Bear in the face.

The Bear felt his head slam into the ground and with his left arm tried to block the next blow.

He failed.

Rossett slammed a fist into his right eye, then lifted him a few inches with the hand on his collar. The Bear struggled for breath, and Rossett punched him again.

The Bear felt the back of his head slap into the mud as the white-hot pain of the punch flashed to his brain. He swiped again with the revolver, grunting with the effort, but the blow was weak, off balance, and took more out of him than it took out of Rossett. He tried to tie Rossett up with his arms. Wear the older man down. The Bear knew he was fitter; it wouldn't take all that long for the Englishman to run out of breath.

Rossett punched him again.

It was like a mule kick. It was the sort of punch that you couldn't take all that many of if you wanted to win a fight.

Maybe the old Lion still had some roar left in him?

The Bear pulled the trigger on the pistol.

The sound deafened him as the round screamed off into the night. The Bear felt Rossett grip his pistol wrist, so he lifted the arm that was across his face and tried to use it to go on the attack.

Rossett read the move and punched him, hard, again in the nose.

The Bear felt it go. For a moment, he couldn't open his eyes, so he tried to cover up again.

He felt Rossett's hand wrap around the pistol, prizing at his fingers, taking control.

He tried to roll under Rossett, who was now straddling him, almost sitting on his chest. Rossett punched him again. This time the blow hit him hard on the right side of his throat. The shock wave shorted his brain for a second. The Bear lifted his shoulder and scrabbled with his free hand, trying to find a way to grip on to Rossett. He failed. Rossett slapped his hand away and punched him again, this time on the fore-head, slamming his head back into the mud with a splash.

The Bear knew he was losing.

He tried to twist his wrist to aim the gun, then pulled the trigger again. The round whistled away with the sound of the shot.

He scrabbled with his heels in the mud, his free arm back across his face in an attempt to block the precision punches that seemed to land every time he left a gap. He lifted his hips in short thrusts, rocking Rossett and then letting him settle again. The heavy lifting of Rossett was energy-sapping work, but it was all the Bear had left to offer.

If he was going to have a chance, he was going to have to get out from under.

He suddenly back-swiped with his right arm, exposing his face. Rossett took the opportunity and went for another punch.

The Bear thrust his hips hard and let the momentum of Rossett's punch do the work for him.

It worked.

Rossett missed with the punch as the Bear drove up with his hips and bucked like a bronco. Rossett fell forward, his fist hitting the mud ten inches above where the Bear's head had been.

The Bear was out.

Round two.

ROSSETT KNEW HE'D made a mistake the second he threw the punch. He'd fallen for the feint, and as the German kicked up under him, it was the best he could to just about manage to keep hold of the Bear's pistol wrist as he went. He tucked his chin, rolled his shoulder, and kicked with his own legs in an attempt to turn the throw back to his own advantage.

Things didn't go exactly as he planned.

Halfway through the roll Rossett felt the Bear's pistol slide through his hand.

He landed in a crouch and rolled again to his left as he went for the Webley in his waistband, eyes on the Bear, who was now right in front of him.

They stared at each other, pistols out, soaked from the rain and the oily mud in which they'd been fighting. The Bear wiped his free hand across his face to clear some blood and rain from his eyes. He smiled at Rossett.

Rossett saw that the German had a tooth missing.

The night hadn't been a waste of time after all.

The Bear's pistol was drifting a fraction as he deep-breathed. Rossett watched as it caught the light and glinted in the rain.

There were worse ways to settle it.

"So is this how it ends, Lion?" The Bear took another breath. "A gunfight?"

"No, Captain." Staff Sergeant Becker answered for Rossett. "It ends with a firing squad."

Rossett dragged his eyes away from the Bear and saw a squad of eleven Waffen SS soldiers, with Becker standing tall at their center.

CHAPTER 25

ET DOWN ON your faces."

"No." Rossett didn't bother looking down at the mud. Instead, he put his hands on his hips and tried to catch his breath after the fight.

"Down now!" The corporal who was shouting the command failed to sound as convincing as he'd wanted to.

"I'm with him." The Bear wiped the blood from his nose and looked over to where they had been ordered to toss their guns. "Besides, I've only just got up."

The corporal jabbed ineffectively at them with his StG 44, then glanced at Becker and the rest of the squad before turning back to Rossett.

"I need to search you," the corporal tried again.

"If you are going to shoot me"—Rossett was staring at Becker's big silhouette—"shoot me standing up, because I'm not lying down to die."

A moment passed, the corporal trapped in no-man's-land, eyes flicking back and forth between Rossett, the Bear, and Becker. Finally, Becker broke the standoff and lowered his gun. He walked toward Rossett and signaled that the corporal should rejoin his mates in the line of soldiers behind him.

Becker slung his assault rifle over his shoulder by its harness and reached under his rubber poncho for his sidearm.

"I was supposed to wait for the major." He struggled to open his holster under the heavy waterproof. "But I don't think that is fair on you."

"You're a coward," Rossett said quietly as he watched Becker finally take out his Walther.

"What I am doesn't count for anything anymore." Becker pulled back the slide as another squall of rain blew in across the yard. "So it's better to just get this over with."

Becker stopped five feet from Rossett, while to Rossett's right, the Bear shuffled a few feet backward.

Becker nodded, planted his feet, and lifted the pistol.

"FIRE!" CAVANAGH SHOUTED, then opened up with his own Thompson at the squad of Germans on the other side of the yard.

The resistance had fanned out a few feet from the end of the tunnel and taken up firing positions behind the various bits of cover that littered that side of the yard.

The rain was making it difficult, but the time they had taken to mark their targets was paying off. At least six of the Germans dropped straight down, while two more lurched and limped away injured. None of the SS returned fire until they found cover, and that gave the resistance a ten-second turkey shoot before they had to start falling back to the tunnel.

Speed: it worked every time.

BECKER FLINCHED, SO Rossett took his chance. He dropped forward to his knees as the resistance rounds fizzed in, and with a twist of the waist, threw a solid right uppercut into Becker's groin. Becker grunted, both hands coming down a half second after the pain went up with his testicles. Rossett reacted fast and grabbed at the pistol as it came into reach.

He missed.

Rossett started to rise and went for the gun again as Becker started to fold above him. This time he managed a slap, just enough to deflect the pistol in Becker's hand, pushing it up and away.

Becker staggered a few paces but managed to grab at Rossett's coat collar as the Englishman launched himself off the ground. Through the pain, Becker managed to use his hold to twist Rossett around a little and throw him off balance.

Rossett was surprised the big man hadn't gone down from the punch to the balls, and as he was dragged to the side, he managed to kick at the inside of Becker's knee, attempting to stretch the joint and make it give way.

It didn't.

Rossett saw the pistol coming back around toward him.

The black and silver world with its gunfire and shadows faded away, and time seemed to slow down.

Rossett needed the gun.

His whole being depended on diverting it.

He reached for the pistol, missed again, but just managed to hook his thumb onto Becker's wrist. He tried to get a solid grip with his wet fingers, but the arm was moving too fast. It felt like it was coated in oil and Rossett felt the tendons straining in his wrist and thumb as they tried to gain purchase. The gun was coming closer, relentless, like a train on a track. Rossett struggled to hold on. Becker shifted his grip a few inches, trying to push Rossett down onto the ground. Rossett took the opportunity to grab at the gun with his other hand, and finally managed to deflect its aim as his left knee splashed down into the mud.

Becker wrapped Rossett's coat tight around his fist, jerked him back, and dragged him nearer like a rag doll.

Rossett was flagging. It was all he could do to hold on. Becker's strength felt inhuman. The German had a curious calm as he ground Rossett down. The fight with the Bear had almost wiped him out. Rossett was running out of options. He couldn't gouge, he couldn't butt, he couldn't punch, he couldn't bite, but most of all, he couldn't lose.

Becker shook him again, trying to free his hand and the pistol, to finally put a stop to the fight. Rossett nearly went fully down as his foot slipped in the mud. He sucked in air, searching for a way, trying to stay calm, trying to focus on what he could do and not what he couldn't. He dug his right heel into the mud, like an anchor in a tug of war. It slipped an inch or two; he grunted, then dug it in again.

This was it.

The last throw.

Rossett twisted, pulling Becker toward him instead of pushing him away. The German almost toppled and his jackboots splashed and slipped as he shifted his footing and tried to regain control. Rossett shifted his weight, lifted his right foot, and then kicked with his heel at right angles to Becker's knee.

This time it worked.

Becker fell like an old tree in a forest, sideways into the mud. He took Rossett with him, but by twisting and turning, Rossett managed to land on top of Becker, one hand still on the pistol, his forearm pushing as hard as he could manage into Becker's throat.

Rossett was as good as finished. His breath was coming in gasps, his legs and arms ruined from the contest of two fights in short succession. Despite his ruined leg, it didn't take long for Becker to work his way out from underneath, and in a second or two, he was on top.

Rossett's hand scratched and slapped at Becker's face as the German clamped down on his throat and stared impassively down at him, sweat and rain dripping off him in fat tears.

Rossett managed a weak left hook, then a right, which ended up flailing and falling short.

Becker rocked forward and squeezed Rossett's throat tighter, all the while staring down at him with dead eyes.

Rossett tried to claw his face, but the German turned it so that Rossett's hand missed its target and had to settle for a pathetic slap on Becker's barrel chest.

"No," Becker said quietly, and shifted forward another inch so that he could lever on a little more weight.

Rossett scratched at Becker's arm and reached up for his face again.

Becker gripped tighter still.

Rossett fought the panic that came with suffocation. He could feel the cold rain falling on his face. The panic seemed to subside a little. The sound of the gunfire was fading.

Rossett was fading.

He tried to twist and apply pressure to Becker's elbow, but the German's arm was like a girder as it locked out, and Rossett felt pathetic for being so weak.

Rossett wanted to cry.

This was it: all the years of pain, all the years of fighting for redemption, and he'd failed.

He finally let go of Becker's pistol and managed a weak punch into the side of the German's head.

The shooting sounded a million miles away now.

He noticed a bead of blood trickling down from Becker's nose, saw it fall toward his own face.

Rossett fell with it.

Darkness called. The ember of fight in Rossett made him flap a last loose fist. It dropped back onto his own chest harder than it had landed on Becker.

The ember flickered, then grew dim.

BECKER WATCHED ROSSETT slipping away with no sense of satisfaction.

He bore the Englishman no ill will.

He just had to die.

He lifted his head. The gunfight was raging all around them. Their moment felt intimate, bordering on peaceful in the chaos. He looked back down at Rossett.

The Englishman looked almost serene in the dirt as the rain splashed onto his face. Becker squeezed a little tighter, eking out the final few drops of life.

The Webley boomed just behind Becker's left ear and blew the top of his head off.

DESPITE LEADING ONE of the largest bands of resistance outside of London, Iris wasn't very good with guns.

Flickering hands and twisted nerves played havoc with her aim.

She normally used an old, battered MP40 on operations, one her father had captured off a tank crew he had killed in the invasion.

She treasured it, but she could barely hit a barn door with it.

Cavanagh had slammed home a magazine and carried the gun for her, the same as he always did. He had pulled back the bolt and handed it over just before the shooting started, same as he always did.

Iris had emptied it in the first thirty seconds of the firefight, same as she always did.

The gun had been hanging loose around her neck as she picked her way across the dead ground, toward where she could see Becker choking Rossett. Her teeth had been gritted tighter than usual as the gap had closed between them.

Despite the bullets buzzing about her like bees around honey, she'd not given up, and kept going, just like she always did.

Rossett's Webley had caught her eye as she struggled with the magazine release of the MP40. The old pistol had glinted in the mud, calling to her like it was desperate to help its master.

She'd picked it up, pulled back the heavy hammer with two thumbs, put its jittery barrel as close to Becker's head as she could get, and pulled the trigger.

Becker was dead.

Now it was time to drop down into the mud to see if Rossett was as well.

ROSSETT COULD FEEL the weight on his chest as he came around. He could smell coal and diesel in the mud, and for a moment, such was the weight pressing down on him, he thought he was trapped in it, sinking into it, going under instead of coming back up.

He could hear the gunfire, and through it, the sound of someone calling his name.

Iris.

He wasn't dead.

He grabbed at the air with a sudden jolt, then tried desperately to get out from under whatever was pinning him down.

Becker.

Brains on the outside. Rossett arched his back as he tried to pull away, and a wave of panicked memory came back as he tried to speak through the pain in his throat.

Becker shifted like a drunk.

Rossett was confused. He thought the German was dead, and yet here he was, all brains on the outside, twitching and trying to turn. Rossett pushed at Becker's shoulder and eased himself out from under. The German rolled and then flopped into the mud with his eyes washed with blood, staring up at the sky. Rossett stared, wiped his face, coughed, and then realized that Iris had been pulling at the dead man's arm trying to move him.

"We need to go!" she was shouting. Rossett knew that, but the words didn't seem to quite make sense. "John." She leaned in close. "We n-need to go."

Rossett retched, lifted his hand to his mouth, and saw that he had put it in something that had leaked out of Becker's skull.

Iris was shouting, pointing toward the tunnels. Rossett stared at her hand instead of the tunnel, then slipped in the mud as she dragged at his arm and tried to get him off his knees and to his feet.

He fell back down. Head next to Becker's, watching the German, waiting for him to move. He didn't, so Rossett rolled, and tried again to stand up.

"J-John, can you hear m-me?" Iris touched a hand to his face.

It was warm, gentle, human.

Rossett blinked.

He was alive. He realized he was snatching and gasping at breaths. He held a hand to his throat and felt the pain of the bruising.

Becker had tried to choke him.

He remembered.

Rossett held out a hand to Iris.

I can hear you, I'm with you again, give me a moment.

They didn't have a moment.

She tried to drag him through the mud, half falling over herself, until finally he was unsteadily on his own two feet.

"We need—" she began, then broke off when Rossett started moving under his own steam.

The sound of the gunfire slammed into his senses as he watched his shoes splash through the mud. His head was moving faster than his feet, and he slowly stumbled into a face-first fall. He lay still, soaked, cold, exhausted, hands open under his shoulders as if he were stuck at the bottom of a push-up.

The mud slipped and slid through his fingers and leached through his trousers.

He was going again.

He felt a kick, hard in his legs, so hard it pulled him back. He rolled onto his side and looked at Iris.

"Get up!"

Rossett held out his hand.

Iris slapped his Webley into it. The gun felt heavy, like some unseen force was trying to slam it through Rossett's palm down into the mud.

The rain was flecking the Webley, and as it ran across the gunmetal, it pooled in his palm and washed the mud away. He looked up at Iris. She was already heading back to the tunnels, slip-sliding lopsided in the mud, as fast as she could manage.

A bullet zinged off a pile of bricks next to Rossett and caused him to dip his head.

He wasn't dead, and if he wanted to stay that way he had to get moving. He climbed to his feet, slowly. Awkwardly, a wobble, and then he finally managed to straighten up.

Another round cut the air.

It sounded like tearing paper as it passed by and made him flinch.

His head ached, his throat ached, and his muscles ached in that familiar way they did every time he had a fight.

He was alive.

He looked back at Becker, thumbed the hammer on his Webley, and followed Iris.

DANNECKER COULD HEAR the gunfire from a quarter of a mile away. He leaned forward in the cab of the truck so he could see out of the rain-skidded windscreen.

It sounded like war.

He heard the dull percussion of a grenade and gestured at the driver to speed up. The driver leaned forward a little over the wide steering wheel but made no effort to increase the pressure on the accelerator. He wasn't an idiot, and somewhere deep inside, Dannecker thanked him for it.

Dannecker checked the magazine of his machine gun, breathed out through his nose, and tried to guess what was happening at the goods yard.

The first message he had received was that Bauer and Rossett were at the yard. Not long after that, Becker had radioed to say he had arrived and was taking control of the situation. Since then, every radio message that had come from the scene had been garbled and panicked.

Panicked.

Dannecker knew the feeling.

He checked his magazine again, then gripped the door handle as the truck lurched around the final corner and stuttered to a halt next to the vehicles that were already there.

He jumped down from the cab as the troops disembarked from the back. Dannecker urged them toward the open gates with a wave of his hand. He could see two squads already in place, crouching outside the yard.

He looked back at the driver, who was busy unhooking an MP40 from the rail behind him.

"You wait here for me, do you understand?"

"Yes, sir."

Dannecker followed his men toward the gates, where they were form-ing up in bottlenecks, too nervous to enter the yard.

"Go! Go! Go!" He pointed into the yard. "Find Bauer! Bring him out alive! Go!"

They were slow to move at first, but gradually, in teams of three and four, they started to filter through the gates into the firefight.

Dannecker dropped down next to Corporal Kohl.

Kohl pushed his helmet back off his eyes and tapped the rim in a weak salute.

"Bauer?" Dannecker got straight to the point.

"In there, sir."

"Becker?"

"Same place."

"Rossett?"

Kohl tilted his head quizzically, so Dannecker tried again.

"The Englishman, the policeman?"

"He killed Bremner, sir."

Dannecker's turn to be confused.

"My driver, sir. The Englishman shot him, and wounded half my men."

"Where is he?"

Kohl nodded his head toward the yard.

"All this shooting for Bauer and Rossett?"

"Fucking resistance have turned up as well, sir."

"Where did they come from?"

Kohl dipped his head as a stray round hit the wall a few feet away.

Dannecker leaned forward and shouted in Kohl's ear.

"Your men know not to harm Captain Bauer?"

"I told them, sir, but—" Kohl was twisting and trying to get back to the cover of the wall.

"Have you told them?" Dannecker slapped Kohl's helmet to get his attention.

"Yes, but there's so much shooting in there . . ."

As proof, Kohl pointed to where his radio operator was lying dead just inside the gates. Kohl flinched again and tried to move back to cover, but was stopped as Dannecker gripped tight hold of his arm.

"Go." Dannecker pushed Kohl forward. "It's time to stop this."

ROSSETT HAD CAUGHT up with Iris, and he was holding her arm by the time he made it to the mouth of the tunnel. Maybe it looked like he was helping her across the rough ground, but despite still being a little dazed, Rossett knew that the closer he got to the resistance, the less likely he was to be shot if he had their leader close at hand.

As soon as they entered the tunnel, the resistance around its mouth started to fall back. Rossett walked with Iris until they reached Cavanagh.

Cavanagh stepped between them, pushed away Rossett's hand, and replaced it with his own.

"The Bear?" He had to shout the question due to the sound of the gunfire echoing off the tunnel walls.

"Gone," replied Iris as she picked her way through the gloom.

"Dead?"

"No, just g-gone."

Rossett stopped and looked at the fighters who were falling back around him. They were firing as they went, covering each other from either side of the tunnel. It was tight, disciplined stuff that impressed him in its efficiency.

He called after Iris, his voice still hoarse. "We can't just let him go."

Cavanagh and Iris stopped fifteen feet farther into the tunnel, near one of the refuges.

Iris turned on a flashlight. The beam danced high on the wall, then down into the alcove, where it found a canvas sack. Cavanagh knelt down and pulled out a reel of detonator cord, a small detonator box, and a plunger.

"We're falling back." Cavanagh looked up at Rossett as he wound the charging key on the box. "And then when they follow us, I'm blowing this. If you want to stick around and carry out a search, feel free."

Rossett stared at the bag for a second, and then took a few paces and swept Iris up off the floor so he could carry her.

"Let's go."

DANNECKER STAYED TO the rear of his men's advance on the tunnel. He'd dispatched a few small groups to search the yard and the surrounding buildings, but a sick sense of dread was telling him that Bauer was either dead or miles away.

Occasionally he dropped to one knee to inspect a facedown corpse, or to question an injured man, but the longer the search went on, the more pointless he felt it was becoming.

One of his men found Becker.

Dead in the mud with half of his head missing. Dannecker stood over his old friend for a moment, then looked toward the tunnel.

"Get this finished." He said it so quietly, Corporal Kohl didn't catch it the first time.

"Sir?"

"Get our men into that tunnel, and kill everyone in it."

Kohl started running across the yard, shouting orders and waving his arms, urging the men forward, pushing them on and into the tunnel.

The resistance inside seemed to give way under this new onslaught. They fell back quickly as Dannecker's men tossed grenades into the darkness.

Dannecker watched for a moment, took another look at Becker, and headed for the tunnel. He wanted to be in on the kill. His blood was rising, his friend was dead, and someone was going to pay.

He was forty feet away when the bomb went off.

He fell backward, then rolled onto his side and curled into a ball. The dust and rubble spewed out of the tunnel like smoke from a chimney. Pieces of stone bounced off him as he buried his head in his arms.

He stayed curled for much longer than was necessary before he finally dared to lift his head. Dust was still belching from the tunnel entrance, and a few confused men stumbled out and collapsed at its mouth like spat-out teeth.

Dannecker climbed back to his feet.

The men who had been searching the yard were running toward the scene of the explosion. He looked around to see if there was anyone else to help the injured and saw five Luftwaffe troop carriers jerking to a halt outside the yard.

They were coming to arrest him.

"Fuck," he said out loud. He started walking back toward the tunnel.

He couldn't keep on fighting. It was over. The Luftwaffe of all people had shot his wild dreams out of the sky and sent them crashing down to earth. Dannecker had raged through Europe for the Führer, then fallen out of love with him when he saw through the sham. He'd committed crimes against mankind, and now it was time he stood before his maker.

His Walther felt like lead in his hand. He couldn't remember pulling it out of his pocket as he looked down at it. Small and black. Deadly. Waiting to do its final duty. He heard someone calling his name. They were coming for him, so he pulled back the slide and took one last look at what was left of his command.

He scanned the yard, full of bodies and blood.

One man, fifty or so feet away, half propped up against some crates, blood on his forehead, blacker than the night, waving to him, saying something he couldn't hear and pointing.

Dannecker lowered the gun, which had found its way up and under his chin.

He stared at the soldier on the ground, tilted his head, and then looked toward where he was pointing.

The other tunnel, the one that led to the Kings Dock.

"There!" the soldier was shouting. The words became clearer as Dannecker took a few steps toward him. "The Bear ran into there!"

CHAPTER 26

THE BEAR WAS running.

A flat-out, fast-as-you-can high-stepping sprint.

It was dark. He was in the Kings Dock tunnel after taking advantage of the fact that when soldiers start shooting, they tended to look nowhere else but down the barrel of their gun. Aside for the one who had tried to stop him just before he made it inside, he'd been able to pass almost unnoticed in the shadows and confusion during the firefight.

The Kings Dock tunnel was the leftmost of the three tunnels. The minute he saw it, he'd known what to do. He'd found a dead resistance fighter, relieved him of a cheap flashlight, then started running.

Three minutes later, the sound of the gunfire was nearly a quarter of a mile behind him and almost drowned out by the sound of his breathing.

He thought about Rossett.

The Englishman had beaten him in hand-to-hand combat. Beaten him easily, if the truth were to be told. The Bear was still alive, though, and that, at the end of the day, meant that he had lost a battle but won the war.

Rossett had his rules, his honor, his Britishness, and all that meant the Bear had nothing left to prove.

"I won," he said out loud between breaths. "I'm free and he got captured, so I beat him."

He fell, picked up the flashlight he'd dropped, then got back to his feet and got moving again.

He ran for another three minutes until he finally broke out into the open air.

The Kings Dock was one of the docks farther up the River Mersey. It was close to the city center, and it was right in front of him.

He followed the train track for another fifty yards as it curved around to meet the warehouses. In the dock basin itself, he could see a few ships' lights shining through the rain.

The tunnel had emerged out of another limestone cliff, its single track breaking out of the wall of rock and then snaking toward the distant quayside. The Bear finally left the track, then ran over to a huge stack of cotton bales. He hid behind them while he got his breath back and assessed the lay of the land.

He inspected the StG 44 he had picked up back at the yard. The magazine was half full, so he slammed it back home and glanced around the corner of the bales toward the dock.

The light breeze was wafting a wet flag and a string of red lights hanging from the mast of an old fishing boat.

The dock looked deserted.

A bell rang in the distance and caused a gull to cry out.

The Bear wiped some blood off his swollen face, then tried to smooth his hair. The longer he remained still, the more his injuries from the fight started to sting. He touched just under his left eye and felt an egg swelling on his cheekbone.

Rossett had a good right hook.

The Bear stood up, tucked the StG tightly in to his side, and started walking. He moved quickly through the dock. The shadows shielded him here and there as he made his way past piles of packing cases toward the dock gates.

To the left of the exit was a gatekeeper's lodge. Outside of it sat an old battered van with PORT POLICE painted on one of the back doors. A yellow light shone through the window of the lodge and splashed some watery light onto the cobbles outside.

The window was angled toward the gates, positioned to allow the gatekeeper a view of what was coming in, not what was going out.

The Bear's original intention was to head straight past the lodge, but then he spotted the telephone line coming off a pole on the roof.

It was worth a try. Sometimes phones could be out in one part of the city and working in the next. It was just like the rest of the country—unpredictable, chaotic, and likely to fail.

He didn't bother knocking.

The port policeman was an old guy who was wearing something that looked like it had once been a smart tunic. He needed a shave, and the collar of his shirt was almost as dirty as his fingernails. He half rose out of the chair as he turned toward the Bear, then fell backward over it as the butt of the rifle slammed into his cheek and shattered it.

The Bear had the phone out of the cradle before the old man had managed to finally slide into the small gap, between a filing cabinet and the table where he had been eating his supper.

"Operator?" The Bear glanced down at the policeman and picked up one of his sandwiches off the table.

"Operator."

"Get me the Adelphi Hotel."

"Putting you through, sir."

The Bear took a look at the sandwich. It was some sort of gray thing that smelled vaguely of fish. He frowned, sniffed it again, then took a bite. He chewed and nodded toward the old man on the ground.

"It's good." He put the sandwich down and noticed there was blood on the white bread from his mouth. He picked up a steaming mug of tea.

"Adelphi Hotel?" The voice on the phone changed as the line worsened.

"Mr. O'Kane's room, please."

"It's very early in the morning, sir. May I take a message?"

"It's urgent. He'll thank you for connecting the call."

"Of course, sir."

The Bear took a sip of tea and felt the sting in his gum where his tooth had been knocked out. He picked up the sandwich again and took another bite as the old man on the floor groaned.

The phone rang once before it was picked up.

"Hello?"

The Bear took note that O'Kane had been awake. He tried to reply, but his mouth was so full he couldn't.

The Irishman called out again. "Who is this?"

"O'Kane?" The Bear's mouth was now half full, but it was still difficult to speak.

"Who is it?"

"Bauer."

"The Bear?"

"The very same."

"Have you got my—" O'Kane paused and collected himself a little. "Do you have what I want?"

"I do." The Bear swallowed the last of the sandwich by craning his neck forward. He picked up the tea again. "Or, rather, I will when I go and get the truck it's loaded on."

"Where is it?"

"Not far from where I am."

"Tell me and I'll get it for you."

The Bear smiled. "Nice try, but I'd rather collect it myself."

"Are you going to give it to me?"

"I want to give it to you, and I want to go with it. I trust that won't be a problem?"

"I don't care who gets the ride, Captain. I just care that the cargo is sitting under them."

"I can trust you?"

"As I explained to the other parties involved in this matter, my organization couldn't work without our word being reliable. People have to trust us or people won't deal with us. If I let you down, and news of that got out . . . well, that would be bad for business, and in turn, bad for me."

"What are you paying me, Mr. O'Kane?"

"Ten percent of what we get wholesale, with approximately five percent immediately on arrival in New York, and the remaining five percent due after we have worked out exactly how much the gold is worth."

"Ninety percent profit seems a steep markup."

"It's a buyer's market."

"Yes." The Bear took another sip of the tea. "I suppose it is."

"You are aware that time is of the essence?"

"How long do I have to make delivery?"

"The ship has to sail in two hours; I can't hold it any longer without it attracting interest. So I'd say you have one and a half hours, if we include loading time."

The Bear looked at the clock on the wall above where the port policeman was bleeding on the floor. "That should be fine. Where do I deliver the cargo?"

"Do you know the Huskisson Dock?"

"Regent Road?"

"The men at the gate will be expecting you. Oh, and Bauer?"

"Yes?"

"Thank you for changing your mind."

"Not at all, Mr. O'Kane. I find it refreshing seeking out new challenges with new people."

"I look forward to meeting those challenges with you."

"As do I." The Bear put down the phone and looked at the old gatekeeper. "May I borrow your van, please?"

DANNECKER WASN'T AS fit as he thought he was. He emerged from the tunnel onto the dock just in time to see the Bear pulling away in the port police van. He dropped to his knees, gasping for breath. It took a full minute for him to be able to get back to his feet and start walking toward the hut.

He guessed he had probably failed, that he'd lost the gold, lost his best friend, lost his reputation and his career. But the despair faded like a wave on the shore.

Dannecker was alive, and he wanted to stay alive.

He wasn't going to give up, not yet, not again.

As he walked along the quayside he considered stealing a boat and making for Ireland. Then a squall of fresh rain dappled the dock's water, slammed into the buildings, and changed his mind for him.

"I don't even know where fucking Ireland is," he said quietly to him-self.

No, he was still in the fight. It was the last round, but he wasn't knocked out yet. He just needed to figure out a way to win.

As he approached the port police hut, he stopped when he saw the overturned chair through the window. He listened, then opened the door and stuck his head tentatively into the light. The policeman groaned as he felt the movement of the air in the room. Dannecker reached in, then pulled the small wooden table across and away from the old man on the floor, who groaned again and weakly waved his hand.

Dannecker considered the old man for a moment, and then finally entered the hut and crouched down. He rested a hand on the old man's shoulder and rolled him slightly so that he could see how bad the injury to his face was.

It was bad. So bad that Dannecker doubted the policeman would be of any use to him, and he started to rise back to his feet.

"Huskisson . . ."

"What?" Dannecker stopped and looked back at the old man.

"Huskisson . . ."

Dannecker crouched again, then set his rifle on the floor. The old man had covered his face with his hand, so Dannecker had to pull it away before he could drag him half up and prop him against the wall.

"What did you say?"

"He is going . . ." The old man's words seemed to bubble out of his broken face. Dannecker gave him a shake and watched a thick gob of blood trickle free from the copper's mouth onto his shirt collar. His head lolled, so Dannecker shook him again and then used the flat of his hand to hold it still.

"What did he say?"

The old man managed to blink open one of his eyes.

"Huss . . ." He trailed off, then tried again. "He is going to Huskisson Dock . . . hour and half . . . he's going there, catch him."

Dannecker let the old man slip back down the wall and stood up. He wiped his hand on his leg, picked up his rifle, and then stepped out of the hut and back into the rain. He took out his Walther, worked the slide, looked back into the hut, and shot the old policeman dead.

The dead were always good at keeping secrets.

THE RAIN HAD eased off, and away across the far side of the city, heading inland, the sky was turning a watercolor dawn of shifting shades of cloud.

Forty minutes after leaving Kings Dock, the Bear fired up the truck on which the gold was already loaded and waiting. He listened to the lumpy idle of the cold engine until it settled into a rough rhythm.

He jumped down from the cab and used the sleeve of his coat to wipe away the thick layer of coal dust that had settled across the windscreen. The warehouse where he'd hidden the gold was next to a coal yard and loading dock.

It was also less than half a mile from where the U.S. Navy ship sat waiting.

He wiped his hands on his damp chest.

He wasn't running away; he was running toward new challenges.

He was the Bear, and bears don't run away.

"Bear's charge," he said out loud, then felt a little foolish and inspected his hands for dirt.

The coal dust had settled everywhere and on everything. It lay like black gold in puddles where the warehouse roof was letting in rain, and it clung like mud to his hands, mouth, and nose as he went around the back of the truck to check the ropes and tarpaulin that were securing the precious cargo.

Once satisfied all was well, he crossed to the heavy wooden sliding doors, set his shoulder to one of them, and eased it back just far enough to be able to stick his head outside. The street was deserted. He leaned into the door again and opened it fully. He ran back to the truck and climbed up into the cab. It was an old beat-up Bedford that sounded like it was running on a couple of cylinders less than it should, and as he sat down another cloud of coal dust puffed up into the air. He revved the engine, crunched a gear, and pulled out of the warehouse.

"Bear's charge," he said again, this time a little louder.

ROSSETT HAD CARRIED Iris almost the entire length of the tunnel after the bomb had exploded.

She was as light as dry kindling and felt almost as brittle.

For all that, when he had stumbled twice in the dark he had dropped her. She hadn't cried out once. Instead, she had simply held out her hands and waited to be taken up into his arms to be carried forward to the next fight.

She was tougher than she looked.

Including Rossett, there were just twelve who emerged into Lime Street station nine minutes after the bomb had gone off. Their faces and clothes were caked with the soot and dust dislodged by the explosion and as they climbed up onto one of the platforms, they could have been mistaken for a band of weary miners on their way home after a shift. The resistance looked exhausted; they were carrying either injuries or each other.

Cavanagh jogged passed Rossett and Iris, then stopped at one of the station exits. He wolf-whistled into the dawn, then turned and signaled that Rossett and the rest should wait. Rossett lowered Iris to one of the few remaining benches left on the station concourse.

Someone brought her a canteen of water, and she sipped some and held it out for Rossett.

He shook his head. "Dannecker will be coming for us. Even if he can't get through the tunnel, he'll know where it comes out." Rossett looked back toward the tunnel and ran his hand around his throat.

"He won't b-be coming."

"He's dead?" Rossett looked at Iris.

"If he isn't, he's to be arrested."

"Who said?"

"That was the Luftwaffe who turned up at the end of the fight. They were coming for h-him."

"Why?"

Iris leaned back on the bench.

"B-because I arranged for one of their men to see the German bodies in the morgue at the hospital. I knew Dannecker would be trying to keep it quiet and that it would make his bosses suspicious if word got back."

Rossett stared at her a moment, then took the canteen and sat down. He took a drink, poured a little of the water into his hand, rubbed it around the back of his neck and his throat, and then passed her the canteen back.

Iris looked at him. "You owe me."

"I owe you?"

She didn't answer straightaway; she was too busy trying to screw the lid back on the canteen. She had to make a couple of attempts to line up the bottle and cap before she was successful.

She looked at him.

"Y-yes, you owe me."

"For what?"

"For betraying me."

"I didn't . . ."

"You were supposed to work with us."

"I never said that."

"I don't c-care what you said, you just were, and you knew it."

The way she said it made Rossett realize there wasn't much point in arguing. He brushed a little mud off his coat and rubbed at the bruises around his neck again.

Over by the exit Cavanagh whistled. This time, another whistle echoed back over the rooftops. He glanced over to Iris and held up his thumb.

"I should have you executed," Iris said quietly.

Rossett looked at her.

She shook her head as she stared off across the station concourse. "I'm not going to, but I should."

"Why not?"

"Because you have honor, and b-because you were trying to do the right thing for the people of this city."

"Save lives."

"Yes," she said. "Save lives."

Rossett leaned forward with his elbows on his knees. "I'm sorry about the gold."

"Say it ten m-million times and I might believe you."

"That much?"

"That much and more." Iris swung the canteen by its thin leather strap a few times. Rossett heard the water sloshing inside as the strap danced in her twitching fingers. She looked at him again. "If you were the B-Bear, what would you do?"

"Hide."

She shook her head.

"You w-wouldn't. Seriously, think, what would you do?"

Rossett stared at the smashed glass scattered all over the floor. A million reflections seemed to offer a million alternate answers. Finally, he replied.

"I'd run."

"W-where?"

"Abroad."

"How?"

"The gold."

She let go with her lopsided grin and nodded.

"Y-you're not as stupid as you look."

He smiled back. "You'd be surprised."

Her smile persisted as Rossett's faded. He asked, "If you couldn't find the Bear and the gold before, what makes you think you can find it now?"

"We didn't know where he had hidden it." She tapped the side of her skull with a thin finger. "But we do know where he has to t-take it if he w-wants to escape the country. The Huskisson Dock."

"When?"

Iris looked up at the station clock, out of habit more than reason. Rossett followed her gaze and saw the clock had been badly damaged during the bombing. Just one hand remained, hanging impotent, pointing at the floor.

"In about an hour, a sh-ship, U.S. Navy, is going to sail."

"U.S. Navy?"

"O'Kane's people have bought the captain."

"You think the Bear is going to catch it?"

"Y-you said he would run with the gold. Where else w-would he go?"

"O'Kane?"

"Even if he hasn't, we've got nothing left to lose. The clock is ticking. If that ship sails in an hour and he is left here, he'll have b-both the resistance and the Germans hunting him down."

Rossett stood up, reached into his coat pocket, and took out his Webley. He cracked it open and six empty shell casings rattled onto the floor. He carefully started to reload it with fresh rounds, and once it was full, he clicked it back shut and looked at Iris.

"The only person Bauer has to worry about hunting him is me."

CHAPTER 27

EVEN THOUGH THE sky was brightening, a soft, smoky gloom hung over the docks like grime on a window. The rain had stopped, but the cobbles still shone like silver turtle backs under the milky last light thrown from the security lamps. The lamps sat on top of the twenty-foot-tall stone wall, which sealed in the Huskisson Dock from Regent Road, which in turn led back to the city center.

Between the wall and the road ran another section of the Overhead Railway. What was left of the Huskisson Dock station sat high up on a platform, like a bombed-out crow's nest floating above the skeleton of an abandoned ship.

The whole place stank of decay.

A few ships loitered at the quayside, waiting for crews, loads, dockers, or the turning of the tide that would take them away from the place they were lost in.

Liverpool hadn't quite woken up yet. Even the dirty gulls stood around with hunched shoulders, waiting for things to look better in the light of a new dawn.

The Bear sat in the cab of the truck and stared at the Huskisson Dock gates. They were set halfway along the tall granite wall that ran along Regent Road. One port policeman in a rain-slick black poncho was flanked by three U.S. shore patrolmen, each of whom was carrying a Thompson machine gun and a smartly strapped sidearm.

The Bear knew from experience that normally there would have been HDT on the gate as well. He guessed they had been dispersed by Dannecker to cover the exits out of the city, either in a search for him and Rossett or maybe to prevent prying eyes from watching Dannecker climb the gangway of a U.S. ship.

One of the shore patrol adjusted his Thompson and stepped out of the gates to look down the road toward the city. The Bear leaned back into the shadows of the truck cab and watched as the SP checked the time, then called back to the others.

The clock was ticking; they were worried he wasn't coming.

The Bear considered the Thompsons the shore patrol were carrying. Normally SP wouldn't carry firearms when they were off their ship in a foreign country. Normally the worst they would be wielding would be a billy club and a bad attitude.

Guns had a habit of changing plans, as the Bear knew only too well.

No HDT was good. But guns and American SP? That was the unknown. Maybe they were there to kill him and take the gold? Maybe they were there to protect him?

He rested his elbows on the steering wheel and watched them.

One of the SP shared a joke and a cigarette with the port policeman.

It looked like everything was normal.

The Bear didn't like normal.

But whether he liked it or not, he had less than thirty minutes until the ship sailed on the high tide, which meant he had about fifteen to decide what to do.

Dannecker made his mind up for him.

The car passed him so closely and so fast from behind, it made the truck rock from side to side. The brakes in the little black saloon slammed on, causing it to dip its nose with a sharp nod before the back wheels locked, and it spun in a 180-degree hand-brake turn in front of the Bear's truck.

Dannecker was climbing out almost before the car had shuddered to a stop.

He fired twice through the Bear's windscreen with his Walther.

The rounds punched through the glass and into the back of the driver's seat, just to the right of where the Bear's spine had been.

DANNECKER'S HEART WAS pounding. He stared at the windscreen of the truck with its fresh bullet holes and its crazed glass.

The Bear had ducked out of sight.

Dannecker had been too slow, and now he didn't know what to do. Move to the right and open a door or move to the left and open a door?

Either option meant he was probably going to end up looking down the barrel of a gun.

Damn.

He fired another round into the metal below the windscreen.

Five rounds left.

Shit.

He took a few steps back toward the car he had hijacked twenty minutes earlier and edged around it, using his free hand to feel the way behind him.

Fuck.

He crouched down on the far side of the car, the pistol held next to his head as he stared through the side windows at the truck. Maybe he had hit the Bear? He took a look toward the dock gates and saw three armed shore patrol officers behind a gatepost.

They weren't intervening, so he turned back to the truck.

"Bear!" He almost surprised himself by shouting out. It felt like some bit of his brain had a plan but hadn't told the rest of him about it.

"What?"

The Bear didn't sound injured.

Dannecker glanced at the SP again. Behind them, through the gap in the gate, he could see a plume of dirty smoke thickening as it rose from the funnel of the American ship.

Dannecker looked back at the truck and saw the driver's door swing open; a moment later, the passenger door opened. The truck sat staring at him like a charging elephant with its ears thrown wide.

"Bear?" he shouted again.

"I already said 'what.'"

Dannecker breathed out and shouted back at the truck. "Looks like we have a problem here, Bauer."

"It does, Major."

"So how do we find a way around it?"

"You could go home?"

Dannecker smiled, then glanced at the SP again. Behind them, he could see O'Kane looking toward him and Bauer. The Irishman must have been on board, heard the shooting, and come to take a look.

Dannecker waved to O'Kane.

He didn't wave back.

"What do you want, Major? I've a boat to catch!" Bauer shouted to Dannecker, forcing him to concentrate.

"How about we put down our guns and let O'Kane decide who goes with the gold?"

"After you," Bauer shouted back.

"I'm serious, Captain, let's both throw out our guns. We could maybe share the reward?"

"Like I said, after you!"

Neither of them threw away their guns. Dannecker took another glance at O'Kane, then knelt and changed the Walther's magazine for a fresh one.

His hand was shaking. He hadn't expected that.

He eased his way back up to a crouch.

"We need to make a move, Bauer."

The Bear didn't respond.

"One of us needs to be the adult here, find a compromise so that we can all come out of the situation on top." Dannecker moved a few inches to get a better view of the truck, crouching low, his left hand on the cold steel of the car, his right on the warm steel of the Walther. "There is enough for all of us to be happy, and I'm sure O'Kane can find a spare berth on the—"

He stopped speaking as he felt the muzzle of a gun pressing against the back of his neck.

O'KANE COULDN'T TAKE it anymore.

He wasn't one of life's watchers, and seeing as the SP had been given orders to remain inside the dock gates unless explicitly under attack, there was nothing for it but to go out there and bring this thing to a close himself.

He was nervous.

Any man who was about to sneak up on another man holding a gun and said he wasn't nervous was a liar.

And O'Kane was many things, but he wasn't a liar.

He took out his Browning, flicked the safety off, and started to head for Dannecker.

And then he saw Rossett.

ROSSETT KNEW IT was easy sneaking up on people who had tunnel vision. Even though he had built a career out of facing things head on, coming up behind Dannecker had been a piece of cake.

"Drop your gun." Rossett was staring over at the truck as he pressed a little harder with the Webley against Dannecker's neck.

"Oh, for God's sake." Dannecker rested his forehead against the car and lowered the Walther to his side.

"Drop it," Rossett whispered.

"Don't you ever give up?"

"Drop the gun." Rossett said it slowly, taking his time to drive home each word.

Dannecker let go of the pistol.

"Now what?" Dannecker's forehead was still resting against the car. "Are you going to tell Bauer to drop his as well?"

"Hands behind your back."

"You don't have a plan, do you? How do you take both of us down?"

"Hands."

"You should have waited till one of us was dead."

"Now."

"Hey, Bauer!" Dannecker shouted to the Bear in the truck.

"What?" Bauer's voice came from the cab.

"Rossett is here."

"Really?"

"Would I joke?"

Rossett saw the Bear's head lift a couple of inches to look over the dashboard and then disappear again.

"Lion?"

Rossett didn't reply.

"Lion!" Bauer tried again.

Rossett was too busy pushing Dannecker down to the ground to answer.

"How are you going to shoot at me while you are fighting with Major Dannecker?"

Rossett set his knee into Dannecker's back, then started to dig around in his coat pockets for the leather strap he had taken from the water canteen back at the station. "Hands behind your back."

The truck's engine fired into life.

Rossett looked up.

THE BEAR KNEW he had a chance the second he saw Rossett staring at him over the roof of the car.

For once, two enemies were better than one.

He knocked off the hand brake, reached up to the ignition button with his free hand, then twisted his leg around so that he could press the clutch in. The engine burst into life and he found first gear with a solid clunk from the transmission.

The release of the hand brake had already started the truck moving, so as he lifted off the clutch the engine didn't stall. Keeping his head down low, he dragged the steering wheel around to the left, and as the truck picked up speed, he aimed it in the vague direction of the dock gates.

He braced himself. Looking up and out of the windscreen, he used the building line as a guide to tell him when to straighten the wheel. He brought his gun to bear and readied himself to shoot at Rossett as the truck completed its turn.

Finally, he looked out of the still-open driver's door toward where he expected Dannecker and Rossett to be.

They were brawling over Rossett's pistol, face-to-face, rolling around, fighting like animals, the kind of fighting that was going to end badly for one of them.

The Bear didn't bother shooting. He had other things to be getting on with.

THE MINUTE THE truck started rolling, Rossett took his mind off what mattered the most.

The immediate threat.

Dannecker.

Rossett lifted his head as the truck started to move, but worse than that, he lifted the Webley. Dannecker didn't wait for a second opportunity. He kicked back with his left heel into Rossett's shin. Even before his foot made contact, he threw back his head, looking to make contact with Rossett's face.

Dannecker missed, but even though his right arm was pinned, he tried to lift his left shoulder to roll under Rossett and into the arm that was holding him down. He didn't get the chance. The Webley swiped him like a brick.

Dannecker's head hit the cobbles hard and saved Rossett the trouble of hitting it again. He was out cold.

Rossett lifted the Webley toward the truck, then lowered it again. He'd missed his chance.

The truck was racing for the open dock gates. The policeman and SP dived for cover, but didn't raise their weapons.

Rossett got to his knees, took a deep breath, and pushed himself up onto his feet. He started walking, then jogging, and then, finally, running after the truck.

He wasn't going to give up now, not while there was still justice to be served.

THE TRUCK HAD clipped one of the dock walls, snagged the gate hinges, then dragged the gate clean off. One of the shore patrol had been caught by the falling gate, hooked on to the tangled metal, and dragged along for twenty feet behind the truck.

The Bear had plowed on in first gear, oblivious to the shouts, sparks, and shore patrolmen following in his wake.

The port policeman pulled his truncheon and held out a hand at Rossett as he ran toward the gate.

Rossett dropped him with a right without missing a step. The SP were too busy with their fallen colleague to notice what had just happened, but O'Kane wasn't.

He started running toward Rossett.

ROSSETT NEEDED TO get to the truck and grab the Bear before the Bear made it to the ship. Rossett knew he wouldn't be able to get to him once he was on the boat, nor would he be able to stop the loading of the gold. If the German could make it up the gangway, he was a free man.

He would lose if the Bear had the U.S. Navy on his side, and Rossett was getting sick of losing.

He was coming up forty feet behind the truck as it stopped near the cargo gangway at the bow of the ship. He saw the back wheels lock and then skid as the Bear threw on the hand brake.

At the head of the cargo gangway Rossett could see several crew members in fatigues already springing into action. The ship's small loading crane swung over the bulwark.

Rossett lifted the Webley and then noticed that the crew were all looking at something behind him.

He stopped, ducked, turned, and raised the Webley in one quick maneuver. O'Kane was charging at him, pulling the slide of the Browning as he ran.

The gap between them was less than ten feet. O'Kane tried to stop but couldn't. He slammed into Rossett hard, and the force of the hit knocked both men over onto the ground.

Rossett was winded as he turned, and saw O'Kane reaching for the pistol he'd dropped in the fall.

O'Kane looked up just as Rossett launched himself at him.

O'Kane was good. He rolled with Rossett and tried to push him off. He threw one, then two, then three punches in a tight, hooking, left-right-left combination, but they landed on Rossett's parrying elbows and upper arms and caused little damage.

Rossett's forward momemtum carried him over and then on top. He managed to throw a weak right at O'Kane's face. It landed, but was barely a tap. They locked arms and rolled once, then once again. Rossett managed a glance over at where he had last seen the Bear, then back at O'Kane as he lifted his forearm.

O'Kane did what Rossett knew he was going to do.

He lifted his head off the cobbles as he tried to get on top.

Rossett head-butted him.

Fatigue meant it was more of a flop than a butt. Rossett was so tired it was all he could do to collapse on the other man and let gravity do all the work.

It was weak, but it was enough. O'Kane's head slammed back on the ground, and his hands dropped limply.

O'Kane was good, but Rossett was better.

BECAUSE THE TWO truck doors were wide open, Bauer couldn't use the wing mirrors to look for Rossett. If he picked the wrong door he was a dead man, so instead, he picked the windscreen.

He emptied half a magazine into the center of the glass in an eighteen-inch spread, braced his back against the seat, and used both feet to kick the windscreen through.

He was out through the hole and onto the hood ten seconds after the truck had stopped.

He dropped to the ground and lay flat against the concrete. He scanned with the MP40 and looked for a sign of Rossett, hoping for a chance to shoot him through the gap under the truck.

He could see O'Kane, flat on his back, drowsily wafting a hand to his bloody nose. He could see the shore patrolmen, tending to their colleague by the fallen gate. He could even see Dannecker, flat on his back, out in the street, fifty yards away by the car.

He could see it all, but he couldn't see Rossett.

"I SWEAR TO God, if you move one fucking inch"—Rossett sucked in a breath—"I will blow your head clean off."

The Bear didn't move.

Rossett had felt completely wiped out back in the goods yard. Now, after the fight with Dannecker, the sprint, the fight with O'Kane, and then, finally, the jump and the climb over the truck, he knew he was running on empty.

He was sprawled on the truck cab's roof, the Webley hanging limp at the end of his arm, being aimed by gravity directly at the Bear, who was lying below it on the ground.

Rossett risked a quick look at the men on the ship. One of them shook his head in disbelief, while another puffed out his cheeks.

They were impressed.

Rossett gulped another breath and looked back at the Bear.

"Slide the weapon under the truck. Do it now."

"Lion, there is—"

"Do it, Bauer."

The Bear considered his options, then slid the MP40 away as instructed.

"Hands out, wide, wide as you can get them, and get your face flat on the ground."

"Lion, you know there is—"

"I swear to God, Bauer, just do it."

The Bear did as he was told.

Rossett slid off the roof of the cab onto the ground next to Bauer. He landed hard, so hard his legs folded underneath him and he ended up on his arse.

He should have known it was never going to be that easy.

He hadn't seen the knife.

The Bear had kept it in the truck cab for when the time came to finally cut the ropes and tarpaulin securing the gold. He hadn't realized he would need it to fight for his life.

He slashed at Rossett, who scurried away from the blade's reach as quickly as his arms and legs could manage.

The Webley clattered on the cobbles as Rossett tried to make enough space to lift it. The Bear chased after him on all fours, the final throw of the dice giving him a spurt of energy and carrying him forward.

Rossett kicked with his feet as the blade flashed, then slashed, left and right. It spun in the Bear's hand, almost too fast to see as he switched his hold to a reverse grip.

The Bear jumped.

Both hands out, the right holding the knife, aiming for Rossett's chest, looking to end it once and for all.

Rossett managed to pat the Bear's knife hand away. He felt the tip of the blade slicing through his coat, jacket, and shirt, then dragging across his skin.

It cut, but it didn't cut deep enough.

The Bear set his left hand onto Rossett's chest and tried to bring the blade back into play.

The Webley was quicker than the knife.

The Bear flinched as he felt the pistol under his chin.

Both men were gasping for breath, staring into each other's eyes, the Bear on top, Rossett underneath.

"Drop it," Rossett said softly.

"Shoot me."

"Let me do my job. Drop the knife."

Bauer blinked. A moment passed. Rossett felt his finger tighten on the trigger, then heard the knife clatter onto the quayside.

The fight went out of Bauer.

It was over.

Rossett rolled out from under him, all the while pushing the Webley into the jaw of Bauer. The German flopped onto the quayside, eyes closed, chest heaving, and Rossett shuffled a few inches back, then pulled out Jimmy's handcuffs. He shook them, snapped the first one on Bauer's left wrist, then dragged the second one around roughly onto his right. Once the handcuffs were tight, Rossett dropped his head a couple of inches and took a deep breath.

After a few seconds, he lifted the Webley and dragged first himself and then the Bear to his feet. It looked like most of the ship's crew had come out onto the deck to watch. A few of the men by the cargo hatch were now waiting on the gangway, unsure of what to do. Rossett used the Bear as a shield as they stared at him.

He stood still, taking in the scene, before looking up to the bridge, where the captain of the ship and two officers were standing.

"I'm a British police officer, and this man is my prisoner!" Rossett shouted toward the bridge over the low rumble of the ship's diesel engines. "I don't want what's on the truck, and I'll not interfere with your passage. I'll just take my prisoner and leave you to go on your way."

Nobody replied.

Rossett slowly started walking toward the gates, all the while still using the Bear as a shield. They managed only five small steps before O'Kane appeared from behind the truck with a bloodstained handkerchief held under his nose.

"You do not give up, do you?"

Rossett angled the Bear so that he was holding him between himself and O'Kane, then made sure O'Kane could see the Webley.

"I just want Bauer. Do what you want with the gold, but give me Bauer and Dannecker."

Finally the Bear spoke. "You made me a promise, O'Kane, remember? You gave me your word."

O'Kane lowered his bloody handkerchief and gestured that the crew on the gangway should start unloading the gold.

The crew looked at Rossett.

He took a few steps back from the truck and O'Kane, gesturing that they could do their job.

The crew leapt into action. They came down the gangway quickly. Rossett took another step backward and then moved to the other side of the truck, putting even more cover between himself and the ship. O'Kane had mirrored his movement, and when Rossett emerged on the other side, he found O'Kane waiting with the two remaining armed shore patrolmen.

Everyone except Rossett had their guns lowered.

"You broke my nose." O'Kane held up his handkerchief as proof. "Nobody ever broke my nose."

Rossett didn't reply.

O'Kane held up the handkerchief for the SP to see, then stuffed it in his pocket. He looked at the SP nearest to him and nodded his head toward Rossett.

"Tell him who you are."

The SP looked at O'Kane. "Are you sure?"

"It's okay." O'Rourke nodded encouragingly. "Tell him."

The SP paused, like he was searching for the right words, and then spoke.

"I'm Sergeant Norris Edwards of the British Royal Marine Commando, and this is Corporal Ian Clark." Edwards nodded his head to his colleague.

"What?" Rossett and the Bear said it in unison.

"We're Royal Marines, and this is a Free British Navy vessel."

"British?" Rossett looked at O'Kane.

O'Kane shrugged. "Most of them, yeah. Some of the officers and crew are American and Canadian, but most are Brits."

"Who are you?" The Bear took a half step forward from Rossett as he stared at O'Kane.

"I'm Lieutenant Colonel Paddy O'Rourke, and you are one genuine pain in the arse." O'Rourke lifted his Browning and fired one shot.

Rossett staggered back as the Bear slipped through his hands and onto the ground. A dot of blood above his left eye gave a small clue to the damage the bullet had done to his head. Rossett limply lifted his Webley as he staggered to the right, then looked down at the Bear as he wiped his own face clean of German blood.

It took him a full five seconds before he looked back at O'Rourke.

"You're English?" was all he could think to say.

"Irish Canadian actually, but close enough." O'Rourke flicked the safety, and slipped the Browning into his pocket. He raised his hand to show Rossett it was empty. "You look done in, Inspector."

Rossett looked up at the truck and saw that the crew had already started to remove the wooden crates from the back of it.

He turned back to O'Rourke, who was still holding up his hand and calming him.

"Put the gun down, John, we're on your side. This is a British operation, organized by the government in exile. You've been fighting your own side."

"Iris?" Rossett wiped his cheek and then looked at his fingertips.

"Her father knew, but nobody else. It was safer that way."

Rossett looked at the gun in his hand, and for the first time in a long time didn't know what to do with it.

O'Rourke nodded. "Please . . . put the gun away."

Rossett dropped the gun to his side and released the hammer with his thumb.

"Dannecker?" he asked quietly.

O'Kane nodded to one of the SP. "Go and see to the major."

The SP drew a razor-sharp commando knife from inside of his tunic and stalked away toward where Dannecker was still lying in the road outside of the dock. Rossett watched him go, then looked back at O'Rourke.

"No loose ends, that's how we prefer it. You understand?"

Rossett thumbed the hammer on the Webley again.

O'Rourke held out his hand and smiled. "No, honestly no, you're amongst friends. You can relax now."

Rossett considered what O'Rourke had said but still didn't drop the hammer. Instead, keeping the gun at his side, he looked over at the men swarming over the truck bed unloading the gold.

"What's going to happen to Iris? Will she get the bounty on the gold?" Rossett turned back to O'Rourke.

"No."

"No?"

"She works for us. She's one of us. This is British bullion. It belongs to the country, the country she is fighting for."

"So all that stuff about paying a bounty and being loyal?"

"If she had delivered the gold to me, she may have got some sort of reward. But the thing is: Iris didn't. You did."

Rossett shook his head and took a few paces over to the truck. He rested his back against the radiator and sank down to sit on the fender. He was exhausted, almost too tired to think. His body ached and his head pounded from the stress and exertion of the last few days. He heard a splash over by the quayside and looked across.

The two shore patrolmen were walking toward the truck. Rossett looked out into the street beyond the gates and saw that Dannecker was no longer there. O'Rourke followed his gaze, then their eyes met and O'Rourke shrugged.

"Like I said, no loose ends."

"What about repercussions? Dannecker dead, Bauer dead, Becker dead, and the soldiers at the bomb site? The Germans will come down hard on Liverpool. Everything I've done has been aiming to prevent that."

"Maybe, maybe not." O'Rourke looked at the back of the truck as the crane swung away with a full load of crates on pallets. "Dannecker lost control here. The shooting of the consul, the bomb, your partner Neumann, and then him disappearing. All of that will make it easy for us to spread disinformation. If we can drag the Americans into it, the Germans will want to keep it quiet, and you never know, a new commander might be good for the city."

"I wish I had your optimism."

O'Rourke nodded, checked the load again, and walked over and took a seat next to Rossett on the fender.

He leaned forward, resting his elbows on his knees, his eyes on the concrete beneath his feet. After a moment, he turned his head and looked at Rossett. "There is an empty bunk on the ship."

"What?"

"You've done your bit here. Why not take it?"

"Go?"

"Yes."

"No."

"What are you going to do here?" O'Rourke straightened a little. "Your partner is dead, and you've been involved in havoc in Liverpool. Even if you can talk your way out of it, you'll just be back to square one, working for the Germans."

"I wouldn't be welcomed by the government in exile."

"You're a hero."

"I'm not a hero."

"You're the closest thing we've got to one. You could do a lot of good, John; you could help rally the troops. Plus, it would give the country a lift to see you standing with the king. Imagine it, the Lion rising again. The papers and the Free BBC would love it. I was ordered to bring back the gold, but if you come back with me, you'd be just as valuable."

"So I just run away?"

"You don't run away." O'Rourke nodded his head toward the back of the truck. "That gold will pay for weapons that will win this war, but they won't win it on their own. Great Britain needs you. If you get on that ship, you'll be back here one day, and when that day comes . . . you'll be on the right side again."

"What about Iris? You could have taken her away from this."

"I would have, if I'd had the chance."

Rossett didn't reply.

"There must be someone over there who you know? Someone worth leaving here for?" O'Rourke said it quietly.

"There is."

"Girlfriend?"

"A little boy I once helped, and the woman who is looking after him."

"They'll want to see you, and you've earned it."

Rossett looked over at the ship and changed the subject.

"How did you get this in here?"

"One navy cargo ship looks pretty much the same as another, especially when it was donated by the Americans at the start of the war." O'Rourke pointed to the numbers painted on the bow. "A splash of paint to convert it back to U.S. markings, a few American or Canadian officers on deck in case anyone gets curious, and a local consul who is sympathetic to what we are trying to do." He paused. "And the right amount of bribery, of course."

"The gold?"

"Enough of it to pay for this operation and one hundred more like it."

A sailor came jogging over to O'Rourke and saluted.

"Captain is ready to sail, sir."

O'Rourke acknowledged him with a halfhearted salute. The sailor glanced at Rossett, then jogged back to the ship, where the cargo gangway was being pulled back on board.

"What'll it be, John? We don't have long. The river pilot is waiting, and the tide's turning."

Rossett looked up at the sky. The morning sun was breaking through the clouds over the city center to his left. Voices were shouting orders on the ship. A gull whirled on the breeze, then became a white arrow as it swooped down and away across the muddy River Mersey.

Rossett noticed for the first time that the rain had stopped. He shivered in his damp clothes and felt the pain of his injuries rattle through his body.

He was tired.

He nodded, just once, to himself, and then looked at O'Rourke.

"I think it's time to go."

O'Rourke stood up and held out his hand.

"Come on, Lion. Let's take you home."

ACKNOWLEDGMENTS

'VE SAID IT before, and I'll say it again:

Just because there's only one name on the jacket of a book, doesn't mean only one person wrote it.

A team put these pages in front of you, and as far as I am concerned, I have the best team there is to have.

Starting with Nat Sobel, my patient agent. He's the one who keeps me going, has my back, lifts me up, but somehow manages to keeps my feet on the ground.

This book wouldn't exist without him, so if you meet him, thank him. He deserves it.

Next up is the manager of the team at HarperCollins: David Highfill.

When I started doing this sort of thing for a living, someone told me that writing was a cutthroat business, one in which everyone was looking out for number one.

I've got to be honest, I was a little intimidated, and then I met David.

He's a gentleman. Old school, like the kind of guy your mother told you to be when you grew up. He's trustworthy, honest, strong, believes in doing things the right way, and is in serious danger of giving publishing a good name. David backed me when there was nobody else, and always worked as hard as he could to make John Rossett a star. I'll always be grateful, and it has been a pleasure working with him. I dearly hope that this isn't the last book we make together.

Every good general like David lives and dies on the strength of his lieutenants, and David has been blessed in that department like no other. Ashley, Julie, Katherine, and the wonderful Chloe have all played their part in bringing these pages to you, so remember them please as you close them for the last time.

The team at Harper360 in the UK have also stood by my side throughout this journey, and I owe them a debt of gratitude.

Along with the bookmakers, a fair few booksellers have been along for the ride too. To them, especially Sarah Hughes, for all the amazing work that they do in putting books in front of you, I say thank you, and keep up the good work.

Now we come to friends and family.

I need to thank my sister, Denise, for the long coffee chats about nothing. They seem to go by so fast, and make me so grateful for having her, and her wonderful family, Jim, Ellen, Alex, and Paul, in my life.

Then there is my brother, Philip, and his boys, David, Karl, and Martin, who I don't see often enough, but think about often.

Now it is time for friends old and new. Terry, Shirley, Tony W., Eddie M., Brian C., Mick W., plus Gina, Donna, and Lisa, et al. Thanks so much for all your support, it means a huge amount to me. St. Aloysius would be proud if he was around to see how we all turned out.

As always, there's a shout out to Jane Buchanan, the woman with the wonkiest spare bed in New York, and whose name has been in more books than Chairman Mao. Mary and Kenny, dear, dear, supportive friends who mean so much to me. Then there are the two Ians, Mitty and Gauckwin, whose efforts to convert me to real ale go beyond the call of duty. Then there are the boys from 'Spoons, who I don't get to see as often as I should: Graham, Rob, Andy, John, Ian, Fran, the dear departed Russ and Cleggy, plus Andy D. and Steve B., I love you all.

I can't forget Tracey Edges, Jo Hughes, Dave Bidwell, Ian Collins, Clare Tiptaft, and Lembit Opik either. You've all helped so much. Thank you.

Now I have to thank you, the loyal followers and friends of John Rossett.

Your support has always brought me joy and made me grateful. I love you all whether we have corresponded or not. Those with whom I have been lucky enough to chat, people like Jacob Perry, Darcia Hale, Elise Cooper, Mark Rubenstein, and the wonderful Barbara and Ron Chennisi. Your efforts to spread the word about John Rossett will always be warmly remembered, and you aren't just readers and reviewers, you are friends.

Now there is Sweeney.

You're a pest. Honestly, you drive me up the wall. I've often thought about a restraining order but I can't see the point, as I'm not sure you would be able to read it. I suppose I'll just have to keep on putting up with you like a bad smell, same as I have done for the last forty-six years. While I am here, I would also like to take this opportunity to say to you that I was right about Kurt Russell and that you owe me a million pounds.

Then there is BooBoo the cat, who purrs on my lap, and keeps me and John Rosset company when all the world has gone to bed. There's only been one other animal who could sleep through the sound of my typing, and BooBoo fills his big shadow beautifully.

Finally, I come to Anna.

The woman I love, and the woman who brought me home.

You've tied up all the loose ends of my life, and given it a happy ever after. I love you.

P.S.

Remember, where you are now isn't where you'll stay, it's just another stop on the road to where you are going to end up.

Keep moving, keep trying, keep fighting, and like John Rossett, never give up, because you don't know what's around the next corner.

Lots of love,

Tony

ABOUT THE AUTHOR

Tony Schumacher is the author of *The Darkest Hour* and *The British Lion,* and was twice a finalist for the Sidewise Award for Alternate History. He has written for the *Guardian* and the Huffington Post, and is a regular contributor to BBC Radio and London's LBC Radio. He has been a policeman, stand-up comedian, bouncer, jeweler, taxi driver, perfume salesman, actor, and garbage collector, among other jobs. He currently lives outside Liverpool.